The
Fingerprint
Story

The Fingerprint Story

Gerald Lambourne QPM
Commander, Fingerprint Department
New Scotland Yard 1975–1980

With a Foreword by
Sir Kenneth Newman QPM

Harrap · London

This book is dedicated to my wife, June,
whose support and encouragement made all
things seem possible.

First published in Great Britain 1984
by HARRAP LIMITED
19–23 Ludgate Hill, London EC4M 7PD

© *Gerald Lambourne* 1984

ISBN 0 245-53963-8

Designed by Robert Wheeler
Printed and bound in Great Britain
by Billings, Worcester

Foreword

by SIR KENNETH NEWMAN, LLB, FBIM, QPM
Commissioner of Police of the Metropolis

The history of fingerprints and of Scotland Yard are inextricably interwoven. Their introduction in the first year of this century as the only really reliable means of human identification was, perhaps more than anything else, the most significant act of my distinguished predecessor Sir Edward Henry. Prior to his appointment as Commissioner of Police of the Metropolis, he had developed fingerprint classification as Inspector General of Police in Bengal.

Fingerprints were destined quickly to supersede internationally all previous methods of establishing beyond question the true identities of criminals appearing before courts and, perhaps as importantly, to translate silent fingermark clues found at the scenes of grave crime, into the single most telling piece of evidence against a perpetrator.

Gerald Lambourne, an old colleague of many years, has spent almost his entire professional police career within the intriguing web of fingerprints, either at Scotland Yard or at the locus of serious crimes. Through merit, he rose steadily and worthily to be head of his Branch. He has now written a definitive and entertaining history of the science of fingerprints, together with its practical application to crime and criminals. The inner story of several infamous crimes are also knowingly described.

Mr Lambourne saw the earliest applications of complex manual fingerprint classification systems and, from this basis of all-round professional experience, was selected to husband the introduction of modern computerization applications to fingerprints. The full potential of this innovation is yet to be seen. He received the Sovereign's Police Medal for Distinguished Service for this devotion to the science of fingerprints and indeed for his discerning shrewdness in criminal matters generally.

His fascinating book deserves all success.

New Scotland Yard
London SW1

Contents

Illustrations

Between pages 128 and 129

The bottle under June Devaney's cot
Comparing prints in the Devaney case
The evidence against Peter Griffiths
    (*Photos Lancashire Constabulary*)
Scars on the chest of Robert Pitts after a skin-graft
Pitt's fingerprints after the skin-graft
The establishment of Pitt's identity
    (*Photos Texas Department of Public Safety*)
Outmoded and modern fingerprint kit (*Photos Metropolitan Police*)
The kitchen at Leatherslade Farm (*Photo Thames Valley Police*)
The ridge structure on an Ancient Egyptian mummified hand (*Photo Metropolitan Police*)
'The Dance to the Music of Time', showing also detail and three enlarged sections (*Reproduced by permission of the Trustees, The Wallace Collection, London*)
Transmogrification (*Photos Royal Hong Kong Police*)
Fixed points on a fingerprint

Between pages 160 and 161

Manual searching in the National Fingerprint Collection (1965)
Fingerprint officers retrieving and comparing scenes-of-crime data on Videofile system)
    (*Photos Metropolitan Police*)
Fingerprint officer making a comparison on a split-screen VDU
Fingerprint expert coding fingerprints, using Datapad
    (*Photos Metropolitan Police*)
The author discussing a glove-print identification with senior fingerprint officer Chris Coombes (*Photo Bersen's International Press Service Ltd*)
The Press heralds the advent of glove-prints
Prints from fabrics, gloves, etc.
Scanned print
Control print
    (*Photos Metropolitan Police*)
Airtight chamber used for treating articles with radioactive sulphur dioxide gas
Postage stamps commemorating fingerprints
Nineteenth-century (1890) and twentieth-century (1967) 'New Scotland Yards'
    (*Photos Metropolitan Police*)

Acknowledgments

The author acknowledges with grateful thanks the assistance received from: The Commissioner of the Metropolitan Police and his staff; the Chief Constables of Thames Valley Police, West Yorkshire Metropolitan Police, and Lancashire Constabulary; the Librarians of The Manuscript Room, University College London, The Royal College of Surgeons, The British Library, Westminster City Library, India Office Library, and Central Library, Newcastle upon Tyne; the Editors of *The Times, Daily Express, News of the World, Nature, The Police Review*, and *The Lancet*; The British Association for the Advancement of Science, The Directors of the Wallace Collection, The Fingerprint Society, The Home Office Scientific Research and Development Branch, The Texas Department of Safety, The Galton Laboratory, The Department of Physics at Southampton University, and The National Portrait Gallery. Last but certainly not least, all fingerprint men and women, past and present, without whom there would not be a story to tell.

The primary object of an efficient Police
is the prevention of crime; the next that
of detection and punishment of offenders
if crime is committed. To these ends all
efforts of Police must be directed. The
protection of life and property, the
preservation of public tranquillity and
the absence of crime, will alone prove
whether those efforts have been successful
and whether the objects for which the Police
were appointed have been attained.

Sir Richard Mayne
First Joint Commissioner
of the Metropolitan Police, 1829

Introduction

As I took the oath of allegiance, on the 28th of January 1946, I fulfilled the ambition of my relatively short life – to become a constable of the Metropolitan Police, the third generation of my family to serve in a police force. At that stage I was the youngest serving policeman in the Force, and couldn't possibly have foreseen that many years later I was also to become its longest-serving member, thereby inheriting the title 'Father of the Force'.

Earlier that day I had entered Peel House in Regency Street, Westminster, which was then the Training School of the Metropolitan Police, with seventeen men and two women, all aspiring members of the Force. It was primarily an austere and functional place, geared to converting ordinary members of the public into guardians of the Queen's peace with a minimum of fuss. As I climbed the worn stone staircase with its metal banisters, I could not help thinking about the many thousands of men who had gone before me. Most of them had served with honour, some with distinction; there were those who had sacrificed their lives in the line of duty, and a few who had brought disgrace upon themselves and the Force.

In the dormitories each man had his own cubicle, which was open at the top and bottom and had just sufficient room for a bed, a small cupboard and a clothes-hanger on the back of the door. Perhaps it was just as well for the women that they slept in another building. The noise at night caused by the snoring and snorting of about twenty men is quite indescribable. This then was to be my home for thirteen hard, tiring, but nevertheless enjoyable weeks.

As well as being sworn in on our first day, we were given our uniforms. I well remember the feeling of putting on that uniform. Not only did I look like a policeman, I felt like one. The high buttoned neck of the jacket and tunic was both very smart and distinctive. With the uniform I wore in my early days no one else had any doubt that I was a policeman. Today, with a modified uniform and a preponderance of flat caps instead of helmets, some policemen look like a cross between a security guard and a ticket-collector. It was good psychology to make us wear our uniforms every day for our three months' stay at the school. The wearing of it became second nature, so that when we made our first appearance on the streets we were no longer self-conscious.

Each day commenced with a run round Vincent Square, then breakfast followed by classroom studies. These were later extended to simulated situations under conditions as realistic as any which could be devised within the confines of the school. The lessons were punctuated with periods of the inevitable 'square-bashing' and saluting – quick march – slow march – left turn – right turn – about turn. It was all rather ironic really, because most of the men had just been demobbed from the armed services.

During that thirteen weeks we were subjected to concentrated cramming about law, police procedures, first aid and basic knowledge of the myriad subjects that a policeman may be called upon to deal with. Quite a lot of the information we were given had to be learned verbatim. I still remember the first piece I had to memorize, probably because at the time – and even now – I consider it embodies the only true function of the police. It was said in 1829 by Sir Richard Mayne, who was one of the first joint commissioners of the Metropolitan Police:

> The primary object of an efficient Police is the prevention of crime; the next that of detection and punishment of offenders if crime is committed. To these ends all efforts of Police must be directed. The protection of life and property, the preservation of public tranquillity and the absence of crime, will alone prove whether those efforts have been successful and whether the objects for which the Police were appointed have been attained.

Our progress was checked every four weeks by a series of tests. Failure to maintain the standard meant being held back for further instruction. Fortunately, the whole of our class took each test in its stride, and at the end of three months we received our individual postings to one of the Metropolitan divisions, which at that time numbered twenty-four.

I was posted to 'F' Division, which had its headquarters at

Hammersmith. On arrival I was assigned to the sub-division of Notting Hill Police Station, and allocated the number ninety-nine. This number – because of its humorous association with a comic book character – was to cause from time to time a certain amount of merriment, both among the public and in the courts.

In those days, when young single policemen were posted to a division they lived in section houses which were appointed in much the same way as Peel House, only with much more privacy. There I became friendly with a young P.C. whose name was Syd Draper, and he joined the Fingerprint Department shortly after I did. When we had been in the Department for a year or two he would say jokingly, 'You for the "Chair", Gerry, and me as your deputy, eh?' He was either a good judge or 'had information', as he might have said, because his forecast became a reality.

An essential part of beat training is to learn the geography of the area. I spent the first two weeks accompanying experienced officers around the sixteen beats of Notting Hill and Notting Dale. During this time I had the opportunity to meet the local inhabitants, most of whom were cheerful, law-abiding citizens. The rest were either out-and-out villains or lived on the fragile edge of respectability. I soon settled down to the shift system: early turn 6 a.m. to 2 p.m.; late turn 2 p.m. to 10 p.m.; and night duty 10 p.m. to 6 a.m. The most difficult shift-change was from late turn to early turn. In other words, to finish duty at 10 p.m. on Sunday and report for duty again eight hours later.

I spent eighteen months in uniform, and I have many memories of those days firmly etched on my memory. One was of the first time I had to deliver a 'dead' message. Informing a wife, husband or parent of the sudden death of a loved one is one of the more unhappy duties undertaken by a policeman. I had learned what I considered to be the accepted conventions of a death in the family: the hushed voices, the comforting arm of a relative or close family friend, the eulogizing of the departed person, the occasional burst of self-recrimination, and invariably the tears. Armed with this worldly knowledge, I made my way to a flat in Notting Dale to tell a woman that her husband had been involved in a street accident, and had died from his injuries. A heavily built middle-aged woman with her hair in curlers, and dressed in a wrapover apron, answered the door. I asked if I might enter her flat, as I had some sad news for her. After we had seated ourselves I told her the unhappy news as gently as I was able. To my astonishment she said, without a touch of remorse or anguish, 'Thank you, but I always told the bastard that he would get his lot one day.'

Then there was Dorothy. She was the first prostitute I ever arrested. It happened on a very hot Sunday afternoon. At a distance she looked reasonably attractive, in a blowsy sort of way. She propositioned potential clients by using the hackneyed 'Have you got a light?' approach. Having watched her for a while, and decided she was a prostitute, I had a quiet word with her and suggested that she stopped plying for hire on my beat. She agreed and left. Needless to say, she returned to her pitch as soon as I walked away.

About half an hour later I returned to the same area to find Dorothy still desperately trying to find a light for her cigarette. When I arrested her she was quite affable, and made various comments about my youth and number. Following my training-school instructions for dealing with an arrested female, I took her to a near-by police box (the blue near-replicas of telephone boxes with the flashing blue lights) and locked her inside, remaining outside to await transport to take her to the police station. When the police van arrived shortly afterwards I opened the door of the police box, and out stepped Dorothy, naked as the day she was born. Smiling, she said, 'Now you won't have to send for the matron to search me, will you, ninety-nine?' Her coat was hastily wrapped around her as she was bundled into the waiting van.

The first serious car accident I dealt with gave me a very sharp lesson about human nature. I was patrolling Shepherd's Bush Green when a taxi pulled in beside me and the driver told me that there was a nasty accident in Holland Park Avenue, and said he would take me there. At the scene I found an Armstrong Siddeley had collided head-on with a Hillman. Both drivers were pinned to their respective steering columns. The passenger of the Armstrong Siddeley had his head through a shattered windscreen, and appeared to be either too stunned or too frightened to move. The taxi-driver said he would telephone for an ambulance and get some help from my station. My first priority was to get the man out of the windscreen. As I opened the car door I was hit by a wave of whisky fumes, and I had no doubt that both driver and passenger were drunk. I removed first the passenger, then the driver, and laid them by the roadside. I started to release the other driver, and shortly afterwards the ambulance, along with a couple of my colleagues, arrived. The second driver was quickly freed and placed in the ambulance. We took the stretchers to collect the other injured men, only to find they had disappeared. All that remained was a pool of blood. I was satisfied that they could not have walked very far, so a search was made – still no trace. The driver was eventually summonsed to answer charges of reckless, dangerous and careless driving. He pleaded guilty, and was heavily fined. After the hearing he told me what had happened. 'You remember the taxi-driver who brought you to the accident?' he said. 'Well, while you were busy with the other driver, he offered to get us both out of it for a fiver. As I was drunk I agreed, so he took us to a hospital on the other side of London.'

I look back on my uniformed service at Notting Hill and Dale with pleasure, because I enjoyed the contact with the public, and my knowledge of human nature was extended considerably during that time. It was a sort of finishing school in human studies.

In the spring of 1947, however, an item appeared in *Police Orders* that was to change my life again. *Police Orders* is a twice-weekly Force publication which gives details of new entrants, retirements, promotions, discipline, transfers, new legislation, and any changes in Force procedure. It is the policeman's 'bible' – if it's not in *Police Orders* it doesn't exist. The particular item which interested me was a request for volunteers to serve in either the Photographic Section or the Fingerprint Branch at New Scotland Yard. As I was a keen amateur photographer, I made an application asking to be considered for the Photographic Section.

I was interviewed by the man who was the head of both sections, Detective Chief Superintendent Cherrill. He had become a legend in his own lifetime as the foremost fingerprint expert in this country. The interview followed a fairly predictable course. 'What had I done before joining the Force? What duties had I carried out since joining the Force? Why did I want to become a photographer? What photographic experience had I? and finally 'Had I used plate cameras?' It was this last question which killed any chance I might have had of being accepted as a police photographer. When I answered 'No', Cherrill told me he could not use me in the photographic section. I thanked him, and turned to leave the room. To my surprise, he called me back and asked me if I would consider fingerprint duties. To this day I do not know why I said 'Yes.' I only know that I never regretted it.

A few weeks later I was told to report for duty in the Fingerprint Department, known as C.3., on the 8th of September 1947. On that day I was to hand in my uniform and become a detective constable of the Criminal Investigation Department.

What a confusing, bewildering yet fascinating world I entered with rows and rows of filing cabinets, filing drawers and people using a language totally alien to anything I had known before – and finger-prints – millions of them. I was one of the ten new entrants to enter the branch on that day. We were issued with the tools of our new trade: a copy of Sir Edward Henry's book, *The Classification and Uses of Fingerprints*, first published in 1900, and a magnifying-glass. I don't mind admitting that I was a little horrified at the smallness of this fixed-focus glass with its one-inch viewing frame. I tried to visualize my life spent crouched peering through it for several hours each day, but apart from some initial discomfort, I quickly adapted to using it.

My biggest surprise at that time came not from within the Branch but outside, among friends, acquaintances, and people to whom I was introduced. I discovered that their attitude towards me was slightly different to that of my pre-Branch days. It appeared that I had taken on some of the mysticism associated with fingerprints, and even palmistry. There would be much rubbing of hands and articles, presumably in order to remove their fingerprints. This performance was usually accompanied by some comment about my new occupation. I soon came to terms with this strange phenomenon by playing along, and on occasions turning fingerprints into a new 'party piece'. I believe most fingerprint men suffer from this occupational hazard.

After six weeks' intensive instruction and indoctrination we at least had some idea of how this unique method of personal identification worked, but it was just the beginning of a seven-year apprenticeship. At the end of that period, if all went well, we would qualify as fingerprint experts and be allowed to give expert evidence in the courts.

We learned that the skin surface on the inner part of the hands differs markedly from that of the general body surface, apart from the soles of the feet. From the tips of the fingers to the flexure of the wrist, and from the extreme sides of the hand, all is covered by a hornier type of skin which takes the form of a system of ridges. Although these run roughly parallel to each other, they change direction, and in so doing form clearly defined patterns on certain parts of the hand. These usually occur where the flesh is mounded, such as the end-joints of the fingers and thumbs, on the palms immediately below the fingers, on the little-finger side of the palm and on the ball of the thumb.

The ridges forming the system are not continuous. There are frequent interruptions in their flow, and where these interruptions occur a ridge characteristic is formed. The ridges and characteristics are formed during the third and fourth month of foetal growth. From birth no changes occur in the detailed configuration of the ridges or characteristics. The only change is that of size. The growth of the ridges matches the growth of the hands.

Identity by finger- or palm-prints is established by comparing the ridge detail in two impressions. With very few exceptions, ridge characteristics are common to all hands, but they appear in the same position, in the same sequence and bear the same relationship to each other only when the impressions have been made by the same finger or palm.

At first we concentrated our attention on the 'clearly defined patterns', known in fingerprint jargon as arches, tented arches, radial loops, ulnar loops, whorls, twinned loops, lateral pocket loops, composites and accidentals. This was the classification system devised by Sir Edward Henry based on these patterns, and it made it possible to search for an individual fingerprint or sets of prints in the national fingerprint collection, which at that time held the fingerprints of about 990,000 persons. It is a sad comment on today's society that when I eventually retired in 1980 the national fingerprint collection held the fingerprints of three million persons.

Having mastered the art of classifying fingerprint forms with ten fingerprints on each, we had our attention directed to the single-fingerprint system, a specialized collection containing the fingerprints of criminals known for breaking into premises. It was the downfall of many careless criminals. The collection consisted of ten separate sub-collections, one for each digit – i.e., all right thumbs, all right forefingers, and so on. Each fingerprint was individually classified and then filed in a logical sequence.

Fingerprints are taken intially to find out if the person in question has a criminal record. If they have not the fingerprint form will be given a unique reference number, and will become the master record form. It is placed in the national records, and will only be activated again if the same person is arrested and charged at some future date.

Providing they consent, a person's fingerprints are usually taken after they have been charged with a recordable offence. Should they refuse, an application will be made to a magistrate for the fingerprints to be taken by the use of reasonable force if necessary. If a person is subsequently found not guilty of the offence the fingerprints taken on that occasion are automatically destroyed.

In 1947 an average of four hundred fingerprint inquiries were received every day, most of them from United Kingdom police forces, but we also received fingerprints daily from all over the world.

On a fingerprint form there are in fact two sets of fingerprints from the same person. One of these – 'rolled' prints – is taken in ten numbered blocks. Each finger is rolled completely from edge to edge in its numbered block. In this way the maximum fingerprint data is recorded. It is essential, because some fingerprint patterns extend around the curve of the finger, and without this data it is possible to arrive at an incorrect classification. The 'plain' impressions are taken simultaneously, without any rolling action. These are taken to ensure that the 'rolled' impressions have been made in the correct sequence (and may possibly be of assistance, moreover, if the rolled impressions are blurred). This precaution was, and still is, vital to prevent a wrong classification. There have been many instances of experienced criminals being 'helpful' to the officer taking their fingerprints by holding out each finger to be printed, and tricking the unwary police-man by presenting them in the wrong sequence. Some have been so clever that on occasion they have conned officers into fingerprinting the same hand twice.

On reception the names on the fingerprint forms are checked through a nominal index. This index consists of cards bearing the name, fingerprint classification and criminal record number of every person whose fingerprints are in the collection, and of course one card for each of their aliases. At the time I joined the Branch this index contained about two million cards. Today it contains in excess of four million cards. If a possible identification is located details are passed to a searching officer, who will make a comparison between the inquiry form and the master set in the collection of the suggested identi-fication. If an identification is established it will be checked by a senior officer before details are passed to the inquiring force. All inquiry fingerprints not linked to a previous record by the nominal index are then classified, and search parameters set for a search in the national collection. A classification formula is created from the type and dis-position of the ten fingerprint patterns on the fingerprint form, coupled with ridge counts and pattern tracings. The final formula has the appearance of a fraction, with numbers and letters arranged in the form of a numerator and a denominator.

In those days all searches were carried out manually. The national records were filed in a classification sequence. The forms themselves were held in bundles of about four hundred compressed between two boards and held in place by a broad strap. Each fingerprint cabinet held sixty-six such bundles, and there were well in excess of two thousand bundles. The searcher would automatically check the work of the classifier, then go to the appropriate part of the collection, open the suggested bundle and make an 'eyeball' check with each form that fell within the search parameters. The magnifying-glass would only be used to check a possible identification. If the fingerprints formed an unusual classification it was possible that only twenty or thirty comparisons would have to be made, but in the common classifications it was a different story. In those cases several hundred comparisons would have to be made, and in exceptional cases several thousands. About one in twenty of the subjects of such searches would be identified, thus preventing the criminal escaping the consequences of his previous record. Once an identification was made, the same validation procedure would be carried out before the result was passed to the inquiring force.

Many months were to pass before we had gained sufficient experience to carry out such searches. These months were filled with the more mundane but nonetheless essential tasks of indexing and classifying. Any errors we made in pattern diagnosis, ridge-counting or classification compilation were rapidly pointed out to us by the searching officers.

For the first few months I was too busy learning my new skills to give much thought to anything other than my day-to-day work, but gradually I found myself becoming absorbed by the power of fingerprint science, and a strong feeling that its full potential had not yet been realized. I had a strong desire to know more about the men who had made it all possible. My knowledge at that time was little more than a potted history.

I had been told that Professor Joannes Evangelista Purkinje was the first person to describe fingerprint patterns in his thesis presented at the University of Breslau in 1823; that Sir William Herschel was the first person to use fingerprints for identification purposes in India between 1858 and 1878; that Sir Francis Galton proved the persistence of ridge characteristics, using material supplied by Herschel; and finally, that it was Sir Edward Henry who had produced the first workable classification system for fingerprints in India in 1897. I also learned of a Dr Henry Faulds, who claimed to be the originator of the fingerprint system. Such frugal information was to be the foundation of a research programme which was to last over thirty years. Strictly speaking, it hasn't finished yet. During this time I visited the Public Record Office, libraries, universities, read many nineteenth-century newspapers, magazines, journals, followed many promising leads which ended all too frequently in dead ends, but the odd cases of serendipity compensated for those. Examples were the day on which I found some letters written by Edward Henry to Francis Galton, and the one on which I found a letter written in 1880 by Faulds to Charles Darwin – especially as Faulds's biographer had stated in 1938 that the letter no longer existed!

It has been a fascinating journey following the historical path taken by the great pioneers of the fingerprint system. They took a concept and converted it into the finest system of personal identification ever known to man. This book traces the history of fingerprints from man's first recorded awareness of them through a period of development to the record-keeping ability and the formation of the Fingerprint Branch at Scotland Yard in 1901. The book then tells how the Scotland Yard Fingerprint Branch has used and developed the system over the past eighty years.

1 Speculation and early interest

Whatever one's beliefs about man's origin, be they theological or anthropological, there can be no doubt that human beings are individualized by their fingerprints. This fact, which has led to man's most perfect of all identification systems, is very much taken for granted today, but the story of how man became aware of this natural phenomenon and developed the fingerprint identification system is far more fascinating than any well-conceived piece of fiction. The fingerprint story falls into four parts, from initial speculation through realization and interpretation to development.

Speculation depends on various artefacts on which fingerprints have been impressed as well as carved configurations which bear a resemblance to fingerprint patterns. The presence of fingerprints on ancient pottery, tiles and tablets has led some theorists to believe that the individuality of fingerprints was understood long before recorded scientific study of the subject. This is unlikely. Undoubtedly ancient potters, like their modern counterparts, were aware of the pleasant designs that were formed when they placed their hands on wet clay.

The carvings on the walls of a Neolithic passage grave on the island of Gavrinis, near Brittany, are described as evidence for ancient knowledge of fingerprinting. The roofing slabs in the grave are held in position by twenty-four large upright rocks. On their surfaces are carved concentric circles, horseshoes, spirals and bending lines. All bear a broad resemblance to fingerprint patterns. Similar patterns are to be found at another Neolithic passage grave at Newgrange, in County Meath, Ireland. The origin and purpose of these markings is unknown, but it is reasonable to assume that they were religious in concept. As most primitive religions of that time were usually closely allied to the natural cycle, the patterns were more likely to be representative of the elements than to be fingerprints.

Many outlined hand stencils, dating back many thousands of years, have been found in some of the famous cave sites in France and Spain. However, one of the most acceptable representations of a hand, from a fingerprint point of view, was found carved into slate rock beside the lake at Kejimkujik Park in Nova Scotia. This carving shows the flexion creases of the hand, and on the tip of the thumb is carved a spiral whorl. Although this carving does not pre-suppose knowledge of fingerprint individuality, it does at least show an awareness of the pattern structure on the fingers. The origin of this petroglyph is obscure, but it is believed to have been carved by an aboriginal Indian, and to be several hundred years old. Records show that tracings of this carving were taken some time before 1873.

The intentional use of fingermarks on legal documents in China and Japan dates back many hundreds of years. In 1894 Kamagusu Minakata drew attention to the old Japanese custom of nail-stamping legal papers by making a mark in ink using the top of the thumb and nail. In the case of contracts accompanied by a written oath, the blood stamp was used: this was a print of the ring finger in blood drawn from that digit. He also quoted Churyo Katsurakawa, a Japanese antiquary, who wrote on the subject:

> According to the 'Domestic Law', to divorce the wife the husband must give her a document stating which of the Seven Reasons was assigned for the action. . . . All letters must be in the husband's handwriting, but in case he does not understand how to write, he should sign with a fingerprint. An ancient commentary on this passage is: 'in case a husband cannot write, let him hire another man to write the document . . . and after the husband's name sign with his own index finger.' Perhaps this is the first mention in Japanese literature of the 'fingerprint' method.

The 'Domestic Law' formed part of the 'Laws of Taiho' enacted in A.D. 702. With some exceptions, the main points of these 'Laws' were borrowed and transplanted from the Chinese 'Laws of Yung-Hwui' (circa A.D. 650–5). Katsurakawa also stated

> That the Chinese apply on divorce papers the stamps of the ends of the thumb and four fingers, which they call 'Shau-mu-ying' (hand pattern stamp) is mentioned in 'Shwui-hu-chuen'.

Minakata stated that *Shwui-hu-chuen* was one of the most popular novels enjoyed by the modern Chinese – it was so popular that he had met many Chinese labourers in the West Indies with a copy of it.

The heroes of this novel flourished about 1160, and its author lived in the twelfth or thirteenth century A.D.

The practice of making fingerprints on legal documents also spread to India, where illiterates signed documents by wetting the tip of one finger with ink from a pen, then touching the document with it. The mark made was called a tep-sai, 'tep' meaning pressure and 'sai' meaning token.

There is no evidence it was known that the marks were individual. As most of them only revealed part of a print or no detail at all, it is most likely that this was a symbolic gesture, in much the same manner that documents are touched when swearing an affidavit or touching the Bible when taking an oath.

The distinction of being the first person to document his findings about the ridges on the hands goes to the seventeenth-century English botanist Dr Nehemiah Grew, Fellow of the College of Physicians and of the Royal Society. In a paper subsequently published in the *Philosophical Transactions for 1684* he wrote:

> For if anyone will but take the pains, with an indifferent glass to survey the palm of his hand very well washed with a ball; he may perceive (besides those great lines to which some men have given names, and those of a middle size called the grain of the skin) innumerable little ridges, of equal bigness and distance, and everywhere running parallel one with another. And especially, upon the hands and first joints of the fingers and thumb, upon the top of the ball, and near the root of the thumb a little above the wrist. In all which places, they are very regularly disposed into spherical triangles and elliptics; as in the hand I have caused to be drawn. Upon these ridges stands the pores, all in even rows, and of that magnitude, as to be visible to a very good eye without a glass. But being viewed with one, every pore looks like a little fountain, and the sweat may be seen to stand therein, as clear as rock water. And as often as it is wiped off, to spring up within them again.

Grew was not to know that over two hundred years later the 'little fountains' would be used to identify criminals at crime scenes.

The ridge formations were referred to again by his contemporary, the Italian anatomist Professor Marcello Malpighi, in the latter's study on the functions of the skin. To this day, the layer of skin below the dermis is named the Malpighian layer.

It was 1823 before anyone described the various patterns formed by the ridges on the fingers. Joannes Evangelista Purkinje, a Bohemia-born professor of physiology at the University of Breslau, presented his thesis, *Commentatio de examine physiologico organi visus et systematis cutanei* (A commentary on the physiological examination of the organs of vision and the cutaneous system) in 1823. In his reference to fingerprint patterns he wrote:

> Our attention is now attracted by the remarkable disposition and flexures of the continuous rugae and sulci in the inner part of the hand and foot, especially in the terminal phalanges of the fingers in general, indeed, some mention of them occurs in every physiological and anatomical handbook. But in an organ of as great importance as the human hand, which serves not only for movements of many different types but especially for the sense of touch, every enquiry, however minute, brings to light some worthwhile information.
>
> After innumerable observations, I have found nine important varieties of patterns of rugae and sulci serving for touch on the palmar surface of the terminal phalanges of the fingers. I present these nine, though the lines of demarcation between types are often obscure; the figures will explain them.

He then described each pattern, and named them: (1) the transverse curves; (2) the central longitudinal stria; (3) the oblique stripe; (4) the oblique loop; (5) the almond whorl; (6) the spiral whorl; (7) the ellipse; (8) the circle; (9) the double whorl. Unfortunately, this 58-page thesis evoked little interest, and remained in obscurity for the next sixty years.

Interest in fingerprints was not confined to anatomists and physiologists. Thomas Bewick, a native of Newcastle upon Tyne, who was a well-known author, naturalist and artist, made a number of wood engravings of fingerprints and printed them in the books he wrote. The first appeared in 1809 in a book entitled *British Birds*. The attention to detail within each print is considerable: even the microscopic pores on the summit of the ridges were included.

Bewick produced two further prints, together with the legend 'Thomas Bewick, his mark' – neither print relating to the other. Whether the prints are copies of his own fingerprints is a matter for speculation; the only positive thing that can be said is that they could only have been engraved by a man with a considerable understanding of the ridge formation of the fingers, and the ridge characteristics within these formations.

In 1975 a painting by Nicolas Poussin entitled *Dance to the Music of Time*, part of the Wallace Collection, was cleaned. The cleaning of the painting allowed a closer technical examination of a feature which had long puzzled students of Poussin. The whole surface of the picture was covered with what appeared to be fingerprints. It had been supposed that these were contained in the varnish, and would disappear if and when the latter was removed. This was not the case. The markings were in fact in the primer.

At the request of the Directors of the Wallace Collection I made a detailed examination of the painting. This revealed that all the finger-prints had in fact been made by the same digit – probably a left thumb – repeatedly pressed into the priming while it was still wet. We shall probably never know if the print belonged to Poussin or one of his assistants, but it is generally accepted that the artist used studio assistants less than any of his contemporaries. What we do know is that this was one instance when fingerprints were employed for a most unusual purpose over three centuries ago.

2 Herschel – the innovator

The individuality of fingerprints was first realized by William Herschel. Born at Slough, on 9 January 1833, he was the eldest son of Sir John Herschel, and grandson of the famous astronomer Sir William Herschel. He spent his childhood in the company of famous scientists, but at his father's request he chose a career other than astronomy. He decided to take up overseas trading. He was sent to Haileybury College, founded in 1809 to educate boys for service with the East India Company. In 1853, when he was twenty, the Company posted him to Bengal. After the Indian Mutiny, in 1858, he automatically became a member of the Indian Civil Service when it took over the affairs of the Company. By the age of twenty-five Herschel was in charge of his first subdivision, with headquarters at Jungipoor, on the upper reaches of the Hooghly river.

In July 1858 he drew up an agreement with a local native named Radyadhar Konai to supply roadmaking material. In order to prevent Konai repudiating his signature, Herschel made him place his right hand-print on the agreement. He later described the scene as follows:

> I dabbed his palm and fingers over with home-made oil-ink used for my official seal, and pressed the whole hand on the back of the contract, and we studied it together, with a good deal of chaff about palmistry, comparing his palm with mine on another impression.

No one knows why Herschel decided to make Konai endorse the contract in this manner. One possible explanation could be that he had heard of, or witnessed, a Hindu suttee ceremony. Suttee was the ritual suicide of a widow on the burning funeral pyre of her dead husband. As she passed through the Suttee Gate on her way to her death the widow would dip her right hand in a red dye and place a print of the inside of it on the gate. Because the elements soon bleached and washed away the dye (and with it the last trace of the dead woman) it became the practice to carve the stonework around the handprint so that it stood out in bas-relief. Although the practice of suttee was outlawed by the British Administration in 1830, many examples of these 'hand-prints' remain to this day. Certainly the 'Konai' handprint looks remarkably like a 'suttee' hand-print.

Herschel was so pleased with this experiment that he carried out a number of trials using his own hands, and soon came to the conclusion that there were advantages in using fingers only as against a whole hand. Shortly afterwards he was transferred to become Magistrate of Arrah, the most north-westerly district of Bengal. He continued his experiments by fingerprinting his colleagues and friends, both British and Indian. Many years later a number of these people were finger-printed again, and the new prints compared with the earlier one. In this way the immutability and persistence of ridge characteristics was first observed.

In 1860 Herschel was sent as Magistrate to Nuddea, a district nearer to Calcutta. There the administration of civil justice was in grave difficulty because of the recent riots caused by the decline of the indigo trade. Indigo, a blue vegetable dye, was no longer in demand. Faced with this situation, Herschel accelerated his fingerprint studies. He eventually sent a letter to the Government of Bengal to suggest administrative action to enforce the use of fingerprints on legal documents. This would prevent false personation and repudi-ation of contracts, the cases that were choking the legal system in that area. Unfortunately, as the situation in this part of India was gradually calming down, it was considered inadvisable to introduce a new system which could raise a new controversy. Although disappointed, Herschel continued his experiments. Early on he had considered the possibility of fingerprints being forged. To test this possibility he sent a number of specimen prints to the best artists in Calcutta and asked them to imitate the prints. Although their efforts were good, they were not good enough to deceive.

In 1864 he married Emma Hardcastle, the youngest daughter of a family who lived near his family home at Hawkhurst, and in 1871, on the death of his father, he succeeded to the baronetcy. His happy married life was cut short after nine years, his wife dying in 1873 at the birth of their fourth child, leaving him with two sons and two daughters.

For a number of years Herschel carried on his interest in finger-prints as a hobby, but the interest and encouragement he received from various people made him determined to give fingerprints an open official trial on his own responsibility. In 1877 he was appointed as Magistrate and Collector at Hooghly, near Calcutta. This appointment gave him control of the criminal courts, the prison and the department for the registration of deeds. He was also responsible for various minor duties, including the payment of government pensions. With such diverse responsibilities, the ground was set for the introduction of fingerprints. His approach, though enthusiastic, was cautious. The memory of the part which cartridges greased with animal fat had played in the Mutiny, so near to Hooghly, was never far from his mind, as he was later to recall:

> I was not a little anxious lest, officially introduced, Hindus might take alarm for their caste. The memory of the greased cartridges of the Mutiny, so near Hooghly, was indelible. In private experiments I had never met any such difficulty, but the old lesson had been a severe one, and I thought it well, when acting officially, to take every precaution. I was careful, therefore, from the first ostentatiously to employ Hindus to take the impressions wanted; using, as if a matter of course, the pad and the ink made by one of themselves from the very seed-oil and lamp-black which were in constant use for the office seals in several departments.

He first introduced the taking of fingerprints of pensioners to prevent their impersonation by others after their death. In general they appeared to approve of the new system. Even the clerks enjoyed the fun of explaining to the pensioners the 'sahib's hikmat [skill]'. He next introduced this system into the office of the Registrar as the final act during the processing of a legal document. After all legal formalities had been completed the Registrar required the person to record the impressions of their right fore and middle fingers simultaneously on the document, and again in a register kept by the Registrar. Many years later Herschel wrote:

> As long as I was at Hooghly I was satisfied that no will or other deed registered there with the new safeguard would ever be repudiated by the actual executant. I have had to think otherwise since then, because many years afterwards a man (in another district) who had given his fingerprint before a Registrar repudiated it. He was summoned to give evidence on oath. It was found that he had cut off the joints of his fingers, hoping to defeat justice by corrupting the witnesses so as to prove that he was not the man they had recognised before the Registrar. The High Court rejected the sworn story of an accident, and confirmed the facts of the registration, with the necessary consequences to the offender for his perjury.

Herschel finally introduced fingerprints into the prison. At that time it was not uncommon for a prisoner or his family to hire a substitute to serve the prescribed prison sentence. Sham death and a conveniently purchased corpse was another method of defeating the rigours of a prison sentence. To ensure that the prisoner could always be accounted for, his fingerprints were placed on the court record, and on the warrant to the gaoler.

Satisfied with the effectiveness and efficiency of the new system, he wrote to the Inspector of Jails and the Registrar-General detailing his ideas, and asked them to give the system a trial. Because of its historic value, the letter – generally referred to as the 'Hooghly letter' – is given in full:

Hooghly, August 15, 1877

MY DEAR B......

I enclose a paper which looks unusual, but which I hope has some value. It exhibits a method of identification of persons, which with ordinary care in execution, and with judicial care in the scrutiny, is, I can now say, for all practical purposes far more infallible than photography. It consists in taking a seal-like impression, in common seal ink, of the markings on the skin of the two forefingers of the right hand (these two being taken for convenience only).

I am able to say that these marks do not (bar accidents) change in the course of ten or fifteen years so much as to affect the utility of the test.

The process of taking the impression is hardly more difficult than that of making a fair stamp of an office seal. I have been trying it in the Jail and in the Registering Office and among pensioners here for some months past. I have purposely taken no particular pains in explaining the process, beyond once showing how it is done, and once or twice visiting the office, inspecting the signatures, and asking the omlah (clerks) to be a little more careful. The articles necessary are such as the daftari [man in charge of stationery] can prepare on a mere verbal explanation.

Every person who now registers a document at Hooghly has to sign his 'Sign-manual.' None has offered the smallest objection, and I believe that the practice, if generally adopted, will put an end to all attempts at personation.

The cogency of the evidence is admitted by every one who takes the trouble to compare a few signatures together, and to try making a few himself. I have taken thousands now in the course of the last twenty years, and (bar smudges and accidents, which are rarely bad enough to be fatal) I am prepared to answer for the identity of every person whose 'sign-manual' I can now produce if I am confronted with him.

As an instance of the value of the thing, I might suggest that if Roger

Tichborne[1] had given his 'sign-manual' on entering the Army on any register, the whole Orton case would have been knocked on the head in ten minutes by requiring Orton to make his sign-manual alongside it for comparison.

I send this specimen to you because I believe that identification is by no means the unnecessary thing in jails which one might presume it should be. I don't think I need dilate on that point. Here is the means of verifying the identity of every man in jail with the man sentenced by the court, at any moment, day or night. Call the number up and make him sign. If it is he, it is he; if not, he is exposed on the spot. Is No. 1302 really dead, and is that his corpse or a sham one? The corpse has two fingers that will answer the question at once. Is this man brought into jail the real Simon Pure sentenced by the magistrate? The sign-manual on the back of the magistrate's warrant is there to testify, &c.

For use in other departments and transactions, especially among illiterate people, it is available with such ease that I quite think its general use would be a substantial contribution towards public morality. Now that it is pretty well known here, I do not believe the man lives who would dare to attempt personation before the registrar here. The mukhtears (Attorneys) all know the potency of the evidence too well.

Will you kindly give the matter a little patient attention, and then let me ask whether you would let me try it in other jails?

The impressions will, I doubt not, explain themselves to you without more words. I will say that perhaps in a small proportion of the cases that might come to question the study of the seals by an expert might be advisable, but that in most cases any man of judgment giving his attention to it cannot fail to pronounce right. I have never seen any two signatures about which I remained in doubt after sufficient care.

Kindly keep the specimens carefully,

Yours sincerely,
W. HERSCHEL

He only received one reply, and that was not particularly encouraging. In 1878, having completed twenty-five years' service in India, and suffering poor health, Sir William Herschel left the country and returned to England.

Twenty-eight years later, at a private dinner party, Herschel was to meet the man who had been the Registrar-General at the time of the 'Hooghly letter', Sir James Bourdillon. It could have been of little consolation to Herschel when Sir James told him that it was his

---

[1]Refers to the case in the late 1860s of an impostor who claimed to be the long-lost son and heir of Sir James Tichborne. The impostor was eventually sentenced to fourteen years' penal servitude.

The Author

Fingerprinting Her Majesty the Queen at Wembley Arena

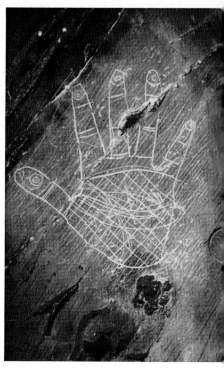

Carvings on a granite wall slab from a Neolithic burial passage at L'Ile de Gavrinis, Brittany

An aboriginal Indian hand-glyph found on slaty rock at the edge of Kejimkujik Lake, Nova Scotia. (The coin at the side indicates the size.)

Gilbert Thompson's order on the camp sutler, incorporating his thumb-print

August 8, 1882.

Mr Jones, Sutter, will pay to Lying Bob seventy five Dollars.

Gilbert Thompson
USGS

his

Thomas Bewick

mark

A wood engraving of fingerprints (possibly his own) by the artist Thomas Bewick

A facsimile of Dr Nehemiah Grew's 1684 description and diagram of the ridges on the hand

For if any one will but take the pains, with an indifferent *Glass*, to survey the *Palm* of his *Hand* very well washed with a Ball; he may perceive (besides those great *Lines* to which some men have given Names, and those of a middle size call'd the *Grain* of the skin) innumerable *little Ridges*, of equal bigness and distance, and every where running parallel one with another. And especially, upon the ends and first Joynts of the *Fingers* and *Thumb*, upon the top of the *Ball*, and near the root of the *Thumb* a little above the *Wrist*. In all which places, they are very regularly disposed into *spherical Triangles*, and *Ellipticks*; as in the Hand I have caused to be drawn *Fig.* 1. Upon these *Ridges* stand the *Pores*, all in even *Rows*, and of that magnitude, as to be visible to a very good Eye without a *Glass*. But being viewed with one, every Pore looks like a little *Fountain*, and the sweat may be seen to stand therein, as clear as rock water, and as often as it is wiped off, to spring up within them again.

Fig. 1

Facsimile reproduction of Grew's description of the papillary ridges and pores and diagram from "Philosophical Transactions for 1684".

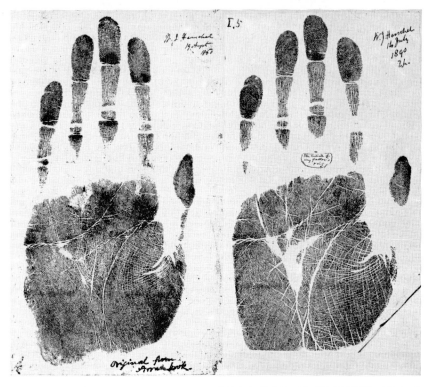

*Two photographs of Sir William Herschel's
left palm-print, taken thirty years apart*

Sir William Herschel

Herschel's Konai Contract (India, 1858)

Francis Galton's first Anthropometric Laboratory (the International Health Exhibition, South Kensington, 1884-5)

ANTHROPOMETRIC
LABORATORY

For the measurement in various ways of Human Form and Faculty.

Entered from the Science Collection of the S. Kensington Museum.

This laboratory is established by Mr. Francis Galton for the following purposes:—

1. For the use of those who desire to be accurately measured in many ways, either to obtain timely warning of remediable faults in development, or to learn their powers.

2. For keeping a methodical register of the principal measurements of each person, of which he may at any future time obtain a copy under reasonable restrictions. His initials and date of birth will be entered in the register, but not his name. The names are indexed in a separate book.

3. For supplying information on the methods, practice, and uses of human measurement.

4. For anthropometric experiment and research, and for obtaining data for statistical discussion.

Charges for making the principal measurements:
THREEPENCE each, to those who are already on the Register.
FOURPENCE each, to those who are not:— one page of the Register will thenceforward be assigned to them, and a few extra measurements will be made, chiefly for future identification.

The Superintendent is charged with the control of the laboratory and with determining in each case, which, if any, of the extra measurements may be made, and under what conditions.

H. & W. Brown, Printers, 20 Fulham Road, S.W.

The description of Galton's Anthropometric Laboratory and its purposes

[*Judy*, July 1, 1891

'... more the prints of hobnailed boots the bobby cute shall gauge
... en forth he starts a crime to track, a criminal to cage.
... matter now how thick and deep the damning footprints fall,
... 'll search for dirty finger-marks upon the tell-tale wall.
... d, having found and studied these, his intellect acute
... ll grasp at once who made the mark beyond the least dispute.
... ce having settled this, he'll start upon the cheerful plan
... taking everybody up—except the proper man.
... tracing crime by finger-marks may very likely come
... much resemble after all the good old rule of thumb.'

The policeman's rule of thumb

A portrait of Sir Francis Galton by Gustav Graef (1882)

The form compiled at the Anthropometric Laboratory

MR. FRANCIS GALTON'S ANTHROPOMETRIC LABORATORY.

...aboratory communicates with the " Western Gallery " in which the Scientific Collections of the South Kensington Museum are contained. Th... ...ern Gallery runs parallel to Queen's Gate, and is entered either from Queen's Gate or from the new Imperial Institute Road. The latter entranc... is close to the Laboratory. Admission is free.

Measurement. Month. Year.	Initials.	Birthday. Day. Month. Year.	Eye Color.	Sex.	Single, Married, or Widowed ?	Page of Register.
12 8⁄9	J.H.S	22 2 70	Brown Grey	m	S	2310

...th, ...n	Head breadth maximum.	Height standing, less heels of shoes.	Span of arms from opposite finger tips.	Weight in ordinary clothing.	Strength of grasp. Right hand. Left hand.	Breathing capacity.	Keenness of Eyesight. Distance of reading diamond numerals. Right eye. Left eye.	Snellen's type read at 20 feet.	Color Sense.
...ths. Inch. Tenths.	Inch. Tenths.	Inch. Tenths.	Inch. Tenths.	lbs.	lbs. lbs.	Cubic inches.	Inches. Inches.	No. of Type	? Normal.
3 5 9½		66 6	67 7	128	93 88	200	19 19	D6	Yes

...sing of	Height of top of knee, when sitting, less heels.	Length, elbow to finger tip, left arm.	Length of middle finger of left hand.	Keenness of hearing.	Highest audible note. (by whistle)	Reaction time. To sight. To sound.	Left Thumb.	Right Thumb.
...s. Inch. Tenths.	5 20 7	17. 7½	4 5	? Normal. Yes	Vibrations per second. 2¹,000	Hundredths of a second. 15	Hundredths of a second. 15	

...e page of the Register is assigned to each person measured, in which his measurements at successive periods are ...n successive lines. No names appear on the Register. Copies of the entries can be obtained through application ...sons measured, or by their representatives, under such conditions and restrictions as may be fixed from time to time.

ARCHES	LOOPS	WHORLS	COMPOSITES

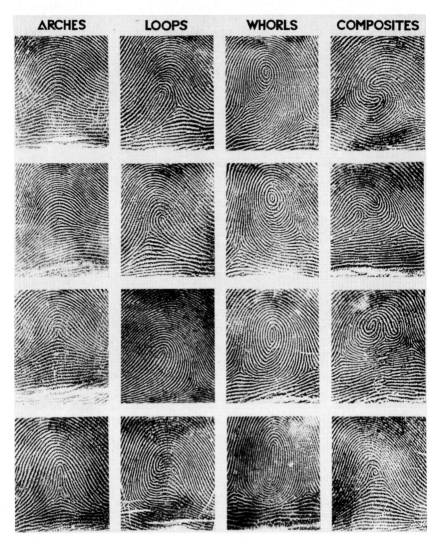

Enlarged photographs of standard types of patterns

constant regret that he let the fingerprint system slip through his fingers. He remembered the letter well, but for some reason he had lost sight of the matter. In any event, the two men became firm friends after this meeting.

In 1879 Dr Henry Faulds, a medical missionary, started to take an interest in fingerprints. He was to become the most controversial person ever to be involved with the science. Faulds was born at Beith, in Ayrshire, on the 1st of June 1843. At the age of twelve he went to Glasgow to work in his uncle's business, and then later he worked for a firm of shawl and dress manufacturers. Determined to improve himself, he attended private classes, and between 1864 and 1867 he attended the Faculty of Arts of the University of Glasgow, studying Latin, Greek, Logic and Mathematics. He later entered Anderson's College, Glasgow, and in 1871 he passed his final examination as a Licentiate of the Royal Faculty of Physicians and Surgeons in Glasgow.

His very strong religious convictions led him to volunteer as a medical missionary to the Foreign Mission Committee of the Church of Scotland. The Committee accepted him, and in November 1871 he was appointed to the Church's Darjeeling Station. His engagement with the Foreign Mission Committee was terminated, however, after one year because of a disagreement between Faulds and the missionary in charge of the station. Undeterred, he applied in the same month – July 1873 – to the Foreign Mission Board of the United Presbyterian Church of Scotland to be sent to Japan, and was accepted. Three months before he sailed to Yokohama he married Isabella Wilson, a lady from Shawlands, Glasgow.

At that time the Japanese Government only allowed foreigners to reside in restricted areas, so Faulds took up residence in the foreign concession in Tsukiji. By 1875 he had opened a missionary hospital there for both Japanese and foreign patients. Its presence was indicated by the flying of a banner on which the red sun of Japan and a white cross were depicted.

The following year he began to set up a medical school. He included himself on the panel of lecturers to teach physiology. He also gave a number of lectures on Darwinism, in which he attacked the atheistic views he believed it fostered. There is no doubt that he endeared himself to the Japanese. Their Government made him honorary Surgeon-Superintendent of the Tsukiji hospital in Tokyo, a post he was to hold from March 1874 until he departed from Japan in 1885. This appointment, however, did not compromise his position as

Medical Missionary. He paid particular attention to those suffering from blindness, and with the co-operation of some Japanese Protestants built a school for the blind.

Early in 1879 Faulds became interested in the fingermarks impressed on prehistoric pottery found at Omori and many other places in the Bay of Yedo. He began to take prints from the paws of monkeys, and later from the hands of people. By 1880 his interest was such that he felt the need of assistance. In spite of his religious convictions regarding the theories of evolution as propounded by Charles Darwin, he wrote a letter to him:

> Tsukiji Hospital,
> Tokio, Japan
> February 16th. 1880

SIR

As an ardent student of your writings I trust I may venture to address you on a subject of interest. I allude to the rugae or furrows on the palmar surface of the human hand. These form singular and intricate patterns which vary in detail with each individual but may be classed according to their leading lines without much difficulty. Now, I have been led to study these in prehistoric pottery and I am engaged in what proves a somewhat difficult task – collecting data from all quarters of such ancient impressions and comparing them with similar impressions of living men of all races. Already I see some glimpses of light but *facts* are hard to get in sufficient numbers. The few monkeys etc. which I have got show similar but *somewhat* different markings and if man's origin has been from organised 'dust' perhaps a comparative study of lemuroids etc. may yield results of real value – I hope for this and bethought myself of your powerful aid – A word or two would set observers working everywhere.

I enclose a filled up form and can send a number to anyone who wishes them. The practical value – and Englishmen will look for that – is in the work of Identification in medico legal studies, thus,

1. Copies of palmar impressions of convicted criminals – as photographs now are used – the latter become unlike the original, the rugae, never.
2. In cases like that of 'Tichborne?' Are his rugae of the Tichborne or Orton type? – for *heredity rules here* marvellously.
3. In cases where mutilated remains are found and various people are missing. The rugae may be compared with that of the parents etc.
4. Where impressions exist of bloody fingers by a murderer, or prints on fresh paint or drinking glasses, windows etc. by a robber –

> Etc.

The Chinese I find since entering on this enquiry, take impressions of this kind from criminals, as our servant girls used to seal their letters with

their *thumbs*. (The Japanese as the ancient Egyptians, use their fingernail.)
Hoping you may find this to be of interest,

I remain
Your obliged reader,
HENRY FAULDS
Surgeon Supt of hospital

It was this letter which led Faulds to claim in his book *Manual of Practical Dactylography*, published in 1923, that 'In 1880 he laid his project of identification by fingerprints before Charles Darwin. . . .' It is interesting to note that in the chronology of the book, which covered a hundred years of fingerprint studies, Faulds makes no mention of Herschel, Galton or Henry.

Unfortunately for Faulds, Charles Darwin was precluded from giving him support, both by reason of his poor health and of the solitary existence which he led in the country. On 7 April 1880 he replied to Faulds[2] in his usual courteous manner, and explained that due to this weak health he was forwarding the letter to Mr F. Galton. True to his word, Darwin wrote to his cousin, Francis Galton, on the same day[3] and suggested that Faulds's letter might be worth taking to the Anthropological Institute. Galton replied to Darwin the following day[4] agreeing with his suggested course of action. This letter gives an interesting insight into Galton's early thoughts on fingerprints:

I myself got several thumb impressions a couple of years ago, having heard of the Chinese plan with criminals, but failed, perhaps from want of sufficiently minute observation, to make out any large number of differences.

Galton sent the letter to the Anthropological Institute, which apparently did nothing with it. Certainly no extract was ever published. Many years later it was found in their archives.

Faulds did not wait too long to see what results his letter to Darwin would bring. He wrote a long and detailed letter to the Editor of *Nature* entitled 'On the skin-furrows of the hand', which was published on the 28th of October 1880,[5] describing how his study of fingerprints on ancient pottery led him to look at the fingerprints of men and monkeys. He commented on the ethnological dissimilarities he had found between prints taken from Japanese and English men,

[2]For full text of letters see Appendix, p.188.
[3]For full text of letter see Appendix, pp.188–9.
[4]For full text of letter see Appendix, p.189.
[5]For full text of letter see Appendix, pp.189–92.

and went on to describe his findings with regard to dominance of heredity. He suggested that a study of these patterns might be useful in several ways:

1. We may perhaps be able to extend to other animals the analogies found by me to exist in the monkey.
2. These analogies may admit of further analysis, and may assist, when better understood, in ethnological classifications.
3. If so, those which are found in ancient pottery may become of immense historical importance.
4. The fingers of mummies, by special preparation, may yield results for comparison. I am very doubtful, however, of this.
5. When bloody fingermarks or impressions on clay, glass &c. exist, they may lead to the scientific identification of criminals. . . .

Many years later this letter, full of interesting observations and suppositions but with a dearth of supporting facts, was to be the cause of a controversy relating to Faulds's claim to be the pioneer of the fingerprint system.

Sir William Herschel, who on his return to England had taken the unusual step of entering the University at Oxford as an undergraduate studying Theology (at the age of forty-five!) read Faulds's letter with interest, and obviously felt that the contributor would be interested in his own 22-year study of fingerprints. His subsequent letter was published in *Nature* on the 25th of November 1880.[6] He outlined his experience of introducing fingerprints into various official areas. He summarized his opinion about their value, referring to them as signatures or sign-manuals, and the persistence of the ridge data in two short paragraphs:

> The ease with which the signature is taken and the hopelessness of either personation or repudiation are so great that I sincerely believe that the adoption of the practice in places and professions where such kinds of fraud are rife is a substantial benefit to morality.
>
> I may add that by comparison of the signatures of persons now living with their signatures made twenty years ago, I have proved that much time at least makes no such material change as to affect the utility of the plan. . . .

When one compares the two letters, the enthusiasm and limited experience of Faulds contrasts with the matter-of-fact approach, based on long experience and practical application, of Herschel. Although neither of them were to communicate publicly on finger-

[6]For full text of letter see Appendix, pp.192–3.

prints for another fourteen years, it is apparent that the contents of their letters reached far and wide. More people began to take an interest in this new concept.

In London in August 1881 at the International Medical Congress, Mr John S. Billing, a surgeon with the United States Army, said:

> Just as each individual is in some respects peculiar and unique, so that even the minute ridges and furrows at the end of his forefinger differ from that of all other forefingers and is sufficient to identify him.

In 1882 Mr Gilbert Thompson was in charge of topographical parties of the United States Geological Survey in the vicinity of Fort Wingate, New Mexico. He made arrangements to pay the members of his party by order of the camp sutler – a camp-follower selling provisions – with whom he had deposited personal funds. In order to protect himself against any alteration in the amount as written, he adopted the additional precaution of making an ink impression of his thumb at the top and bottom of the orders on the left-hand side. He wrote in ink on the upper impression the number of the order and on the lower the amount in figures corresponding to the written value of the order. This was a perfect guarantee against fraud, for not only could he identify his own thumb-mark, but the slightest change or erasure would be detected.

In 1883 Samuel Langhorne Clemens (who wrote under the pen-name 'Mark Twain') had his book *Life on the Mississippi* published simultaneously in London and New York. One story in it tells of a fortune-teller who made use of thumb-prints:

> My apparatus was simple: a little red paint and a bit of white paper. I painted the ball of the client's thumb, took a print of it on the paper, studied it that night, and revealed his fortune to him next day. What was my idea in this nonsense? It was this: When I was a youth, I knew an old Frenchman who had been a prison-keeper for thirty years, and he told me that there was one thing about a person which never changes, from the cradle to the grave – the lines in the ball of the thumb; and he said these lines were never exactly alike in the thumbs of any two human beings. In these days, we photograph the new criminal, and hang his picture in the Rogues Gallery for future reference; but that Frenchman, in his day, used to take a print of the ball of a new prisoner's thumb and put that away for future reference. He always said that pictures were no good – future disguises could make them useless. 'The thumb's the only sure thing,' said he; 'you can't disguise that.' And he used to prove his theory, too, on my friends and acquaintances; it always succeeded.

In 1886 Mr I. W. Taber, a photographer of 8 Montgomery Street, San

Francisco, discovered fingerprints by chance. He accidentally inked his thumb, and noticed that the impression left on a blotting-pad was singularly lined. He photographed and enlarged this thumb-print. With his interest aroused, he took thumb-prints of a number of people, including members of the local Chinese community, and made photographic enlargements of these prints and exhibited them outside his premises. At that time the Chinese Restriction Act was operative, so Taber sent copies of these enlarged thumb-prints together with a letter to the United States House of Representatives suggesting that thumb-prints be used in identifying Chinese immigrants. After a careful examination of the whole subject, it was determined that the best identification was by the whole photograph of the face, and that was the judgment of the best detectives in the country.

3 Galton – the interpreter

The interpretation of fingerprints for general use as a method of identification was to be the work of Francis Galton, one of the greatest scientists of the nineteenth century. He was born at The Larches, near Sparbrook, Birmingham, on 16 February 1822. Of Quaker origin, he was the last of nine children born to a successful and wealthy banker. Even as a child he displayed a remarkable level of intelligence, and eventually his parents decided he should study medicine. At sixteen he became a House Pupil at Birmingham General Hospital, and a year later went to King's College, London. While on a visit to Germany to attend lectures on chemistry he developed an insatiable desire to travel, and promptly embarked on a tour of south-east Europe. In October 1840 he went up to Trinity College, Cambridge, to study mathematics, and in spite of a breakdown in his health he took his BA in January 1844. He then continued his medical studies. Before they were completed, his father's death gave him the necessary financial independence to enable him to abandon the medical profession and embark on further foreign travel.

Having partaken of leisurely expeditions up the Nile and in the Holy Land, he organized an expedition into an unexplored area of South-West Africa. These efforts were recognized in 1853, when he was elected a Fellow of the Royal Geographical Society, and three years later, at the age of thirty-four, of the Royal Society.

In his time he was to write nine books and over two hundred papers on many diverse subjects such as foreign travel; statistics; meteorology; the efficacy of prayer; mental imagery; burial in the Abbey; psychometric experiments; pedigree moths; and three generations of lunatic cats. Overall, his principal scientific passion, undoubtedly encouraged by his cousin Charles Darwin, was people: how their minds worked, how their bodies worked, could the human race be improved by artificial selection – or, in his terms, the science of human eugenics. In order to quantify his theories he needed a large amount of data. An opportunity to obtain some of this came at the time of the International Health Exhibition held in London in 1884. He equipped and maintained a laboratory there to take various measurements, such as: keenness of sight and hearing; colour sense; visual judgment; breathing-power; reaction time; strength of pull and squeeze; force of blow; span of arms; height, both standing and sitting; and weight. At the end of the exhibition Galton was so encouraged with the results that he asked for, and was given, a room in the Science Museum at South Kensington. He maintained a laboratory there for about six years.

Galton's interest in fingerprints did not surface until 1888. In that year he was requested to give a Friday-evening lecture at the Royal Institution on what was briefly called 'Bertillonage', a system devised by M. Alphonse Bertillon for identifying people by the measurements of their bodily dimensions. Dubbed 'The Anthropometric System' by its inventor, it had been introduced in Paris on an experimental basis late in 1882 to identify French criminals who had been previously convicted. The first identification was made on February the 20th, 1883, and by the end of the year a further twenty-six prisoners were identified. Bertillon's success was eventually rewarded in February 1888, when he was appointed Director of the police Identification Service.

Galton was quite prepared to give an account at the Royal Institution as requested, but since he was an original thinker, he also wanted to introduce new work of his own. He recalled that finger-prints had been written about at some time in the past. A letter to the editor of *Nature* soon put Galton in communication with Sir William Herschel, who was very happy to impart his fingerprint knowledge to Galton and provide him with material from his own collection. To this and other miscellaneous information on fingerprints Galton added his own observations, and presented it together with an appraisal of 'Bertillonage' to the Royal Institution under his modified title 'Personal Identification and Description'.

It was at this meeting that Galton gave the first public demon-stration of the persistence of ridge characteristic data by producing prints of Sir William Herschel's right forefinger and right middle finger made in 1860 and prints of the same two fingers made twenty-eight years later in 1888. Copies of these prints and an account of Galton's lecture appeared in *Nature* the following month.

In the following seven years Galton was to do more than any other man of his time to promote and popularize – if that is the right word – fingerprints. The taking of thumb-prints was added to the list of measurements taken at his laboratory in the Science Museum, but this was soon varied to the securing of prints from all ten digits, when he noticed the variable distribution of patterns on each. He amassed a vast collection of fingerprints, not only of Englishmen but also of Welsh, Hindus, Jews, Negroes, and special groups of idiots and criminals. He published his first authoritative book on the subject, entitled simply *Fingerprints*, in 1892. It was a masterpiece of analysis and understanding. Acknowledging the contribution by Faulds, he nevertheless wrote of Herschel:

> If the use of fingerprints ever becomes of general importance, Sir William Herschel must be regarded as the first who devised a feasible method for regular use, and afterwards officially adopted it.

The following year Galton published a supplement to his book entitled *Decipherment of Blurred Finger Tips*.

Galton's studies of personal identification were most timely, as considerable disquiet was being voiced about the unsatisfactory methods available for identifying criminals. Many were avoiding the consequences of previous criminal convictions by the simple expedient of giving false names when arrested. They knew it was unlikely that they would be recognized as recidivists.

Earlier attempts at maintaining criminal records date back to 1755, when Sir John Fielding established at Bow Street a central register of burglars, housebreakers and receivers. These records were presumably of a local nature, and unfortunately faded into obscurity after a while. A likely explanation for this was the large-scale transportation of criminals to the colonies during the last half of the eighteenth century and the first half of the nineteenth which lessened the need for such records.

The Habitual Criminals Act 1869 first established the Habitual Criminals Register. This was the only agency especially established by Parliament, and was intended for general use throughout the country in the work of identifying old offenders. This Act was very soon repealed, and partially re-enacted by the Prevention of Crimes Act 1871. Section 6 of that Act stated that:

> Registers of all persons convicted of crime . . . shall be kept in such form and contain such particulars as may from time to time be prescribed . . . by the Secretary of State. . . . The Register for England shall be kept in

London, under the management of the Commissioner of Police of the Metropolis, or such person as the Secretary of State shall appoint.

At first the register included all persons convicted of crime, but it was soon found that the registration of criminals was being carried out on far too large a scale. A large proportion of the persons registered were not habitual criminals in any ordinary sense of the term; many of them were first offenders, and children convicted of trivial thefts. By Lord Cross's Regulations of 15 March 1877, the register was confined to 'every person convicted on indictment of a crime, a previous conviction of a crime being proved against him'.

The Habitual Criminals Register was published annually, and contained all habitual criminals and convicts who had been liberated between 1 January and 31 December of the previous year. All the names were in alphabetical order, and gave, in columns opposite to each name, the prisoner's full description at the time of his discharge, including his distinctive marks, the particulars of his last conviction, his destination on discharge and the number of his previous convictions, with references to entries in previous registers. From details gleaned from the Habitual Criminals Register, a Register of Distinctive Marks was also produced. This register was published annually, but contained details of criminals who had been released in the preceding five years.

The work of identifying criminals in the Metropolitan Police District was managed by the Convict Supervision Office, a department originally formed to deal with convicts and others under sentence of police supervision within the Metropolitan District. It gradually increased its activities to deal with the whole of the crime records within the District. The Office maintained albums of photographs of all convicts and other habitual criminals. In the early volumes, photographs were arranged chronologically as they were received. Gradually they were subdivided according to the age and stature of the person concerned and the type of crime committed. A very elaborate register of distinctive marks was maintained, and supplementary to this was an alphabetical register of tattooed initials and names.

Although these methods of identifying criminals had limited success, it was quite apparent by 1893 that a more effective method of identifying criminals was urgently needed. One Chief Constable was so impressed by the difficulties of identifying criminals that he suggested the desperate solution that the arm of the criminal about to be discharged should be tattooed with a letter, a number and the year of his discharge.

In June 1893 the influential Council of the British Association for the Advancement of Science communicated its concern regarding the poor system of identification then prevailing to the Secretaries of State for the Home Department, Army, Navy, India and the Colonies:

> Considering the recognised need of a better system of identification than is now in use in the United Kingdom and its dependencies, whether for detecting deserters who apply for re-enlistment, or old offenders among those who are accused of crime, or for the prevention of personation, more especially among the illiterate, the Council of the British Association express their opinion that the anthropometric methods in use in France and elsewhere deserve serious inquiry, as to their efficiency, the cost of their maintenance, their general utility, and the propriety of introducing them, or any modification of them, into the Criminal Department of the Home Office, into the Recruiting Departments of the Army and Navy, or into Indian and colonial administration.

Galton was not present when the original resolution was framed, but was appointed a member of the committee to whom the Council referred it for a report. Although he agreed with it, he did not believe it covered all the options available. To make his views known, he wrote a lengthy letter to *The Times*, in which he referred to the Association resolution and the Anthropometric system. The rest is worth quoting in full:

> The results of my own inquiries are that we may consider it to be almost proved, that Anthropometric Records, including measures of the head and limbs, bodily marks, and fingerprints, admit of being so classified that a register, or rather a collection of assorted cards, consisting of considerably more than 100,000 different records may be searched with surprisingly little trouble, somewhat on the principle of a dictionary, in order to learn whether a record of any suspected person is contained in the collection or not.
>
> Another safe conclusion is that, leaving fingerprints for the moment out of consideration, there can be little doubt whether or no two different records refer to the same person, it being supposed that both were taken when the person was adult and by operators who have been instructed in their duties. If, however, fairly clear impressions of the fingers are included in the records, the strong probability becomes changed into practical certainty, at whatever age the first impression may have been taken and however long may have been the interval between its date and that of the second one. The evidence of this is published in my two books as above.

The trustworthiness of these conclusions may safely be accepted provisionally, so far as to justify two preliminary inquiries, which Government could easily make, but which are almost beyond the powers of private persons. They have merely to frame appropriate questions to their own officials, and ask for brief reports in reply. The first is as to the various economies which would result from a sure and easy method of identification such as the Paris method professes to supply. . . . Under our present system a considerable total of annual expenditure appears to be incurred, partly in summoning police from a distance as witnesses to previous convictions, partly through prolonging the period of detention of prisoners before the required evidence of identity can be collected to justify the case being sent for trial. It ought not to be difficult to obtain through official inquiries a useful approximation to the annual cost under these heads. Again, the opinions might be gathered of persons well versed in conducting prosecutions, as to the annual number of cases in which justice has presumably failed, where, under the Paris system, always supposing it to be as efficient as is said, there would have been a conviction, together with the cost of these futile prosecutions. I have asked lawyers, but failed to obtain a trustworthy estimate of the average cost of each criminal trial, taking into account the shares of the paid-for time of all the officials concerned in it, from the Judge down to the policemen, and, further, including the average cost of the prisoner during his imprisonment before the trial, and such other items as may fairly be put down to the score.

Lastly, the probable gain has to be considered that would be due to the deterrent effect of increased probability of identification. According to Bertillon's statement, foreign pick-pockets now frequent Paris in steadily diminishing numbers; the statistics of crime show it, and the prisoners themselves acknowledge it on the ground that their previous careers are more easily traced under the present system than heretofore. Leaving moral considerations aside, each crime that is prevented is a money gain, inasmuch as the expense of prosecution and imprisonment is also prevented. In other words, each crime that is committed which a better system of identification would have prevented, is to be counted as so much cost. The cost due to desertions in the army and navy, and that due to the personation of deceased pensioners, could similarly be traced out. As to India and some of the colonies, the hindrances in the way of justice, and the consequent cost of an ineffective means of identification, are greater than here. This is partly due to the large proportion of their illiterate populations, who make marks but cannot write, partly on account of the difficulty felt by most Europeans in accurately distinguishing the features of men of the darker races, and partly on account of the prevalence of false witness among them. I have published evidence of all this in my book on fingerprints.

So much for one side of the account; we have next to consider the other side to which the second branch of the inquiries would be directed –

namely, the cost of an effective system of identification. That of the French method is, of course, procurable officially; it is given in part in the pamphlet above mentioned, and which is stated to be taken from official sources, together with the allotment of the times of the officials to the several portions of their work. It is not possible to go far into this in an already too long letter, so I will dwell only on broad facts – namely, that the clerks, who work eight hours a day, are engaged during the morning half of their time in making measurements and during the afternoon half in verifications, searches, copyings, and correspondence. Again, the time occupied in measuring is such that two clerks, working together, the one being engaged in making the measurements or observations, and in calling them out, the other clerk being occupied in registering them, can thoroughly deal with six prisoners in the space of an hour. Consequently it costs the third part of the hourly pay of a single clerk to measure a man, say 4d. The cost of the afternoon time would be the same, and let an additional 4d. be thrown in for all kinds of additional expense, including that of superintendence, these amount to a total of 1s. per prisoner. These are the two preliminary inquiries that are much needed; then, since one of them will afford a rough estimate of the gain that would follow a more efficient system of identification than we possess in England, and the other would tell us the cost of Bertillonage, with or without modifications, we can strike the balance between them. I do not myself doubt that the estimated gain will be found to exceed the estimated cost very considerably. . . .

As to fingerprints, my collection is ample. Only a few days since I received complete sets of the impressions of all ten digits of no less than 964 natives of India, mostly prisoners, that had been very kindly taken for me by Surgeon Lieut.-Col. Hendley at Jeypore. They are printed in water colour, which is a less good method than that of printer's ink; nevertheless, although they are blurred, nearly all of them can be surely classified by entering each successive digit under one or other of three or four very distinct heads, in the way I have published. I possess between two and three thousand complete sets of English prints, made at my laboratory, and some 300 repeated impressions, all of which are beautifully printed, and, in consequence, very easy to deal with and excellent for purposes of sure identification. It occupies my assistant about one minute to take one complete set of impressions of the ten digits of each person. This collection affords abundant material for testing the powers of fingerprint classification, the addition of which to Bertillonage would multiply the registering power of the latter by considerably more than a hundredfold. Whatever small trouble the existing form of Bertillonage may give to hunt out a required record from a collection of 10,000, less than that same small amount of trouble certainly suffices to hunt out a particular set of fingerprints from a collection of 100 of them. As the measures and the patterns of the fingerprints are proved to be wholly unrelated to one another, it follows that two doses of the same small trouble would suffice to hunt out any one complete record from a collection of a million different ones, in each of which the fingerprints had been included.

Galton once again demonstrated his talent for reducing great difficulties to the most simple terms. This masterly summary of a possible solution to a very unsatisfactory situation could not fail to impress anyone who had responsibilities in this particular field. Just over three months later the Home Secretary appointed a committee to carry out the inquiries Galton had suggested. The terms of the warrant were:

I hereby nominate and appoint –
   Charles Edward Troup, Esquire, of the Home Office;
   Major Arthur Griffiths, Inspector of Prisons, and
   Melville Leslie Macnaghten, Esquire, Chief Constable in the
      Metropolitan Police Force;
   as a Committee to enquire (a) into the method of registering and
   identifying habitual criminals now in use in England; (b) into the
   "Anthropometric" system of classified registration and identification in
   use in France and other countries; (c) into the suggested system of
   identification by means of a record of finger marks; to report to me
   whether the anthropometric system or the finger-mark system can with
   advantage be adopted in England either in substitution for or to
   supplement the existing methods, and if so, what arrangements should
   be adopted for putting them into practice, and what rules should be
   made under section 8 of the Penal Servitude Act, 1891, for the
   photographing and measuring of prisoners.

I further appoint the said Charles Edward Troup, Esquire, to be
Chairman, and Harry Butler Simpson, Esquire, of the Home Office, to
be Secretary of the said Committee.

Given at Whitehall, this twenty-first day of October, 1893.

                                        H. H. Asquith

4 The Troup Committee and compromise

The Troup Committee tackled their task with determination and enthusiasm. Within two weeks of being formed they sent a questionnaire to twenty-one police forces seeking information on their identification procedures and the value of the registers produced by the Habitual Criminals Registry. The replies revealed a curious combination of inefficiency and apathy, coupled with a partisan approach by a number of forces.

The provincial forces relied heavily on the 'route form' to identify travelling criminals. The route form was a document which displayed a photograph and a written description of the prisoner charged with a criminal offence, and a list of police and prison authorities most likely to have had the prisoner in custody on some previous occasion. The form was passed from one authority to another until it was completed and returned to the inquiring force. In spite of this cumbersome procedure, most route forms could complete their journey in one week.

The Metropolitan Police did not rely solely on the Convict Supervision Office for all its identifications. They also carried out an inspection of remand prisoners in Holloway Prison. To this prison were sent all persons committed for trial or remanded by magistrates within the Metropolitan Police District. Here three times a week prison warders from Wormwood Scrubs, Pentonville, Wandsworth and Chelmsford prisons, together with detectives from the then twenty-two Metropolitan Police Divisions, an inspector from New Scotland Yard and six officers from the City of London Police, viewed the unconvicted prisoners as they exercised. In this way a prisoner (whose identity was unknown) would often be recognized either by a warder who had known him in prison or by a police officer who had had him in custody on some previous charge. During 1893, 1,949 such identifications were made at Holloway.

In spite of this procedure the proportion of criminals identified in London was smaller than in any other part of the country, with the exception of Dorset, Devon and Cornwall. In the first three months of 1893 the percentage of prisoners tried in London known to have been previously convicted was only 47 per cent, while in Lancashire, the West Riding of Yorkshire and Staffordshire it was about 70 per cent, in Liverpool, Birmingham and Bradford 79 and in Norfolk and Suffolk it was 61.

The Committee travelled extensively, talking to Chief Constables, detectives, prison governors and prison officers, as well as representatives from the Home Office and the office of the Director of Public Prosecutions. They also visited the Habitual Criminals Registry of the Home Office and the Convict Supervision Office of the Metropolitan Police, and discussed their working methods with the staff of each. A picture of a very unsatisfactory identification system emerged. They heard of cases of wrong identifications. One case in particular was sufficient to raise doubts about the safeguards available to prevent such errors. In the early hours of the 4th of May 1893 Percy Albert Blake had been found in a pawnbroker's shop in the Strand in circumstances which pointed strongly to a deliberately planned burglary. He gave a rambling and incoherent account of himself, and it became evident that he was either a lunatic or a clever and dangerous burglar.

The police constable who arrested Blake had searched the collection of photographs at the Convict Supervision Office, and he believed that his prisoner could be identified with one Henry Steed, alias John Blake, who had been convicted of attempted burglary in July 1881. Persons who had known Steed agreed that the person held was the same man. Evidence to this effect was given at Bow Street Magistrates Court by the police constable who had had charge of the case against Steed in 1881, by another constable who was present at Steed's conviction, by a retired police constable who had also been involved in the Steed case, and by a retired prison warder who had seen Steed daily at Pentonville Prison while he was serving his sentence of eighteen months' imprisonment. The description in the Convict Office of Steed, however, stated that his right leg showed signs of a fracture. At Bow Street a surgeon gave evidence that there were no signs of a fracture on either of P. A. Blake's legs, though expressing the opinion that all signs of a fracture might disappear in time. There was also evidence given on the prisoner's behalf showing that he could not be the man who was convicted under the name of Steed in 1881.

Blake was committed for trial. The prosecution was undertaken by the Treasury, and careful inquiries were at once made in various directions to test the truth of the statements made in his defence. As the result of these inquiries, evidence was obtained of Blake's having been at liberty at the time when Steed was undergoing the sentence passed on him in 1881. Blake was acquitted, but sadly only to be committed to an asylum. Subsequent investigations left no doubt that he was entirely innocent of this previous conviction at first ascribed to him.

The Committee felt that in this case the personal description of Steed was too vague to establish an identification even had there been no discrepancies. It was too uncertain to prevent a misidentification when discrepancies occurred. The mistake arose either from a very strong resemblance between P. A. Blake and Steed or from a very defective recollection on the part of no less than four persons. It was only corrected by what may be described as evidence of an alibi – evidence which might not have been available if a similar mistake were to occur in another case.

As well as cases of wrong identifications, the committee also heard of failures to identify old offenders. One case was singled out, and described as remarkable. A convict under sentence of five years' penal servitude was released on licence in London in August 1892. In October he was brought up at the Mansion House Police Court for stealing a watch. Not being recognized, he was convicted summarily and sentenced to six weeks' imprisonment. On reception into Pentonville his identity was discovered, and the Secretary of State thereupon revoked his licence. In the ordinary course of events he was released on a new licence in August 1893. In November he was again charged at the Mansion House Police Court, again treated as a first offender, and sentenced on this occasion to a term of three months' imprisonment. It was only on his reception into Pentonville that his real name and antecedents were again brought to light.

In order to obtain a greater understanding of the anthropometric identification system, the Committee visited Paris. They had discussions with M. Louis Lepine, the Prefect of Police, M. Gordon, the head of the Sûreté and, of course, M. Alphonse Bertillon. Although Bertillon was not noted for his social graces, he received his visitors and discussed his system with them in a most cordial manner.

The principle of the anthropometric system was the unique combination of measurements obtained from the length of 'bony structures' in the body which, in the case of adults, remain stable.

Cards bearing this data were then filed in such a way that it was possible to take the measurements of any person and identify them if they had been previously measured, even if that person had given a false name and particulars. Although Bertillon took many measurements, the five most important – which formed the basis of the classification in the Anthropometric Register – were the length and width of head, and the lengths of the left forearm, left foot and left middle finger, these being selected as the most constant measurements in individuals. The Committee was impressed with the apparent simplicity and efficiency of the system but they were quick to recognize that this apparently infallible scheme had an Achilles heel, the skill and integrity of the measurer.

Back home the English champions of anthropometry added their support to the French system. Dr John George Garson, a vice-president of the Anthropological Institute, after giving supporting evidence to the Committee, concluded by saying: 'I consider the adoption of the anthropometric method of identification in England is very desirable, and would mutually be of advantage both to ethnological science and to criminal anthropology.' Mr Edmund R. Spearman, a Justice of the Peace, also gave supporting evidence. He had resided in Paris for a number of years, had studied the Bertillon system, and in fact had been the first person to bring it to the notice of the Home Office in 1887.

Troup and his colleagues paid several visits to Galton's laboratory, and were impressed with the accuracy and clearness with which fingerprints could be taken, together with the simplicity of the method. Galton, together with his assistant, Sergeant Randal, accompanied the members of the Committee to Pentonville prison and superintended the taking of the fingerprints of more than a hundred prisoners. In every case perfectly clear and complete fingerprints were obtained, the only two exceptions being two prisoners with amputations.

Galton demonstrated his ability to classify a collection of 2,645 cards using three pattern 'descriptors' – arch, loop and whorl, with an added descriptor for loops on forefingers of radial or ulnar. He also demonstrated his ability to identify a person within this collection. Unfortunately, fingerprint patterns do not occur in equal numbers – in other words, there are more loops than the combined total of arches and whorls. This produces an imbalance between various groupings, which even in a small collection was quite noticeable. Some sections had only one card in them, while the largest section had 164 cards.

The Committee would have liked to have adopted Galton's system as the sole basis of identification, but they recognized (as did Galton) that the weakness of the system lay not in the concept but in the classification and filing. Although suitable for a small collection, it probably would be totally inadequate for a collection of many thousands.

Eventually the Committee recommended a compromise: to take the five major measurements of the Bertillon system and use them for a primary classification, and to employ Galton's fingerprint system for the subdivisions. They further recommended that the measurements and fingerprints should be taken in prisons by prison warders and should afterwards be classified and used for identification through a central registry for the whole of England.

Now that they had proposed a new Anthropometric Registry, the Committee attached it to the Convict Supervision Office of the Metropolitan Police. They also suggested that ultimately it might be found convenient to transfer the Habitual Criminals Registry to New Scotland Yard. The Committee produced its report for the Home Secretary on the 12th of February 1894, and on the 4th of July in the same year the new Anthropometric Registry was formed with Mr R. Anderson, the Assistant Commissioner of Police for the Criminal Investigation branch, as its first Registrar and Dr J. G. Garson as scientific adviser.

The publication of this report stirred an adverse reaction in at least two people. The first person hid behind the pseudonym of 'Observer' when writing to *The Times* regarding an article on the 'Troup report'. Having introduced his subject, he continued:

> . . . but it seems that the taking of nice measurements is to be intrusted to police officers and prison warders, as is the 'deciphering' of the 'papillary ridges which cover the tip of the human finger.' These officers, the vast majority of whom are most excellent men, are to become 'experts' in distinguishing between the various types of 'arches, loops, radial loops, ulnar loops, or whorls.' And upon their accuracy in making distinctions of this character are to depend the reputation and liberty of incriminated Englishmen who may possibly be innocent. An Englishman charged, by some mistake, with having committed some crime, and with being an old offender, might object to the indignity of being submitted to the 'five primary measurements' of M. Bertillon, and might see fit to resist attempts of police officers and warders to 'reckon him up' in this way. A very slight amount of resistance would involve inaccuracy in taking the measurements. Accuracy could be obtained, in such a case, only by placing the supposed culprit under some sort of restraint – restraint of the kind that could be effected by the muscles of the constables and warders. That may

answer very well on the Continent, where everyone submits patiently to the inevitable, but it would not do in England, and I trust the recommendations of the committee – opposed as they are to the sentiments and principles of Englishmen – will not meet with the approval of the Secretary of State.

The second angry person was Dr Henry Faulds. Upon his return to this country he had settled as a medical practitioner at Fenton in Staffordshire. He objected to the 'Troup committee' report, stating that the fingerprint system had been first suggested – and to some extent applied practically – by Sir William Herschel. Faulds wrote to the chairman of the committee asking where they had obtained their evidence on this point. The chairman's reply referred him to Galton's book *Fingerprints*. Although Faulds had not taken any active part in the development of fingerprint science for fourteen years, he was obviously offended that his one contribution – his letter of 1880, also mentioned in Galton's book – had been ignored. In a long letter to *Nature* published on the 4th of October 1894[1] he drew attention to this apparently deliberate omission from the report, and continued:

> As priority of publication is generally held to count for something, and as I knew absolutely nothing of Sir W. Herschel's studies, nor even heard of anyone in India who did, some little evidence on the point of priority would be of interest even now. . . .

Herschel obliged – on the 22nd of November 1894 Herschel's reply was published in *Nature*[2]:

> I have been quite unable, since I saw Mr. Faulds' letter in your issue of October 4, to take the matter of it in hand hitherto; and I do so now only because I think Mr. Faulds is entitled to raise the question if he pleases. To the best of my knowledge, Mr. Faulds' letter of 1880 was, what he says it was, the first notice in the public papers, in your columns of the value of fingerprints for the purpose of identification. His statement that he came upon it independently in 1879 (?1878) commands acceptance as a matter of course. At the same time I scarcely think that such short experience as that justified his announcing that the finger-furrows were 'for-ever unchanging.'
>
> How I chanced upon the thing myself in 1858, and followed it up afterwards, has been very kindly stated on my authority by Mr. Galton, at whose disposal I gladly placed all my materials on his request. Those published by him are only a part of what were available. (See his

[1]For full text of letter see Appendix, pp.193–5.
[2]For full text of letter see Appendix, pp.195–6.

'Fingerprints,' page 27, and his 'Blurred Fingerprints.') To what is there
stated I need now only add, at Mr. Faulds' request, a copy of the
demi-official letter which I addressed in 1877 to the then Inspector-General
of Jails in Bengal. That the reply I received appeared to me altogether
discouraging was simply the result of my very depressed state of health at
the time. The position into which the subject has now been lifted is
therefore wholly due to Mr. Galton through his large development of the
study, and his exquisite and costly methods of demonstrating in print the
many new and important conclusions he has reached. . . .

Galton drew the attention of Faulds to the letter, and received the
following reply:

> Fenton 'Potteries'
> December 3rd. 1894

DEAR SIR,

I have just got a copy of "Nature" containing Sir W. Herschel's
letter and I am much obliged to you for calling my attention to it. The
matter of indexing to which you allude was simply that the incorrect
spelling was repeated in the index to your book, which by the way I got a
copy of and appreciate very greatly. I have lent it to all our Sergeants and
Inspectors in this district and they have been much interested. My address
has always been correctly given in the medical dictionary. As I may do
something with my material by and by, please excuse me from lending it
for your publications. You must always deserve the greatest credit for your
lucid and masterly exposition of the subject.

> I am dear sir,
> Yours sincerely,
> H. FAULDS

As this epistle was written fourteen years after Faulds's original letter
on the subject, his remark 'As I may do something with my material
by and by' could indicate that he had not made much progress in his
fingerprint studies since 1880.

In later years Faulds was to claim that in 1889 (five years before his
letter to Galton) he offered to create a small bureau at Scotland Yard,
free of expense, in order to test its value and practicability. The fact
that he met with Inspector Tunbridge of Scotland Yard at some time
is not in doubt, and that they discussed fingerprints is highly
probable, but from the wording of Faulds's letter to Galton there can,
however, be little doubt that he did not have a system available to
operate a fingerprint collection.

5 Henry and Vucetich – the developers

Meanwhile, overseas, the son of an English doctor in India and a Dalmatian immigrant in Argentina were both already very involved with fingerprints.

The English doctor's son was Edward Richard Henry, who was destined to be the person who finally developed the fingerprint identification system. He was born at Shadwell on the 26th of July 1850, educated at St Edmund's College at Ware, and in 1867 he became a junior clerk at Lloyds. Having a strong desire to improve his capabilities, he became a part-time student at University College, London, the following year. Within two years he had passed for the Indian Civil Service at an open competitive examination. After spending two years at Haileybury College he went out to India, in the North-Western Province Civil Service. Towards the end of 1873 there were indications that Behar and parts of Bengal were about to endure a period of famine. The signs became so evident that the Indian Government decided to strengthen the Bengal administration by drafting additional officers from other provinces. Edward Henry was sent, among others, and was placed in charge of the Darbhanga famine circle. At the conclusion of the famine operations he was permanently transferred to the Lower Provinces.

Between 1874 and 1890 Henry held a wide range of posts, each with increasing responsibility, within the provinces. He served in Champaran, a region as much famed for opium-production as for indigo. Later he returned to Behar to cope with another period of the near-famine which was experienced in several districts of the division during the cold weather in 1888–9. The following year he was appointed as Secretary to the Revenue Board and deputed to investigate land tenures.

With such a variety of experience and responsibility, Henry was an admirable choice, in 1891, for appointment as the Inspector-General of Police for the Lower Provinces, Bengal.

It was the case with most law-enforcement agencies of that time that the ability to identify previous offenders was very rough-and-ready, relying heavily on tattoos and scars for indexing criminals. By the beginning of 1892 Henry had started experimenting with the anthropometric system, using ten measurements and noting the colour of the eyes. In January 1893 he refined this system to only six measurements and the inclusion on the record card of the left thumb-print. The left thumb was chosen because it was assumed that as most persons were right-handed the ridges on the left hand would not be as worn, and would therefore give a clearer impression.

Although he was reasonably satisfied with this modification, Henry did have strong doubts about the accuracy of the measurements being submitted, as strict supervision was extremely difficult. He was convinced that a record system based solely on fingerprints would solve many difficulties. To increase his knowledge of the subject he wrote to Galton, and thus started a friendship which was to last for many years. In the latter half of 1894, when he returned to England on leave, he lost no time in visiting the Convict Supervision Office, Galton's laboratory and of course Galton himself.

When Henry returned to India he was determined to find a formula which would enable a fingerprint collection of many thousands to be formed. His first action was to arrange for all ten fingerprints of each prisoner to be taken in addition to the anthropometric measurements. Fortunately, among his staff at the Central Anthropometric Office were a number of Indian officers who took a keen interest in fingerprints. Among them were Azizul Haque and Chandra Bose, who were to make a substantial contribution to the development of the fingerprint system.

In a report dated the 24th of June, 1896, to the Government of Bengal Henry detailed the effectiveness of the anthropometric system during 1895, but then continued:

It has been claimed for the Anthropometric system that the probability of all six measurements of any two persons coinciding is so small that a fraction with a denominator of five figures is required to represent it arithmetically. The assertion would be correct if no allowance had to be made for the 'personal equation' error. But, in practice, such allowance, and a considerable allowance, has to be made, the result being that coincidences in measurements are not infrequent. In the Central Office no positive deduction as to identity from measurements is considered safe or is made, reliance being placed exclusively in determining identity, upon similarity in the innumerable details which make up the pattern of the thumb-impressions.

A system of identification by means of finger impressions would have the following amongst other advantages over Anthropometry. The accessories, a piece of tin and some printer's ink, are inexpensive and procurable everywhere; the impressions are self-signatures, free from possible errors of observation and transcription; any person of ordinary intelligence can learn to take them with a little practice after a few minutes instruction; no objection can be raised on the score of religion or caste, or rank in society or even sex; their characteristics being persistent throughout life, the finger impressions of a child could be used to identify the same person when he had reached middle or old age; the patterns which appear on these impressions are easily recognizable and are susceptible of such succinct and exact definition that the most complicated pattern can be described in four or five words with sufficient completeness for purposes of comparison; and last, the evidential value of identity obtainable from the scrutiny of the prints of two or three fingers is so great that no person capable of weighing it, would deem it necessary to seek for confirmation elsewhere.

The problem which remains to be solved is whether it is possible to devise a system of classification based solely upon finger impressions, which will give sufficient power of differentiation to enable duplicates to be unerringly traced in a collection of the finger impressions, say of 20,000 persons. This problem is now being worked at, and so far, results are not unpromising, serious difficulty being experienced in respect of only two combinations. With extended experience, these difficulties may be overcome, but as, up to the present, the impressions of only about 5,000 persons have been classified, it would be premature to express an opinion as to whether a solution is probable.

Being impressed with the advantages which a system of identification by finger impressions would possess over Anthropometry, I have endeavoured to popularise amongst police officers a knowledge of the subject by issuing a Circular which explains by means of diagrams, the details of patterns, their classification, and the points to be kept in view when attempting to decipher them. . . . A number of police officers have acquired a good working knowledge of the details of finger-print decipherment, and their number is being added to, as it is one of the subjects of the Training School curriculum.

Henry sent a copy of this report to Galton with a covering letter:

Inspector General Police, Bengal
Writers' Building,
Calcutta
28.6.1896

DEAR MR. GALTON,

I enclose a copy of my last report to the local Government regarding the results obtained during 1895.

You will see that I am anxious to substitute a system based upon fingerprints solely from anthropometry if we can hit upon a system of classification. I think what we have done so far, in that direction will lend itself to tabulation, if so, I will send you results for criticism.

My difficulty is want of time. I have a very heavy Department to run and can only give my attention fitfully to special projects.

I am satisfied with our results from anthropometry but the supervision used to ensure success is a strain and possibly my successor may take less interest in the subject. I am anxious to substitute a system which affords less scope for errors. We measure now at about 120 centres, so exercising supervision is no light task.

I am afraid these papers will arrive too late to be of any use but I send it all the same, knowing the interest you take in the subject.

Yours sincerely,
E. R. HENRY

In this letter it is interesting to note Henry's recognition of team-work by the use of 'we' as against the temptation to use 'I'.

Eventually, after much hard work, Henry and his team of dedicated police officers were successful. A classification which allowed all fingerprints to be filed into 1,024 primary positions with secondary and tertiary subdivisions within each of the primary positions was devised. Although Galton was pleased with Henry's success, he was a little sceptical, and indicated that he would like to see the system tested on a really large collection of 100,000 fingerprint forms. In years to come he was to see the system tested many times in many countries.

Early in 1897 Henry made application to the Government of India for the appointment of an independent committee to inquire into and report upon this system. In March of that year General Strahan, RE, Surveyor-General of India, and Mr A. Pedler, FRS, Director of Public Instruction, were selected to form a Committee. They inquired into both systems, and submitted a report to the Government of India, the concluding paragraph of which stated:

In conclusion, we are of the opinion that the method of identification by means of fingerprints, as worked on the system of recording impressions

and of classification devised by Mr. Henry, may be safely adopted as being
superior to the Anthropometric method; (1) in simplicity of working; (2) in
the cost of apparatus; (3) in the fact that all skilled work is transferred to a
Central or Classification Office; (4) in the rapidity with which the process
can be worked; and (5) in the certainty of the results.

On the 12th of June 1897 a Resolution signed by the Governor-
General in Council directed that the system of identification of
criminals by finger-impressions be adopted generally in British India.
Needless to say, the two systems had to operate side by side until full
sets of fingerprints were obtained for all those persons with an anthropometric record only. At the time of the changeover it was estimated
that between 150,000 and 200,000 anthropometric cards had been
collected.

In the Argentine a Dalmatian immigrant, Juan Vucetich, was
employed as a statistician in the Central Police Department at La
Plata. A bureau of Anthropometric Identification had just been established in Buenos Aires, and another was also set up at La Plata. The
then Chief of Police of La Plata, Capitan Guillermo J. Nunes,
appointed Vucetich as head of this bureau. Later Captain Nunes
called his attention to an article by Henry de Varigny in the French
Revue Scientifique of May 1891. Basically, it reproduced, with due
credit, Galton's lecture on 'Patterns in thumbs and finger marks'.

It did not take Vucetich long to recognize that fingerprints could be
a more effective means of identification than Anthropometry. By
September 1891, using Galton's basic material, he had formulated a
ten-finger classification system. With considerable enthusiasm, he
arranged for prisoners to be fingerprinted. Some of these early sets of
fingerprints still exist in the Vucetich museum.

In 1892 Vucetich played an important role in the first murder case
in which fingerprints formed part of the evidence. In the Buenos Aires
provincial town of Necochea the two sons of Francesca Rojas were
found murdered, and she herself had a throat wound. She accused a
near-neighbour of this grisly crime, and he was arrested, although he
protested his innocence. Fortunately, the police officers examining
the crime scene noticed what appeared to be fingerprints in blood on a
door adjacent to the place where the bodies had been found. Portions
of the door bearing these marks were cut out and sent to La Plata
identification bureau, together with the fingerprints of the accused
man and the woman Rojas. It was quickly confirmed that the marks
were in fact fingerprints, and that they had been made by the woman.
Faced with this damning evidence, Francesca Rojas confessed to

the murder of her sons, and was sent to prison.

In spite of this success, Vucetich was not to receive any official recognition of his fingerprint work for many years. During these years, certain of the eventual acceptance of his fingerprint system, he carried on his researches, improving his classification formula and meeting all costs incurred out of his own pocket. Eventually he published his system at the second Latin-America Congress of Science, held in Montevideo in March 1901, and on the 8th of September 1901 he lectured on 'The Dactyloscopic System' in the Halls of Acts in La Plata. Although it received an enthusiastic reception, it was to be another four years before an independent fingerprint bureau was formed in the Argentine. Total recognition came to Vucetich in 1909 when he was honoured with the title 'Perito Identificator' – 'Skilled in Identification' – which was confirmed by decree of the President of the Argentine Republic.

6 The first National Fingerprint Bureau

The newly formed fingerprint bureau in Calcutta had by June 1898 established nearly three hundred identifications by fingerprints alone. In this year Henry added another dimension to his success – like Vucetich, the solving of a crime using a thumb-print in blood. Henry's own description of the case makes vivid reading, even today.

The manager of a tea garden situated in the district of Julparguri on the Bhutan frontier was found lying on his bed with his throat cut, his despatch box and safe having been rifled and several hundred rupees carried away. It was suggested that one of the coolies employed on the garden had committed the deed as the deceased had the reputation of being a hard taskmaster, or that his cook, upon whose clothes were some blood spots, might be the culprit. There was suspicion also against the relatives of a woman with whom the murdered man had a liaison, also against a wandering gang of Kabulis of criminal propensities who had lately encamped in the neighbourhood. A representation was also made that the deceased had an enemy in an ex-servant whom he had caused to be imprisoned for theft. Inquiry, however, satisfied the police that there was no evidence to incriminate the coolies, or the relatives of the woman, or the Kabulis, and it was ascertained that the ex-servant had been released from jail some weeks before, and no one could say that he had since been seen in the district. The cook's statement that the marks on his clothes were stains from a pigeon's blood which he had killed for his master's dinner was supported by the Chemical Analyst's report. Fortunately amongst the papers in the despatch box was found a calendar in book form. It is printed in the Bengali character, with an outside cover of light blue paper on which were noticed two faint brown smudges. Under a magnifying glass one smudge was decipherable as a portion of the impression of one of the digits of some person's right hand. In the Central Office of the Bengal Police, the finger impressions of all persons convicted of certain offences are classified and registered, and the impression on the calendar when compared there was found to correspond exactly with the right thumb impression of

Kangali Charan, the ex-servant above referred to. He, in consequence, was arrested in Berbhum, a district some hundreds of miles away, and brought to Calcutta, where his right thumb impression was again taken, and the police in the meantime set about collecting corroborative evidence. The Chemical Examiner to Government certified that the brown marks on the calendar were mammalian blood, the inference being that the actual murderer or some associate had knocked his blood stained thumb against the calendar when rummaging amongst the papers in the despatch box for the key of the safe. The accused was placed on his trial before a native judge and assessors, charged with murder and theft, and finally was convicted of having stolen the missing property of the deceased, the assessors holding that it would be unsafe to convict him of murder as no one had seen the deed committed, but recording their opinion that the charge of theft had been conclusively established against him. This conviction was upheld by the Judges of the Supreme Court to which the case was taken on appeal.

In the same year the special qualities and abilities of Henry were recognized by the Government of India, when he was made a Companion of the Most Exalted Order of the Star of India.

Back in England, however, the Anthropometric Office was not as successful as had been hoped. A desire to retain the old cumbersome hit-and-miss system to which the police had become accustomed meant the new system was often misunderstood or treated with suspicion. When two police officers, Sergeant William White and Constable Frederick Hunt, were assigned to assist Dr Garson to set up the new Office, their enthusiasm helped his pioneer efforts. Prison warders were trained to take accurate measurements and fingerprints. Methods were set up to register, classify and search through the records.

Apparently satisfied with the progress being made by the Anthropometric Office, the Home Secretary transferred the Habitual Criminal Registry from the Home Office to New Scotland Yard, and in 1896 it was amalgamated with the Anthropometric Office. Dr Garson became the 'Expert Adviser to the Commissioner of Police and Instructor of Prison Warders on methods of identification by means of measurements and fingerprints', and by 1898 he had become a familiar figure in various courts, where his expert testimony was required to prove a criminal's identification.

Justification for the new system of identification came in January 1898. At Clerkenwell Sessions a waiter named James Coots was called up for sentence, having been convicted of stealing a clock, valued at five shillings, from the Lord Raglan public house. At the previous sessions it had been thought that Coots was a man named Egerton, who at the Liverpool Assize some years previously had been sentenced to twenty years' penal servitude for manslaughter. Because James Coots denied this identification he was remanded for his photograph to be circulated. A prison warder recognized the photograph and subsequently the man as Frank Foley, a criminal who had served three sentences of penal servitude. Once again Coots denied this identification. Unfortunately for him, Garson was able to produce the measurements and fingerprints of 'Foley' which matched exactly the measurements and fingerprints of Coots. He was sentenced to a term of three years' penal servitude. Distraught, the prisoner attempted to commit suicide by tying his necktie round the iron bars over his door cell and hanging himself by it.

In spite of such a success Melville Macnaghten, head of the CID at New Scotland Yard (who had been a member of the 1894 Troup Committee), was far from satisfied. In his view, accurate measurements were difficult to obtain, and although prison Governors and warders did their best – as did the police – the results seemed pitifully small. The British Association for the Advancement of Science, however, heard of Henry's success, undoubtedly through the good offices of Galton. They invited him to address the Association meeting to be held at Dover in 1899. He prepared a comprehensive paper entitled 'Finger Prints and the Detection of Crime in India'.[1] In it he recalled the historical aspects of fingerprints, giving due credit to Galton. He compared the anthropometric system with the fingerprint system, and outlined his method of fingerprint classification. He also described the practical use of fingerprints in crime detection, and detailed the extent to which fingerprints were being utilized in various branches of public business in India. They were a means to stop relatives drawing military and civil pensions fraudulently after the death of the pensioners. They helped settle cases of disputed property transfers. In the department controlling opium-cultivation, fingerprints helped to stamp out frauds by middlemen and moneylenders. They were even used to help enforce quarantine laws on pilgrims to Mecca.

Henry's paper was well received by a most appreciative audience. Galton too presented a paper to the same meeting and on the same day as Henry. His paper was entitled 'Finger prints of young children'. The subject had been prompted by a request for an opinion from a police authority which had received information that a baby who was

---

[1]See Appendix, pp.197–8.

heir to a great title and estate might be kidnapped. Fears were expressed that if a stolen infant were restored after a lapse of some time doubts and legal difficulties could arise as to the true identity of the baby. Galton was asked whether the prints of the fingers of a baby would serve for ever afterwards to identify him, and prove that he was not a changeling. To demonstrate his view that fingerprints remained constant Galton used a series of fingerprints sent to him by an American lady – Mrs John Gardiner of Boulder, Colorado. She had fingerprinted her own daughter Dorothy numerous times from her birth until the age of four and a half years. Ironically, as it later transpired, Garson also presented a paper to the same meeting, only this was not about fingerprints but Anthropometry.

The next few months were busy ones indeed for Henry. The Government of India requested him to write a text-book on his method of classifying fingerprints. Later, when the South African War led to the occupation of the Transvaal, the Colonial Office requested him to travel to South Africa to organize the civil police of Johannesburg and Pretoria.

At about the same time the disquiet that was being voiced about the ineffectiveness of the combined measurement and fingerprint system prompted the Home Secretary to form a committee of inquiry. Under the chairmanship of Lord Belper, this five-man committee was to investigate 'the working of the method of Identification of Criminals by Measurements and Finger Prints, and the administrative arrangements for carrying on the system'. They were to include in their report suggestions for changes and to consider how best the information could be made available to the courts.

The committee found that only 18,000 sets of anthropometric measurements had been registered in the five years that the system had been in use, and some of the methods of identification in use before the 1894 Troup Committee inquiry were still being employed. Many reasons were advanced to account for the situation: that a Home Office circular recommending adequate discretion in the use of the system had been misunderstood; that some prisoners were remanded into police custody because the nearest prison was too far away, and police were not authorized to measure prisoners; and that some magistrates were reluctant to grant remands for the purpose of obtaining any possible previous record of persons charged with petty theft, even though such persons might be confirmed criminals, preferring to deal with such cases summarily.

Fortunately, Henry was able to give evidence to the Committee before he sailed to Africa. He gave a short account of his system, and then gave them a practical demonstration, using a fingerprint collection of about seven thousand persons. They were obviously impressed with the ease and rapidity of picking out any required record.

Shortly after Henry had given his evidence, his book – entitled *Classification and Uses of Fingerprints* – was published by Messrs Routledge and Sons. Fifteen thousand copies were printed of the first edition. He sent one to his friend Galton a few days before he sailed, and his covering letter[1] reveals the very high regard he had for Galton with a most descriptive turn of phrase:

> I feel sure you will be gratified and realise that I have done my best to 'stand upon your shoulders' – very broad shoulders they are.

The rest of the letter contained a brief description of the ease with which the fingerprint system had been introduced into India, and its benefits. He expressed the hope that the Belper Committee would realize the imperfections of the existing system.

The Belper Committee finalized their report in December 1900. In spite of Garson's attempt to divert them away from a fingerprint-only system, the Committee obviously saw that the future for an infallible identification system was in this direction. This was reflected in their recommendations:

> Our recommendation, therefore, is that the present system should be maintained for such reasonable time as may be necessary to enable the department to decide how far Mr. Henry's system, with or without any modifications, could safely be adopted, and the present system gradually superseded, but that active steps should be taken towards the immediate introduction of the Henry system. For this purpose the fingerprints on the Henry form should be taken in every case registered. (This would not occupy more than one or two minutes, and more time than this might be saved by reducing the number of distinctive marks described and measured on the arms and body.) These prints should be classified according to the Indian system, which should be used concurrently with the other for the purpose of tracing the identity of criminals, and if the number of the records taken is increased to the extent which we shall recommend there will soon be enough to show which system is the easier to work and gives more certain results. Unless this experience shows a decisive advantage in the English as compared with the Indian system, the latter will ultimately be adopted, for other things being equal, the ease with which the finger prints can be taken in any place, at any time, and by untrained officers, inclines the balance of advantage in its favour.

[1]For full text of letter see Appendix, pp.196–7.

7 The formation of the Fingerprint Department at New Scotland Yard

The decision to implement most of the recommendations made by the Belper Committee was taken early in 1901. By good fortune this coincided with the pending retirement of Dr Robert Anderson CB, an Assistant Commissioner of the Metropolitan Police, who had been the head of the Criminal Investigation Department for thirteen years. This paved the way for the recall of Edward Henry and his appointment as Assistant Commissioner. Although his appointment was welcomed by many, within the Force – particularly the CID – doubts were expressed regarding his suitability to be the head of such a specialist branch. The dissenters obviously did not appreciate that Henry was able to place in their hands one of the most efficient detection systems of all time – fingerprints. On the 1st of July 1901, within one month of taking office, Henry selected three men from the Anthropometric Office – Detective Inspector Charles H. Stedman, Detective Sergeant Charles Stockley Collins and Detective Constable Frederick Hunt – to form the Fingerprint Branch. Dr Garson paid the penalty of failing to recognize, or not wanting to recognize, that fingerprints were far more reliable as a means of identification than anthropometry, and he was removed from office. Stedman was appointed the first head of the Fingerprint Branch.

The relationship between Henry and the three officers was one of mutual respect and enthusiasm. He instructed them in fingerprint classification, using many fingerprint forms he had brought from India. When fingerprint patterns were encountered which did not conform to one of the various definitions for basic patterns they would discuss them, and draw out the salient features before arriving at a conclusion. Such discussions were important, because the resulting decision provided criteria for the next time a similar pattern was encountered. The staff soon mastered the new technique and set about converting the fingerprints on the anthropometric records to their new role. They also travelled to various prisons all over the country, instructing prison officers how to take fingerprints on the new fingerprint forms. So successful were they that the Home Office implemented another recommendation of the Belper Committee – that of extending the class of criminal to be recorded. Hitherto only habitual criminals were recorded in the anthropometric collection. 'Habitual criminals' were defined as those being convicted on indictment of a crime, a previous conviction being proved against them. Fingerprinting was now extended to all persons convicted at assizes or sessions who were sentenced to a term of imprisonment exceeding one month. This was later extended further to include persons sentenced at any Petty Sessional, Police, or Stipendiary Magistrate's Court to more than one month's imprisonment without option of a fine. The offences for which fingerprints could be taken included:

Arson	Frequenting
Attempts to break into houses, shops etc	House breaking
Bankruptcy offences	Indecent assault upon females
Being found on enclosed premises	Indecent exposure
Burglary	Killing or maiming cattle
Coining	Larceny
Conspiracy	Malicious injury
Embezzlement	Possessing housebreaking tools etc
Entering with intent to commit felony	Receiving
Extortion	Robbery
False pretences	Sacrilege
Forgery	Shopbreaking
Fraud	Unlawful possession

The police forces responded to this new, and demonstrably more efficient, method of identifying criminals with a willingness they had not shown with other methods. Within months of the Fingerprint Branch starting operations it was necessary to increase the staff by another five officers: Detective Constables Herbert Leman Alden, William Thomas Bell, John Kenneth Ferrier, Jesse Charles Dumper and Detective Sergeant Charles Munro. In the first six months 93 identifications by fingerprints were effected. The Commissioner, Colonel Sir Edward Bradford, was so impressed with the efficiency of this new branch that he stopped the practice of sending police officers to Holloway Prison to view the remand prisoners.

Although all the staff worked with considerable enthusiasm and utter dedication to master their new skills, one man, Detective Sergeant Collins, emerged as a natural leader and innovator. One of his principal aims was to emulate Edward Henry, and use fingerprints not only as a means of linking criminals to their past criminal record but also to their present, and as yet undetected, crimes. He attended classes at the Battersea Polytechnic, and studied photography, so that when the opportunity presented itself he would be able to record chance fingerprints left at a crime scene.

He had to wait until the middle of 1902 for this particular triumph. On the 27th of June 1902 a house at Denmark Hill was entered by a burglar, and some billiard balls stolen. The investigating detective (named Haigh) noticed a number of dirty fingerprints on a newly painted window-sill at the point where the burglar had entered the house, and passed the information to the Fingerprint Branch. Collins went to the scene, and after a meticulous examination of the marks decided that the clearest had been made by a left thumb. Having checked that the mark had not been made by any member of the household, he photographed it, and returned to Scotland Yard with high hopes of identifying the burglar, even though he knew that many thousands of comparisons would have to be made. His colleagues, with equal enthusiasm, rallied round him to assist with this massive search of all criminals whose fingerprints were on record with a similar loop pattern on the left thumb. Eventually Collins made the identification he so desperately wanted – a 41-year-old labourer named Harry Jackson, who had several previous convictions recorded against him. Luckily, when Jackson was arrested he was found to be dealing in property stolen from a house in Dulwich that had been broken into on the 30th of July.

This identification, however, was only the first hurdle that Collins had overcome. The next, an even greater one, was getting a court to accept the identification of a single chance thumb-print as the sole means of proving that Jackson had in fact committed the crime. This could have proved more difficult. Up till then a fair amount of scepticism had been displayed by the public, and even some of the magistrates and judges, about the true accuracy of the fingerprint system. After some discussion between Edward Henry, the Director of Public Prosecutions, Detective Inspector Stedman and Detective Sergeant Collins, it was decided to arrange for the prosecution to be conducted by Richard Muir – later to become Sir Richard – a well-established Treasury counsel. Muir spent many hours with Collins learning the intricate details of the relatively new investigative technology.

In due course, when Muir was satisfied with his new-found knowledge, Jackson was arraigned on the 13th of September, and pleaded not guilty to all charges. Muir opened the case for the prosecution by stating that the case was an ordinary one but for the fact that fingerprints would be given in evidence for the purpose of connecting the prisoner with the burglary at Denmark Hill. He also mentioned that this system of identification had been tried on a large scale for the purpose of identifying habitual criminals in India. He went on to outline the case against Jackson. He then called Collins to the witness-box, who explained in simple terms the basic principles of fingerprint identification to the jury and then produced photographic enlargements of the thumb-mark on the painted window-sill and the left thumb-print of Jackson which had been taken after his arrest. He also produced tracings of the ridges on both prints, and indicated ten ridge characteristics which were present in both prints and in the same coincident sequence. The jury were both interested and intrigued, and spent some considerable time studying the photographs. They also heard evidence regarding the breaking in at Dulwich and about a bag containing burglar's tools which had been dropped by a man who had been disturbed on the roof of the billiard room of a public house in Kennington. It was alleged that these tools belonged to Jackson. Surprisingly, there was no strong attack on the fingerprint evidence by the defence. Jackson was found guilty of all charges by the jury, and thereby set a profound precedent. The Common Serjeant, F. A. Bosanquet Esq., KC, sentenced the prisoner to a term of seven years' penal servitude.

The euphoria in the Fingerprint Branch following this conviction was slightly deflated a few days later when Collins had to attend the Guildhall and explain to Mr Alderman Burnett an alleged failure in a fingerprint identification about which much had been published in the Press. On the 12th of September Mr Alderman Vaughan Morgan was informed that the Fingerprint Office had stated that the fingerprints of William Ward were identical with those of a criminal named Hopkins. Fortunately, this was not a fingerprint identification error but a clerical error. The fingerprints of Ward had been correctly identified for a criminal of the same name, but in copying down the reference number from the master set of fingerprints an officer had recorded the number as 2,392 instead of 2,393. The Alderman accepted the explanation, and said he was glad to learn – and the public would be equally pleased – that the error referred to was a clerical one, and in no degree a fault of the fingerprint system.

By the end of 1902 the superiority of the fingerprint system began really to manifest itself. In that year 1,722 fingerprint identifications were established, almost 400 more than all the identifications made during the six years of the anthropometric system.

On the 4th of March 1903 the Commissioner, Colonel Sir Edward Bradford, retired. Edward Henry was appointed Commissioner the next day. Henry was succeeded as Assistant Commissioner in charge of the CID by Melville Macnaghten, who had been the Chief Constable CID for the previous thirteen years. Macnaghten was a staunch supporter of Edward Henry and the fingerprint system and readily agreed to a suggestion that the Fingerprint Branch should take positive action to deal with criminals who for many years had plagued the numerous racecourse meetings up and down the country. Hitherto, those persons arrested were detained overnight and then dealt with summarily by the Petty Sessional court the following morning. This limited period of detention gave insufficient time for the prisoners to be correctly identified and their previous convictions obtained. Most of those arrested realized this and usually gave false names.

The Epsom Derby meeting was chosen for 'positive action'. Fingerprint experts were sent to Epsom, and there fingerprinted sixty men who had been arrested for a variety of offences. Later the same evening these fingerprints were taken to Scotland Yard, where two more fingerprint experts processed them through the system. Twenty-seven of the men arrested had previous convictions, and their records were available in court the next morning. Macnaghten described the first case:

> The first prisoner on this occasion gave his name as Green of Gloucester, and assured the interrogating magistrate that he had never been in trouble before, and that a racecourse was, up to this time, an unknown world to him. But up jumped the Chief Inspector, in answer to a question as to whether 'anything was known,' and begged their worships to look at the papers and photograph, which proved the innocent to be Benjamin Brown of Birmingham, with some ten convictions to his discredit. 'Bless them fingerprints,' said Benjamin, with an oath; 'I knew they'd do me in!'

The 'positive action' was repeated successfully at the Ascot race meeting that year. Everyone was so satisfied with the results from both of these meetings that the attendance of fingerprint experts at them continued for many years.

In 1904 Henry's fingerprint system went to North America. It was in May of that year that the World's Fair and Exposition was held in St Louis, Missouri. The British contribution was, by the gracious permission of King Edward VII, to be a display of Queen Victoria's diamond jubilee presents. Arrangements were made for six Metropolitan policemen, five uniformed and one detective, to be seconded for duty in the Royal Pavilion at the Exhibition.

At the same time, the International Association of Chiefs of Police under their president Major Richard Sylvester, of Washington DC, arranged to move its whole bureau to St Louis for the six months of the exhibition and to arrange an International Police Exhibition within the main exhibition complex. Police forces around the world were invited to submit exhibits for display. The contribution from Scotland Yard naturally related to the fingerprint system. To ensure adequate explanation of the system and exhibits, the Commissioner arranged for John Kenneth Ferrier of the Fingerprint Branch to be the detective to accompany the five uniformed officers to the Royal Pavilion. The uniformed officers were Sergeant James Prockter and Constables: Mark Parnell, Henry Andrews, William Shepherd and William Fulcher.

While in St Louis, Ferrier addressed the members of the International Association of Chiefs of Police on the virtues of the Henry fingerprint system. He was inundated with inquiries, both in person and by letter. During his six-month stay, he answered no less than 403 letters of inquiry. There can be little doubt that Ferrier's visit to North America converted many law-enforcement agencies, including the United States of America, from anthropometry to the Henry fingerprint system.

In his book *Crooks and Crime* Ferrier recounts one particular incident which occurred during his St Louis visit:

I was introduced to a police official of high position in New York who interrogated me as to the merits and demerits of fingerprint identification. He deemed my explanation of the system as too near approach to the infallible mark, and scoffingly remarked: 'Scotland Yard has nothing on us, we are more go ahead than sleepy old England.' I ascertained that he was sailing for England the following week, and persuaded him to permit me to take two sets of his finger impressions. One he kept, the other he marked and I sent it to Scotland Yard, requesting that it might be classified and placed in the collection, and that a person might call one day and claim it. About a month later the American officer called at the Yard and refused to disclose his identity, but produced his fingerprints and said: 'Here are my fingermarks; tell me who I am.' To his astonishment he had within two minutes placed in his hands the two sets of his fingerprints. He was so impressed at what he saw in connection with the fingerprint system that on his return to the United States he soon converted other sceptics and established a fingerprint department in New York. . . .

Ferrier returned to duty at Scotland Yard on the 5th of January 1905, and was promoted to detective sergeant the same day.

Ferrier's visit to St Louis was to be recalled during the very first case in the United States dealing with fingerprint evidence, which was decided by the Illinois Supreme Court on the 21st of December 1911. It was the case of The People *v*. Jennings.

Clarence B. Hiller lived with his wife and four children in a two-storey house on West 104th Street, Chicago. At about 2 a.m. on the 19th of September 1910 his wife noticed that the gas-light at the head of the stairs was out. She told her husband, and he went to investigate. At the top of the stairs he encountered an intruder, and in the ensuing struggle they both fell to the foot of the stairway, where Hiller was shot twice and died in a few moments.

Shortly afterwards, a man named Thomas Jennings was stopped by four police officers about three-quarters of a mile away from the murder scene. The officers searched Jennings, and upon finding a loaded revolver in his trouser-pocket, and being dissatisfied with his explanation, detained him. At this time they had no knowledge of the murder.

The murder scene was examined for clues. It appeared that the assailant had entered the house of the deceased through a rear kitchen window from which the window screen had been removed. A porch near the window had been painted on the previous Saturday, and on the railings of the porch, in fresh paint, were the impressions of four fingers from someone's left hand. The railing was removed and taken to the Chicago Police Department Bureau of Identification, where the fingermarks were speedily identified as belonging to Thomas Jennings. Jennings was indicted for murder, and stood trial in the criminal court of Cook County. A considerable amount of evidence was forthcoming, including the finger impressions in paint on the railing. To prove the identity of these finger impressions the prosecution called four fingerprint experts: William M. Evans, who began to study fingerprints in 1904 and had been connected with the Chicago Police Department Bureau of Identification on fingerprint work for about a year; Edward Foster, an Inspector of Dominion Police, Ottawa, Canada, connected with the Bureau of Identification, who began to study fingerprints in St Louis in 1904 under a Scotland Yard man, and had a good deal to do with fingerprints for six years or more; Mary E. Holland, who began her investigation of fingerprints in 1904, and had studied the subject at Scotland Yard in 1908 – she started the first Bureau of Identification for the United States Government in Washington; Michael P. Evans, who had been in the Bureau of Identification of the Chicago Police Department for twenty-seven years, and had studied fingerprints since 1905 or 1906.

All the experts agreed that the fingerprints on the railing had been made by Jennings. He was found guilty by the jury and awarded the death penalty. He appealed to the Illinois Supreme Court, basing part of his appeal on the inadmissibility of the fingerprint evidence, but in a lengthy judgment the Supreme Court rejected his appeal and confirmed the death sentence.

In reporting this case the *Chicago Daily Tribune* stated, 'The circumstances of the negro's conviction were dramatic enough to furnish the "big scene" in a sensational novel.'

8 Fingerprints and murder

It was not until 1905 that a fingerprint featured in an English murder trial.

The victims, Thomas Farrow and his wife Ann, who were both nearly seventy years of age, lived at 34 High Street, Deptford, where Thomas Farrow was the manager of a shop called 'Chapman's Oil Shop'. Farrow had been employed by George Chapman for twenty-four years, and it was the practice of the latter to visit the Farrows every Monday morning to receive the takings of the shop for the previous week.

The Farrows were a well-liked couple in the neighbourhood, and were noted for their helpful and considerate ways. For instance, painters who required paint would sometimes call at the shop before the official opening time, knowing that Farrow would quite happily serve them.

A young man, William Jones, was employed at the shop to assist with the heavier tasks. At half-past eight on the morning of the 27th of March 1905 Jones arrived there as usual, but was unable to gain entry. As he had never known this to happen before, he became most concerned, and hastily went to Chapman's shop in Greenwich to tell the owner. Chapman sent one of his assistants back to Deptford with Jones. Upon their arrival they banged on the front door, but with no result, so they went to the rear of the premises and forced an entry.

To their horror, when they went into the parlour they found Thomas Farrow lying dead on the floor, with his head severely battered. His wife was upstairs on the bed, her head also savagely battered. Incredibly, she was still alive, but only just. She was taken to the Seamen's Hospital at Greenwich where, four days later, she died.

Meanwhile a murder investigation, led by Detective Chief Inspector Fox, had started with a thorough examination of the premises. On the floor in the bedroom was an empty cash-box, and the inner tray of this was lying close by, as were a sixpenny piece and a penny. Also in the bedroom was a mask which had been crudely made with a piece of material cut off the top of a long black stocking. Two similar masks were found in the shop parlour. The investigating officers formed an early opinion – based on the fact that only money and no other property had been stolen – that the perpetrators of the crime had local knowledge about Chapman's habit of calling on Farrow every Monday to collect his money. While local inquiries were being made the cash-box and tray were taken to the Fingerprint Branch, where an application of fingerprint powder soon revealed a fingerprint on the tray. As a precaution the fingerprints of every person, including the deceased, were taken to see if the fingerprint had been made by one of them – fortunately, it had not.

An early break in the inquiry came when a milkman, Henry Jennings, and his eleven-year-old assistant, Edward Russell, told police that about quarter-past seven on the morning in question they had seen two men leave Mr Farrow's shop. The men slammed the door behind them, but it had flown open again. Although Jennings had called to them, they ignored him and continued on their way towards Deptford Broadway. One of the men was taller than the other. The taller one, who was dressed in a blue serge suit and bowler hat, walked quickly and stiffly. His companion was wearing a dark brown suit, cap, and brown boots.

How the door to the shop came to be closed again was solved by a painter named Alfred Purfield. He had been waiting for a friend opposite Mr Farrow's shop before catching the 7.35 a.m. train to London, when he saw an old gentleman with blood on his face, shirt and hands come to the door, which was open. He told the police that the old gentleman stood at the door in a vacant kind of way and then closed it. As Purfield was unable to find a policeman, he departed to catch his train.

Henry Littlefield, a professional boxer, provided the next link. At half-past two on the morning of the 27th of March he was on his way home when he met the brothers Alfred and Albert Stratton. Whilst he was speaking to them he noticed that Albert was fumbling with his coat as if he had something under it. He recalled that Alfred was dressed in a brown suit, check cap, and brown boots and that Albert was wearing a dark blue serge suit and bowler hat.

Another witness was found, named Ellen Stanton. She remembered that at about quarter-past seven on the morning of the murder at the corner of the High Street and the Broadway she saw two men running from the High Street in the direction of the New Cross Road. She recognized one of them, who was dressed in a dark brown suit and cap, as Alfred Stratton, but was unable to identify the other man, who was wearing a dark overcoat and bowler hat. At this stage the investigation polarized on the Stratton brothers.

Mrs Kate Wade, with whom Albert had lodged at 67 Knott Street, Deptford, was interviewed, and recalled that one day Albert had asked her if she had an old pair of stockings she could give him, to which she replied no. Some time later she found between the mattresses on the bed some stocking-tops; one of them had strings and holes in it, and the other a piece of elastic.

Hannah Cromerty, who had lived with Alfred Stratton in a down-stairs front room in Brookmill Road, Deptford, remembered that on the morning of the murders Alfred's trousers had smelt of paraffin, but he had put it down to spilling some while filling the bedroom lamp. When she had missed his brown overcoat the next day he told her he had given it to one of his destitute friends. She had also noticed that on the day of the murders he had blacked over his brown boots.

When Alfred Stratton was arrested in a public-house, on the 3rd of April, he was asked the whereabouts of his brother. He replied that he had not seen him for a long time, and thought he had gone to sea. The following day Albert Stratton was arrested in the street. The brothers were fingerprinted by Detective Inspector Collins, who later established that the fingerprint on the cash-box tray had been made by the right thumb of the older brother, Alfred. The brothers were eventually charged with wilful murder and brought before the magistrates at Greenwich Police Court, who remanded them in custody.

The committal hearing was eventually transferred to Tower Bridge Police Court, where during the lunch adjournment on the 18th of April the pressure on the younger brother, Albert, began to tell. The brothers had been placed in separate cells. Albert called to the gaoler, Police Constable Giddens, and said, 'How do you think I shall get on?'

The gaoler replied, 'I don't know.'

Albert said, indicating his brother, 'Is he listening?'

The gaoler looked through the aperture of Alfred's cell and said to Albert, 'No, he is reading a newspaper.'

Albert then said, 'I reckon he will get strung up, and I shall get about ten years. He let me into this. He is the cause of my living with that woman. Don't say anything to him. I shan't say anything until I can see he has got no chance, and then –'

Albert broke off at that point, walked round his cell, and then said to the gaoler, 'I don't want to get strung up. He has never done any work in his life except about a month. They tried to get that Brixton job on him, but they found that he was at work at the time. I have only been out of the Navy about seven months.'

They were committed for trial at the Old Bailey on the 25th of April, in spite of an attempt by their legal representative, Mr Budden, to obtain a further remand before committal. He addressed the magistrate, and said that the most important evidence was that relating to the fingerprint. He was in the awkward position of defending two exceedingly poor men, and the case raised a most highly scientific point – that the system adopted at Scotland Yard was an erroneous one. He asked the magistrate to adjourn the case to give him an opportunity of calling a gentleman to give evidence in favour of the prisoners upon this point. If he were called at the police court the court would pay his reasonable expenses. When the magistrate said the name of the gentleman to whom he referred had not been given Mr Budden handed him a letter. The magistrate, having read the letter, said, 'He does not mention what his fee is, and that is a matter for you to consider. I do not say this gentleman is a faddist, but any faddist might ask to give evidence in a trial of this nature.' The prisoners were then formally charged with the murders of the Farrows. The brothers reserved their defence, and called no witnesses.

Their trial commenced on the 5th of May before Mr Justice Channell. Mr R. D. Muir, Mr Bodkin, and Mr J. F. Vesey Fitzgerald prosecuted on behalf of the Director of Public Prosecutions; Mr H. G. Rooth and Mr Curtis-Bennett defended Alfred Stratton; and Mr Harold Morris appeared for the defence of Albert Ernest Stratton. Both prisoners pleaded not guilty.

In his opening address Richard Muir presented the prosecution case in his usual clear and concise manner. He courteously but firmly coaxed the evidence from the prosecution witnesses. One disappointment was that neither Jennings the milkman nor his youthful assistant could identify the accused as the men they had seen leaving the shop. The fingerprint evidence now became a most vital factor in the final outcome of this trial.

In his evidence, Detective Inspector Collins described in detail the method of identification by fingerprints, and stated that there were 80,000 to 90,000 sets of fingerprints at Scotland Yard, which meant between 800,000 and 900,000 individual impressions of digits. He had never found two such impressions to correspond. The highest number of characteristics he had ever found to agree in the impressions of two different fingers was three, and there were only two or three such instances. He described the method of classification, first by types and sub-types and then by counting and tracing the ridges when there were complete prints of the whole finger. He further described the method of comparing the characteristics. He told the court that he had photographed the fingerprint on the tray of the cash-box found in the Farrows' bedroom, and that until the prisoner Alfred was arrested he was unable to find any print which agreed with it. After the arrest of the prisoners he had fingerprinted both of them, and was satisfied that the right thumb-print of Alfred agreed with the mark on the tray, as there was a total of twelve characteristics which agreed in both prints. He then produced photographic enlargements of the prints and handed copies to the jury. Using a prepared chart, he described each matching characteristic and its relationship with other matching characteristics. He also pointed out that there were no characteristics which did not agree. At the request of the jury he took a number of impressions from a digit of a juryman to demonstrate the effect of varying pressures during printing. Collins likened this effect to that of a soft rubber stamp which had been applied unevenly – the appearance changes slightly, but not the data.

During a very strong cross-examination by Mr Rooth, Collins reaffirmed his opinion about some of the disputed characteristics. When it was suggested to him that he had been a pupil of Dr Garson Collins replied that he was not exactly a pupil of Dr Garson, and explained that Garson had been attached to the Anthropometric Office simply as an adviser to the Commissioner. When pressed by defending counsel about the fingerprint expertise of Dr Garson Collins replied that he had no experience of his ability on the question of fingerprints, but on the question of body measurements he would value any opinion expressed.

The evidence given by Collins was then corroborated by Detective Inspector Stedman.

After Alfred Stratton had given evidence on his own behalf – needless to say, denying his involvement in the murders – Mr Rooth called Dr Garson to the witness box. Garson told the court that he had given special attention to medico-legal work, and had had a large experience of the fingerprint system. He had seen a photograph of the fingerprint on the cash-box tray, and one of the print of Alfred Stratton's right thumb, and had made a thorough examination of the two prints. He went on to describe what he considered were dissimilarities between the two. He said it was possible that they were of the same person, but he was of the opinion that they were undoubtedly different fingers. They might be the fingers of the same person, but not the same finger; they were two distinct fingers.

During cross-examination by Muir, Garson admitted he had no experience of identification by fingerprints since 1901. He said that he had written to the solicitor for the defence on 26 April. At that time he had not seen copies of the fingerprints, but he saw that Inspector Collins had spoken a great deal of nonsense in the police court. Garson said he was prepared to swear that the impression on the cash-box was not made by the right thumb of Alfred Stratton.

Muir then read to the court a letter written by Garson to the solicitor for the defence:

> I am not quite sure whether the Treasury are going to call me. Should I not be called I shall be pleased to arrange with you to give expert evidence for the defence. It (the fingerprint system) is a splendid means of identification when properly used, but I have no hesitation in saying that the way it is being used by the police is that which will bring it into disrepute.

When asked by Muir if he had also written a letter on the same day to the Public Prosecutor offering to give evidence on his behalf, Garson replied that he had. This letter was also read to the court, the crucial passage being:

> I would be glad to know whether you intend to call me as an expert in the trial of the Stratton brothers on the fingerprint impressions which are to be brought forward, I understand, as evidence against them. I feel the Government has, perhaps, the first claim on my services. I may say that, if I am not retained by the Treasury as an expert, I shall probably give evidence as such for the defence.

When asked how he could justify writing two such letters on the same day Garson stated he was an independent witness. At this point the judge commented that he thought Garson was an absolutely untrustworthy witness after writing such letters. Garson assured the court that he would have given the same evidence whether for the Treasury or the defence. This, however, did not placate his Lordship, who made the observation that in neither letter did he say a word about wishing to see the impressions before giving evidence. The court could have understood it if he had. Garson said that he meant in his letters that he wanted to see the impressions, and that he would form his opinion after seeing them. Unwittingly, Curtis-Bennett exacerbated the fragile situation by putting further questions to Garson. This provoked further comment from the judge, who asked tartly, 'Is there not a limit to whitewashing this gentleman? It has done your client a lot of harm.'

In his final speech for the defence, Rooth made a desperate attempt to rectify the damage Garson's evidence had caused with an emotional attack on the fingerprint evidence. He suggested that it was unreliable, and savoured more of the French courts than of English justice.

In his summing-up of the case the judge was more than fair to the defence. He emphasized that the finger-mark on the tray was due only to perspiration, and it was not so satisfactory as it would have been if the material with which it was made had been of a kind which would give a better impression. If it was correct that people's hands and fingers varied so much, there was at any rate an extraordinary amount of resemblance between the two marks, and therefore to a certain extent it was corroborative evidence in regard to Alfred, though he did not think the jury would like to act upon it alone.

What effect the thumb-print had on the jury's decision no one can tell, but at ten minutes past ten on the evening of Saturday the 6th of May the jury, after deliberating for two hours, returned guilty verdicts on both brothers. They were both sentenced to death. The executions were carried out on the 23rd of May – and, strange to relate, by two brothers.

Garson, still smarting from the verbal attack on his integrity, wrote letters to various newspapers in which he tried to justify his actions. These met with very little sympathy, probably as a result of the judge's comments.

As one observer put it:

> Medical men are most valuable expert witnesses in countless cases before the Courts; but we know of no other instance of a medical man writing letters inviting his retention to give such evidence, even on one side, not to say both. Professional etiquette alone would debar this practice.

Although he did not give evidence, Dr Faulds was active on behalf of the defence. He apparently formed his opinion by making careful measurements in court. Quite what he was measuring he does not say. Predictably, he later attacked the fingerprint evidence by stating:

> A smudge of this quality should not be presented in court as evidence . . . it is likely that in an old man's well fingered cash-box there were more than one smudge to be found. Scotland Yard possibly got hold of the wrong one.

As a matter of record, copies of the fingerprints from the Stratton case still exist, as indeed does the cash-box, and there is no doubt that the print on the cash-box tray was made by the right thumb of Alfred Stratton.

Perhaps Dr Garson truly believed the fingerprints were not identical. He had, after all, given evidence in court on many occasions of identity based on fingerprints and anthropometric measurements during the years 1895–1901. Various theories have been put forward in an attempt to explain his actions. We shall probably never know the truth.

As for Faulds, the kindest construction that one can place on his attitude is that, in spite of his many claims, his knowledge and experience of fingerprints as a means of identification may have been more limited than he would have us believe. His various books, published in 1905, 1912 and 1923, sadly lack good, solid, progressive fingerprint data and techniques.

Even before the trial of the Strattons, the medical profession commenced to close ranks regarding the giving of expert evidence in fingerprint identifications. The *Medical Press and Circular* commented:

> It is a matter of regret, however, that delicate scientific work of this kind is entrusted to Police Officers, who have shown themselves to be untrustworthy where prosecutions are concerned. In the interests of the public, work of this kind should be performed by men of medical education, whose evidence would be not only technically accurate, but also absolutely above suspicion of professional bias.

An editorial published in *The Lancet* one week after the trial, and entitled 'Identification by Fingerprints', continued this theme. After describing the ten-finger system of recording a person's criminal record the following comment was made:

> It is therefore, perhaps, somewhat an open question whether, in the interest of the public, in cases where previous conviction is to be proved against a prisoner, the data should not first be submitted for confirmation to some independent authority possessed of anatomical and physiological knowledge.

The editorial went on to describe identification by a chance fingerprint at a crime scene, and concluded with the following:

> . . . and for the due consideration of the matter it seems to us that the person called upon to examine and to advise as to identity or non-identity should possess thorough and practical knowledge as well as trained mental

powers of discrimination. To entrust the duty to partially skilled persons is in the highest degree dangerous from a public point of view.

The Chief Constable of Staffordshire probably had the last word on who should give evidence of fingerprint identification, the police or the medical profession. In his letter to the *Express*, published on the 28th of July 1905, the final paragraph stated:

There is one objection to the employment of medical men for this particular purpose. With the very best intentions, nine doctors out of ten make the worst witnesses in the world.

9 The growth of public interest

Fingerprint activity in 1905 was not confined to the courts. Following hard on the heels of the publicity generated by the Strattons' trial, the *Daily Express* launched a 'fingerprint' competition. This took the form of a serialized murder story with fingerprint clues. As the story unfolded fingerprints found at the fictitious crime scene were published, followed by the fingerprints of various characters who appeared in the story. The object was to discover the murderer by comparing their fingerprints with those found at the crime scene. A prize of £100 was offered to the competitor who correctly solved the mystery and gave the best reasons for his deduction.

In the same year the first of Henry Faulds's three books was published, entitled *Guide to Fingerprint Identification*. Unfortunately for him, the Editor of *Nature* invited Francis Galton to review it. Galton, in a very fair review, did not spare Faulds when he wrote:

> Dr. Faulds in his present volume recapitulates his old grievance with no less bitterness than formerly. He overstates the value of his own work, belittles that of others, and carps at evidence recently given in criminal cases. His book is not only biased and imperfect, but unfortunately it contains nothing new that is of value, so far as the writer of these remarks can judge, and much of what Dr. Faulds seems to consider new has long since been forestalled.

Galton was scrupulously fair when he referred to Faulds's 1880 letter by stating it was apparently the first printed communication on the subject. He reminded the reader, however, that it appeared years after the first public and official use of fingerprints had been made by Sir William Herschel in India.

William A. Pinkerton, head of the Western branch of the world famous Pinkerton Detective Agency, after a tour of all the principal

European cities was so impressed with the fingerprint system that he is reported to have said in 1905:

> It is twelve years ago since I was in England, but in that time I was astonished at the progress Scotland Yard has made. We in America believe we are progressive and up to date, but, make no mistake, there are no modern methods of capturing and identifying criminals that Scotland Yard doesn't investigate and, if they are worth anything, adopt at once. There is no red tape, no delay about taking on something that will improve the efficiency of the service.
>
> The one thing at the Yard which interested me the most was the high state of efficiency which the fingerprint system of identification has reached. The Bureau of Fingerprints there is one of the most marvellous departments I have ever examined. The identification of criminals has been reduced to practically a matter of book-keeping. To get a fingerprint and then simply turn up your indexes and you know your man at once.
>
> A criminal may shave or grow his beard, become stout or thin, alter his appearance to a considerable extent, but the one constant factor in his makeup is his fingerprints. They never change, in fact the only safe way for criminals nowadays is to wear gloves when they go out on a job, for the impressions of the fingers are found by the detectives on glasses, on newspapers, on dusty tables – in fact, the slightest impression of the fingers upon even a damp table or paper can by the process in use at the Yard serve as an adequate means of identification.
>
> One imagines that the romantic days of a detective's calling have passed, but with this fingerprint system the romance is far greater, far subtler, far more scientific and intellectual than it ever was.

Obviously inspired by the success being enjoyed by Scotland Yard, the provincial police forces started to maintain their own local fingerprint collections. The first were the East Suffolk Constabulary; Blackburn Borough; Blackpool Borough, Bradford City; Cardiff Borough and York City. Without doubt the most successful of these was Bradford City, led by an enthusiastic Detective Inspector Talbot. He presented the first provincial case, based on fingerprint evidence alone, to a court in December 1903.

One of Talbot's cases which occurred in August 1904 must have caused a certain amount of amusement. It started when two men were arrested in possession of property believed to be stolen. Their explanation was the one used by criminals since time immemorial: it had been given to them by an unknown man. Inquiries revealed that the property had come from the house of a minister who had been on holiday.

Entry to the house had been effected by the removal of tiles from the roof over the bathroom. As the intruders lowered themselves through the bathroom ceiling they supported themselves by holding the top of the open bathroom door. When Talbot examined the scene he found a clear fingerprint on the top of the door. As the latter was seven feet in height he was unable to photograph this print in situ. Undeterred, he had the door removed and carried through the streets to the police photographic studio, on a cart. The fingerprint was found to be identical with that of one of the men originally arrested. They were then charged with housebreaking. Although they pleaded not guilty, the jury thought otherwise, and they were sentenced to imprisonment with hard labour.

Although there was a gradual acceptance of identification by fingerprints, there were still many sceptics. A number of juries acquitted persons who had been identified by this method. In one such case at the Central Criminal Court a burglar had been identified by his thumb-print on a pane of glass from a laundry. The prisoner's defence was an alibi which the jury believed, so that he was found not guilty. The Common Serjeant, Mr Bosanquet, when discharging him gave him good advice, and at the same time gently rebuked the jury when he said, 'The jury, fortunately for you, did not know, as I now do, the absolute identification of your fingerprints possessed by Scotland Yard, where they are remarkably well known. You had better take care another time, because you may not again escape.'

Another Doubting Thomas was the mayor of a Northern city who dealt with the case of a riveter who had stolen twopence from a young miner. At the conclusion of the case the Chief Constable intimated that the accused had a bad record, and put in a list of convictions, some of which, however, the prisoner denied. When the Chief Constable told the court that the identification had been made by fingerprints the Mayor said, 'We cannot go into probabilities in this matter. We must have facts.' He was not impressed when the Chief Constable said, 'I have no doubt about them. They are fingerprints.'

The Mayor was eventually satisfied when the Chief Constable produced a number of prison documents previously signed by the prisoner for comparison with one that he wrote in the court.

The magazine *Punch* naturally saw the funny side of fingerprints when it wrote:

> We hear that the fingerprint experiments have proved so successful in tracing criminals that the police authorities will in future oppose any proposals for the erection of more public baths and wash-houses, as the cleaner the criminal the worse the fingerprint.

The fingerprint system was vindicated in a most unusual manner at the Rochester Quarter Sessions on the 7th of July 1905. A few weeks previously a man had been charged with burglary at a house in Strood. When he appeared before the Rochester magistrates he said his name was 'John Smith'. He went on to admit this was not his true name, and although he intended to plead guilty to the charge, he would withhold his identity because he wanted to test the value of the Scotland Yard fingerprint system. He told the magistrates that he had been convicted twice before, but he wanted the police to tell him who he was. 'Smith' was then committed for trial. At the Rochester Quarter Sessions the police explained that 'Smith' had given every facility for having his fingerprints taken. They had been sent to Detective Inspector Collins, with the result that 'Smith' was found to be Frank Cotton, who had previous convictions for theft and housebreaking. He was sent to prison for ten months.

In June 1906 a new dimension was added to the use of fingerprints for identification. An unknown man had committed suicide in Birmingham by cutting his throat with a knife. Detective Constable Parrack, the official photographer of the Birmingham force, was sent to the mortuary to take photographs of the body. He also examined the belongings of the dead man. On the buttons of the man's trousers he noticed the word 'Pentonville', while an examination of his hands revealed that skin on the fingers and in the middle of the hands was chafed. This was the sort of marking one usually associated with the making of mats or mailbags, a well-known prison occupation in those days. The thought struck Parrack that the deceased might have a fingerprint record, so, assisted by P.C. Hickman, he recorded the man's fingerprints and sent them to Scotland Yard. The fingerprints were quickly identified as belonging to a discharged convict.

This method of identifying bodies has been used successfully many thousands of times since. Such a system has come into its own during the last twenty or thirty years, when disasters occur with our mass transport by air, rail and sea: often the only satisfactory method of identifying the numerous mutilated corpses has been by fingerprints, or by the more recent addition of dental records.

A dead person does not have to have a criminal record to be identified by fingerprints. Providing the police have some idea where someone lived, a fingerprint examination for latent prints at that address can quite often produce prints of sufficient quality for them to be able to state that a particular person has at some time been in the premises. It is not quite as satisfactory as having a properly recorded set of fingerprints, but it is the best method available at the moment.

One of my last non-criminal cases before I retired was to assist in such an identification. An ocean yachtsman's boat had capsized, and he was drowned. His body had been washed ashore in a foreign country, and the authorities buried it within twenty-four hours. Fortunately, they had recorded an impression of the dead man's right forefinger before doing so. Meanwhile, in this country the executors of his will were unable to proceed with the administration of his estate because there was no death certificate or any authoritative document which proved beyond doubt that the deceased was the person they believed him to be. Once we received a copy of the fingerprint taken from the dead man, an officer was dispatched to the home of the victim so that he could make an examination for a matching fingerprint. He was successful, and the executors were able to complete their task. However, if the officer had not been able to find a particular matching print, the unfortunate widow would have faced the possibility of having to wait a number of years for a presumption of death before her husband's executors could settle his estate.

On the 2nd of March, 1908 the first head of the Fingerprint Branch, DCI Stedman, was forced to retire through ill health. He was succeeded by Detective Inspector Charles Stockley Collins. Ironically, Stedman was to survive his successor by the best part of twenty years.

The first stated case involving fingerprint identification in this country occurred the following year. A 'stated case' is one in which a new idea or proposal is placed before the courts and thoroughly argued, the court finally giving a ruling, which is then used as a yardstick in later cases.

This stated case arose when Thomas Herbert Castleton was tried for burglary. It was heard at the West Riding Quarter Sessions on the 21st of October 1909. The only evidence offered by the prosecution was a candle which bore fingerprints and which had been found at the crime scene. The detective superintendent identified the fingerprints on the candle as those of Castleton. No evidence was led for the accused, and he was found guilty and sentenced to three years' penal servitude. He sought leave to appeal against this conviction, but the trial judge refused. Castleton then successfully appealed against this refusal.

The appeal was heard on the 12th of November 1909 at the Court of Criminal Appeal before Lord Chief Justice Alverstone, and Justices

Darling and Bucknill. Counsel for the appellant claimed the conviction was bad, as the only evidence against his client was that of fingerprints upon a candle left behind, and that there was no other evidence against him. He suggested that even supposing the prints on the candle were those of Castleton, the evidence was not sufficiently weighty. He concluded by reminding the Court that the appellant was an associate of thieves and that the fingerprints might have been put there by someone else.

When Mr Justice Darling inquired if the prisoner could find anybody whose fingerprints were exactly like his, counsel explained that he was not instructed as to that. He finally suggested that someone else might have used the candle, although it belonged to Castleton.

Giving judgment, the Lord Chief Justice said:

> We are clearly of the opinion that this application must be dismissed. The suggestion has been made that these fingerprints may have been put there by someone else, but that suggestion was disposed of by the jury, who decided upon the evidence before them. Our attention has been drawn to the photographs of the impressions of the fingerprints. Looking at the middle finger particularly, as well as to the index finger of the right hand, we agree with the evidence of the expert at the trial.

This was the forerunner of a number of 'stated cases' relating to fingerprints. A particularly interesting judgment was given in Scotland in 1934. The case was H.M. Advocate *v.* Hamilton. The Lord Justice General Clyde in his judgment said:

> Fingerprint evidence is undoubtedly competent, that is settled. . . . The value of fingerprint evidence depends upon the reliance which can be placed on the result of expert investigation and experience. . . . to the effect that identity is never found to exist between the skin ridges on two different persons' fingers. This is what leads the expert to claim infallibility for the finger mark method. I deprecate the use of the word infallibility in this connection at all. What the experts obviously mean is not absolute but practical infallibility – that is to say a presumption of truth, the reliability of which may be accepted, not because it is irrebuttable in its own nature, but because long and extensive experience is shown to provide no instance in which it has ever been successfully rebutted.

By 1909 public interest in the fingerprint system was such that the Commissioner was invited to prepare a fingerprint exhibition for display as part of the Imperial International Exhibition to be held in London. The popularity of this display was undisputed, and an invitation was received from the organizers of the Japan-British Exhibition for it to be made available again in 1910. This particular exhibition was under the auspices of the Imperial Japanese Government.

In his Annual Report for 1910 the Commissioner wrote of the fingerprint system:

> The Fingerprint Department recorded no less than 10,848 identifications as against 9,960 in the previous year. It is, however, apparent that high water mark has now been reached, and it is unlikely that the total of 1,910 will be surpassed.

What halcyon days! In 1979 the fingerprint collection held the fingerprints of 2,905,203 convicted persons; 487,462 sets of inquiry fingerprints were received during the year from police forces; 285,456 identifications were made, and over 200,000 sets of fingerprints from newly convicted persons were added to the collection. One vast step backward in human integrity.

10 The Criminal Record Office

In 1911 Sir Edward Henry – who was knighted in 1906 – accompanied the newly crowned monarch, King George V, to India as equerry. On 6 January 1912 he was entertained at dinner by the members of the Bengal Police. During the evening he was presented with a large silver salver, and was garlanded, Indian-style. It was during his address to this assembly that Sir Edward presented to the assembled company his former Sub-Inspector Azizul Haque, and paid tribute to his unsparing efforts, which helped perfect the fingerprint system.

Haque did not stay in the fingerprint branch when Henry left India. He transferred to general police duties, as he felt there was no possibility of attaining promotion to the higher ranks if he remained in the identification bureau. In 1913 he received the title of 'Khan Sahib', and eventually rose to the rank of superintendent before he retired in 1923. The following year the Government of India decorated him with the personal title of 'Khan Bahadur', and awarded him an honorarium of 5,000 rupees in recognition of the special services he had rendered in connection with the fingerprint system.

It is not known whether Sir Edward met Chandra Bose during his visit to India, but I think it was highly probable. Bose had remained in the Bengal Fingerprint Bureau, where over the years he introduced various improvements. He was a deputy superintendent when he retired. He also was decorated with a personal title of 'Rai Bahadur', and received an honorarium of 5,000 rupees in recognition of the services he had rendered in connection with the development of fingerprints.

In November 1912 a 25-year-old barman attempted to assassinate Sir Edward Henry. The attack came as Sir Edward was leaving his car to enter his London house. His assailant, Albert Bowes, who had been loitering in the vicinity for several hours, approached him and said he wanted to speak to him. Sir Edward replied that he was busy and that the man should call at his office. Bowes then pulled out a revolver and fired three shots at the Commissioner. One bullet entered his right groin and travelled across the stomach, coming out at the other side, while the second bullet went through his leg. Mercifully, the third bullet missed Henry and was found later embedded in a piece of hall furniture. The Commissioner's driver seized the man and held him until help arrived.

Apparently Bowes had applied to the Carriage Department at Scotland Yard for a licence to drive a bus, but because of his record it was not granted. He had made several other applications, all with the same result, until he was sent a formal letter stating that the matter could not under any circumstances be reconsidered. Bowes considered this refusal an injustice. In the Latymer Arms public house, Notting Hill, where he worked, he had told George Billings, a tram-driver, of his grievance. Billings suggested that another application in six months' time might be more successful, whereupon Bowes announced his intention to kill the Commissioner if he didn't get it. Billings's dry response to this was that it wouldn't do him any good, because he wouldn't get a licence at all then.

At his trial Albert Bowes pleaded not guilty to attempted murder. His defence counsel tried to show that he was of unsound mind when he carried out the attack. Two of his sisters were called to give supporting evidence. One of them stated that he had heard voices urging him to do something dreadful. This line of defence was soon disposed of by Dr Dyer, the medical officer of Brixton Prison, who was of the opinion that Bowes was sane at the time. He also mentioned that the prisoner had told him that he had drunk nine pints of ale on the morning of the day in question. The jury did not take long to find him guilty.

After the verdict Sir Edward Henry asked Mr Justice Darling if he might address the court. The judge agreed, and Sir Edward said:

> I wish to throw myself on the mercy of the Court in the peculiar
> circumstances of the case for venturing to take the unusual course of
> making a personal appeal. The members of my family, one of whom was
> quite a small child, arrived on the scene so soon after the shots had been
> fired as to have been almost spectators of what happened. The impression
> made on their minds of what they saw has been a lasting impression, and
> they have been moved to pity by consideration of the prisoner's youth and
> the conditions of his home. When their thoughts in years to come travel
> back to the events of that evening, as they inevitably must, the pain of

recollection will be mitigated if they could feel that I have pleaded, and not ineffectually, to induce your Lordship to mercifully weigh the sentence you think it is your duty to pass on the prisoner.

When passing sentence the judge commented that although he had not the slightest doubt that the prisoner was sane at the time, he believed he was not so stable in his intellect as the ordinary run of people. But for that fact, and the appeal made by Sir Henry on his behalf, he would have sentenced the prisoner to penal servitude for life, an awful sentence to pass on anyone so young. As it was, for the protection of the public the sentence he would pass must be a severe one. He then sentenced Bowes to fifteen years' penal servitude.

The *Police Review* in an editorial stated:

Every member of the force therefore, as a part of the great body of Police that exists for the preservation of law and order, is identified with Sir Edward, just as the Commissioner has felt himself to be identified with each individual Constable who has similarly suffered at the hands of some reckless and vicious desperado. The tendency in this direction of assaulting, wounding and murdering the Police has apparently grown in recent years, and the necessity for more stringent measures of protection is cumulative and urgent. The possession of hand firearms is evidently too great a danger in the hands of impulsive law-breakers to be tolerated. Doubtless regret comes to the criminal soon after the event, especially when the consequences come home to himself. . . .

We trust therefore that the numerous instances of attacks upon the Police, which have now so tragically culminated in this flagrant example, will lead the authorities to enact some preventive restrictions with regard to the carrying of firearms, as one of the means for making the life of a Policeman less liable than it now is to the vagaries of lunatics or the savagery of brutes.

Seventy years later, and actively encouraged by the abolition of capital punishment, criminals are still murdering and maiming policemen with firearms.

That particular episode had a sting in the tail. When Bowes was released from prison Sir Edward helped him to emigrate to Canada, where he would be able to start a new life. In 1924 Albert Bowes was killed at Rossburg, Florida, when he was shot by a sheriff. It would appear that Sheriff Lyle had been called to Rossburg, where it was alleged that Bowes had shot and injured a man. Some hours later the sheriff and his men found Bowes at a farm. As they approached Bowes rushed towards them, brandishing an automatic pistol, whereupon the sheriff took refuge behind a tree and shot him through the head.

Gradually throughout the world the fingerprint system of identification was replacing the outmoded anthropometric system. In 1910
at the annual convention of the International Association of Police
Chiefs held at Birmingham, Alabama, it was reported that, out of four
hundred police establishments in the United States consulted by the
Association, there were ninety-seven departments who applied the
Bertillon method for the identification of criminals, sixteen who used
the fingerprint system alone, and seventy-six who worked a
combination of the two methods.

In 1915 a small group of Americans, all engaged in fingerprint
identification, met in California to exchange views and to discuss
experiences in their specialized field. Such was their enthusiasm that
they formed an organization called 'The International Association for
Criminal Identification'. The word 'Criminal' was later dropped from
the title. This was to be the first professional body of identification
experts to be formed. The IAI (as it is commonly known) has gathered
strength and prestige over the years, and today its many thousands of
members are scattered throughout some forty countries.

For many years the criminal record-keeping section of the Criminal
Investigation Department at Scotland Yard had been known
variously as the 'Convict Supervision Office', the 'Habitual Criminals
Registry', and the 'Fingerprint Department'. Each title had been
correct at the time, but by 1913 the changes had become confusing.
The confusion had been compounded by the passing of the
Prevention of Crimes Act 1908, which gave a precise legal definition to
the words 'Habitual Criminal', and the definition was unrelated to the
record-keeping function. The situation was rationalized on the 20th of
September 1913 by the abolition of all former titles, and the
substitution of 'Criminal Record Office' in their stead.

With a stable and competent method of identifying criminals now
firmly established, serious concern began to be experienced about the
administrative loopholes which made the fingerprint records in-
complete. Under the Prison Standing Orders of that time, for
instance, persons sentenced to one month's imprisonment and under
by a summary court were exempted from having their fingerprints
taken. Although this had no real detrimental effect when the original
order was made, by 1913 it was noticed that the courts were showing a
marked reluctance to commit offenders to prison except in the last
resort, preferring instead to make probation orders, give bind-overs
and to pass prison sentences of one month or less even for offences of a
serious nature.

As the Prison Service was at that time the only source of criminal fingerprints, the concern being shown had a very real basis. The obvious solution was applied the following year: the staff of the fingerprint department started to train divisional detectives to take the fingerprints of their prisoners. This had an immediate impact, as the detectives were able to obtain knowledge of the criminal status of their prisoners faster than under the old remand system. The magistrates were pleased with the result because they could deal with a large number of cases on the first appearance of the prisoner, as against remanding them in custody for inquiries to be made, while the prison service was also glad that the number of remand prisoners was reduced considerably. The fingerprint department was satisfied that the fingerprints of most criminals were now being obtained, thus making the fingerprint collection far more comprehensive, and, in a perverse sort of way, some prisoners benefited by not having to be remanded in custody in order to have their fingerprints taken. The innovation was so successful that by 1917 the fingerprint collection was approaching 300,000 persons, and being added to at a rate of about four hundred new criminal sets of prints a week.

In fact, it was almost too successful, for it came at a time when the department was short on experience. It had lost the services of three experienced men. In October 1917 the size of the collection was reduced by removing the fingerprints of all persons previously convicted at Police or Petty Sessional Courts and sentenced to not more than a month's imprisonment for petty offences, and for men who had not been re-convicted for a period of five years. The records of persons known to have died, and those apparently too old to commit further crime, had already been removed. This was a continuing process.

1918 was to see the resignation of Sir Edward Henry. For a man who had done so much for the police service in general, and policemen in particular, it was a very sad year. The storm-clouds had been gathering for several months in the shape of the (unrecognized) police union, which had been campaigning for better pay and conditions and recognition.

The storm erupted when Henry and his wife were visiting his wife's relatives in Ireland. On Sunday the 25th of August a police constable named Thiel was dismissed the service for indulging in union activities. Three days later the illegal police union sent an ultimatum to the Commissioner. It not only demanded that Thiel should be reinstated immediately, and that pay together with pensions should be increased, but more importantly, that there should be recognition of the police union. A reply was demanded by midnight on Thursday. This was rejected by the acting Commissioner. The following day, the 30th of August, 6,000 policemen went on strike.

When Henry heard the news he returned to London immediately. Meanwhile the Prime Minister, David Lloyd George, had invited delegates of the striking policemen to a meeting on Saturday. Also present were the Home Secretary, Sir George Cave, and the Commissioner. The Prime Minister conceded two of the demands, the reinstatement of Thiel and pay increases. On the third demand, of recognition, he managed to persuade the delegates that it was not the right time to pursue this particular matter. This satisfied the strikers, and the following day London had full police coverage again. Sir Edward Henry felt his position was untenable, and promptly resigned.

On his resignation the *Police Review* commented:

> In the retirement of Sir Edward Henry from the Commissionership of the Metropolitan Police the rank and file of the London constabulary have lost a very sincere and devoted friend. . . . There may be different opinions in regard to the methods of Police government and administration for which he, as Commissioner, was held responsible, and in any case the present is not the time to anticipate the final judgement of history, but we would assure Sir Edward that he carries with him into his retirement the good wishes of the Metropolitan Police, who have long recognised in their chief the qualities of a Christian gentleman.

In recognition of his distinguished service, the King conferred on Henry a baronetcy. The honour pleased him, because it was hereditary, and he imagined that it would eventually pass to his son, John, then aged ten. Fate, however, was to deny Henry's hopes. His son died before him, at the age of twenty-two.

When Detective Inspector Frederick Hunt retired on the 29th of April 1918 and returned to his native Devon it left only one of the original trio, Collins, who was to remain as head of the Branch until 1925. In 1920 two new men joined the Department, Detective Constables Arthur Henry Dutch and Frederick Rupert Cherrill. The latter was destined to become a legend in his own lifetime.

11 From Telegraphic Code to single fingerprints

The 1920s were a period of innovation and change, and included one small panic.

As more and more countries adopted the fingerprint system some fingerprint experts directed their energies to finding a suitable way of sending fingerprint data from one country to another. Detective Superintendent Collins was one of them. His booklet *A Telegraphic Code for Fingerprint Formulae* was published in 1921. The code allowed for pattern descriptions, ridge counts between fixed points and the reading of ridge characteristics by using a specially prepared window with parallel lines set at six millimetres apart. Collins quite rightly pointed out that any recognition made solely by coded information would only supply a 'strong suspicion', which had to be confirmed by comparison of the actual finger impressions. He had to wait until 1924 for it to be tested operationally, and then it happened twice, once to Australia and once to New Zealand. In both instances replies were received within forty-eight hours, and both indicated that the subjects in question had criminal records. It is reported that when one of these men heard how his criminal record had been obtained he said, 'If you can send my fingerprints from one end of the earth to the other, I might as well commit suicide.'

Although it was a most satisfactory situation to have a more or less comprehensive fingerprint collection of the criminal population, the growth of this collection was counter-productive as far as solving crime by fingerprints was concerned. During the early days of the system any chance fingerprints found at a crime scene were searched against the ten-finger collection. This was accomplished by deciding which digits made the fingerprints found at the scene of a crime; then by using the pattern data these prints revealed it was possible to select certain areas of the collection containing fingerprints of persons which revealed similar patterns on those digits. With relatively small collections, such searching is not particularly arduous, but as the collection grows the number of records in each section to be consulted increases proportionately until the results obtained are disproportionate to the effort expended. This counter-productivity was amply illustrated in 1918 when with a collection of fingerprints from 300,000 criminals not one crime in London was solved by fingerprints. The following year was not much better, with only four crimes solved in this manner.

The natural solution was to create a much smaller, separate collection of those people who specialized in the type of crime capable of being solved by fingerprints – i.e., housebreakers and shopbreakers – and classify their fingerprints in such a way as to make the searching of them relatively quick and productive.

Collins saw within the framework of his 'Telegraphic Code' the possibility of its modification for use as a single-fingerprint system. Unfortunately, he did not consider each digit in complete isolation; although he was able to classify individual digits, he filed them according to the numerical value produced by the code. As the code only related to characteristics appearing in a restricted portion of the print, it was possible to have prints from different digits with wide ridge-count variations filed next to each other. This produced a cumbersome searching routine which eliminated only about a quarter of the collection. The Department persevered with this collection, which eventually contained the fingerprints of 4,000 persons – that is, 40,000 single impressions – for seven years before abandoning it.

On the 4th of January 1924 fingerprints were reproduced in Supplement 'A' of the *Police Gazette* for the first time. This publication is probably the most famous of all police publications – it is certainly the oldest. Before it received its present title in 1828 it was known as the 'Hue and Cry', and listed details of offenders wanted in various places. The *Police Gazette* has a number of supplements dealing with specialized subjects, Supplement 'A' dealing with travelling criminals. A front and profile photograph of the subject was reproduced, together with a copy of his right forefinger print.

Detective Superintendent Collins, the last of the original trio, retired on the 27th of February 1925. Three months earlier, on the 17th of November 1924, he had the pleasure of seeing the Fingerprint Department obtain independent status – a Department in its own right, and not just a section of the Criminal Record Office. Collins's successor, the newly promoted Detective Chief Inspector William Bell, only held the post for fourteen months before he retired on the

Charles Stedman

Sir Edward Henry

Frederick John Hunt

Charles Stockley Collins

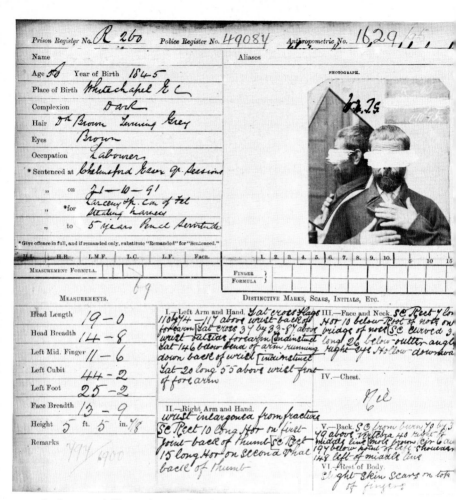

| Prison Register No. | *R 260* | Police Register No. | *49084* | Anthropometric No. | *1629, ,* |

Name		Aliases	
Age *56* Year of Birth *1845*			
Place of Birth *Whitechapel E C*			PHOTOGRAPH.
Complexion *Dark*			
Hair *Dk Brown Turning Grey*			
Eyes *Brown*			
Occupation *Labourer*			
*Sentenced at *Chelmsford Essex Qr Sessions*			
„ on *21 — 10 — 91*			
„ *for *Larceny &c. Con of Fel Stealing harness*			
„ to *5 years Penal Servitude*			

* Give offence in full, and if remanded only, substitute "Remanded" for "Sentenced."

| H.L. | H.B. | L.M.F. | L.C. | L.F. | Face. | | 1. | 2. | 3. | 4. | 5. | 6. | 7. | 8. | 9. | 10. | 5 | 10 | 15 |
| MEASUREMENT FORMULA. | | | | | | FINGER FORMULA | | | | | | | | | | | | | |

MEASUREMENTS.

Head Length	*19 — 0*
Head Breadth	*14 — 8*
Left Mid. Finger	*11 — 6*
Left Cubit	*44 — 2*
Left Foot	*25 — 2*
Face Breadth	*13 — 9*
Height	*5* ft. *5* in. *78*
Remarks	

DISTINCTIVE MARKS, SCARS, INITIALS, ETC.

I.—Left Arm and Hand. *Sat cross flags 110&74 — 117 above wrist back of forearm. Sat cross 34 by 33-84 above wrist outscar forearm (indistinct) Sat 146 below bend of arm running down back of wrist (indistinct) Sat 20 long 55 above wrist front of forearm*

II.—Right Arm and Hand. *wrist inlarged from fracture SC Rect 10 long Hor on first joint back of thumb. SC Rect 15 long Hor on second Phal back of thumb*

III.—Face and Neck. *SC Rect 7 long Hor 10 below Root of nose on bridge of nose. SC curved 3 long 26 below outter angle right eye. Hollow downwards*

IV.—Chest. *Nil*

V.—Back. *SC from burn 70 by 3 49 above vertebra 40 right of middle line mole brown Cir 6 au 197 below point of left shoulder 148 left of middle line*

VI.—Rest of Body. *Slight skin scars on tops of fingers*

Anthropometric/fingerprint record card (front)

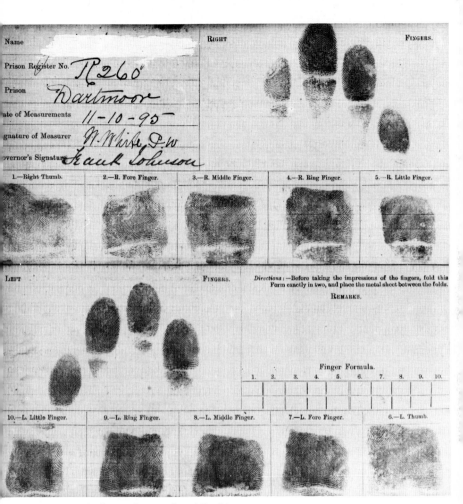

Name

Prison Register No. *R 260*

Prison *Dartmoor*

Date of Measurements *11-10-95*

Signature of Measurer *N. White, P.W.*

Governor's Signature *Frank Johnson*

RIGHT

FINGERS.

1.—Right Thumb. | 2.—R. Fore Finger. | 3.—R. Middle Finger. | 4.—R. Ring Finger. | 5.—R. Little Finger.

LEFT

FINGERS.

Directions:—Before taking the impressions of the fingers, fold this Form exactly in two, and place the metal sheet between the folds.

REMARKS.

Finger Formula.

1. | 2. | 3. | 4. | 5. | 6. | 7. | 8. | 9. | 10.

10.—L. Little Finger. | 9.—L. Ring Finger. | 8.—L. Middle Finger. | 7.—L. Fore Finger. | 6.—L. Thumb.

Anthropometric/fingerprint record card (back)

First crime-scene fingerprint proved by the New Scotland Yard's Fingerprint Department in 1902

Top left: *Thumb-print on window-sill at No. 156 Denmark Hill*

Top right: *Left thumb-print of Harry Jackson*

Bottom left and right: *Tracings of prints above, showing characteristics in agreement*

Members of the Metropolitan Police sent to guard the Jubilee presents of Queen Victoria at the St Louis Exhibition, USA, 1904. (Detective Sergeant Ferrier is second from left.)

Fingerprints in the Deptford murder case

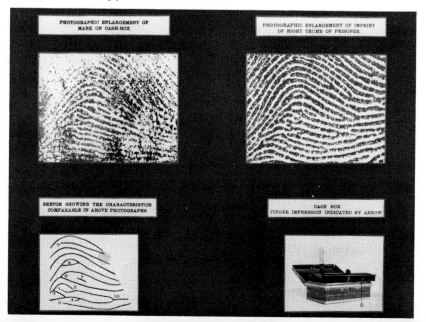

PHOTOGRAPHIC ENLARGEMENT OF MARK ON CASH-BOX.

PHOTOGRAPHIC ENLARGEMENT OF IMPRINT OF RIGHT THUMB OF PRISONER.

SKETCH SHOWING THE CHARACTERISTICS COMPARABLE IN ABOVE PHOTOGRAPHS.

CASH BOX
FINGER IMPRESSION INDICATED BY ARROW

FOR DETECTIVE WORK

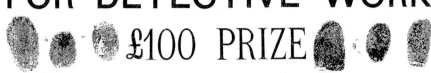

£100 PRIZE

TO WHOM DO THESE FINGER-PRINTS BELONG?

A prize of **ONE HUNDRED POUNDS** is offered by the Editor of the

"DAILY EXPRESS"

for the best solution of the mystery WHO DID THE DEED? in connection with a novel and thrilling **DETECTIVE STORY**, which is to commence in the

"DAILY EXPRESS" on JULY 21st.

The interest of the story is centred upon the mysterious death of a solicitor, and the heroic efforts of his daughter to discover who did the deed. The clue is

A FINGER-PRINT

on a tumbler, and, in the course of the story, the finger-prints of all the characters are given, and by comparing them the problem can be solved.

On the day preceding the opening of the Story (JULY 20th) an interesting illustrated article by Dr. J. G. Garson, the celebrated finger-print expert, will appear. In the course of this article the writer explains the various patterns in the finger-print. Ridges (Fig. 1), Arches (Fig. 2), Whorls (Fig. 3), and Loops (Fig. 4).

(Figure 1—RIDGE). (Figure 2—ARCHES). (Figure 3—WHORLS). (Figure 4—LOOPS).

In the competition for the hundred pounds Police Officers stand a splendid chance. Their experience in dealing with crime must materially assist them in solving the mystery. The story and the problem form a practical lesson in a branch of detective work that is coming more and more into prominence.

READ THE

Daily Express

On Thursday, July 20th.

Fingerprint competitions conducted by the 'Daily Express' (above) in 1905 and the 'News of the World' (right) in 1939

*T*O test that infallibility which is officially claimed for the Finger-print System, the "News of the World" makes the substantial offer of £2,000 to-day.

The sum of **£1,000** will be paid to the man reader who can reproduce a finger-print identical with **any one** of the five reproduced at the top of this page.

Similarly the sum of **£1,000** will also be paid to the woman reader who can reproduce a finger-print identical with **any one** of the five reproduced at the bottom of the page.

The finger-print illustrations, it should be explained, have been photographically enlarged for the purposes of clarity.

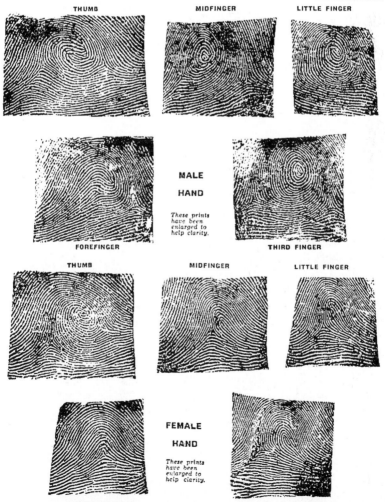

THUMB   MIDFINGER   LITTLE FINGER

MALE HAND

These prints have been enlarged to help clarity.

FOREFINGER   THIRD FINGER

THUMB   MIDFINGER   LITTLE FINGER

FEMALE HAND

These prints have been enlarged to help clarity.

FOREFINGER   THIRD FINGER

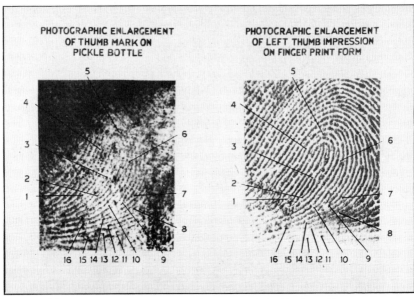

The thumb-print used to establish the identity of murder victim Mrs Irene Manton

(Below) *Detective Chief Superintendent Cherrill with his senior officers, three of whom later became heads of the Fingerprint Department. The front row, left to right, shows Jack Livings, Frederick Cherrill, Leonard Witt; the back row, left to right, has Maurice Ray, Dermot Carrigan, Harold Squires, Herbert Nicholls, Ted Holten, Sydney Drew, John Dobson, John Godsell and Percy Law*

31st of May 1926, to be replaced by Detective Chief Inspector Harry Battley, who was to remain considerably longer.

Shortly after he retired Collins travelled with Sir Edward Henry to Windsor, Ontario, to attend the eleventh annual convention of the International Association for Identification, held between the 26th and 29th of August 1925. Sir Edward gave the opening address on the discussion about fingerprints, and Collins presented a paper entitled 'The Fingerprint as I Know It'. Very little was recorded about this convention, but an article by Mr T. D. Cooke, Editor of the *Fingerprint and Identification Magazine*, the official organ of the IAI at that time, described what the body stood for. He wrote:

> Ten years, as time goes, is not an extensive period for a great work to be accomplished. And yet in ten years the IAI has accomplished a great work. It has brought Maine closer to California, Nova Scotia nearer to Mexico. It has introduced identification officials of South America to peace officers of Canada; it has helped Mississippi sheriffs by teaching them what British constables have learned; it has given detectives in the Philippine Islands the opportunity to profit by the experience of police chiefs in New England. It has brought the spirit of friendship and fellowship into the work of the identification expert; it has elevated the standards of identification work in the minds of the public and the minds of its members. . . .

The small panic had its innocent origins in 1926, and manifested itself in 1927. Dr G. P. Crowden, of the Institute of Physiology, University College, London had a paper entitled 'A Comparative Study of the Development of Physiology of Identical Twins' published in the Guy's Hospital reports in October 1926. The paper was an extremely detailed study of 25-year-old male identical twins. He detailed their anatomical and physiological similarities, and he also analysed their school reports, which their father had carefully preserved. These showed a remarkable similarity in scholastic attainment and behavioural pattern. Naturally, he referred to their fingerprints. On these he wrote:

> Their fingerprints are particularly interesting. Without exception all are loops, and in some cases the number of friction ridges between the delta and the centre of the loop is the same.
>
> From their fingerprints it can be seen that in the case of the right middle finger of each there is almost perfect mirror imaging. In one case the loop turns towards the radius, in the other towards the ulnar, while the number of friction ridges is the same in each, namely three.

What Dr Crowden failed to draw attention to in the body of the report (although it was shown in one of his analysis tables) was that one twin had seven ulnar-loop and three radial-loop patterns on his fingers, whereas the other twin had nine ulnar loops and only one radial loop on his. The *Lancet*, in its issue dated 25th December 1926, mentioned the work of Dr Crowden in an article about identical twins.

On the 24th of December 1926 a national newspaper published a potted version of this fifteen-page report. There is always an inherent danger when a person from one discipline tries to make a précis of a report written by someone in a different discipline because they usually fail to recognize some of the more subtle nuances, as happened in this case. One paragraph of the newspaper version read:

> Their resemblance extends not only to their size, shape and appearance, but to their blood pressure and fingerprints – indeed, to everything that can be measured.

Within a week a northern newspaper had gone the whole hog with a sub-paragraph heading:

EXTRAORDINARY TWINS
FINGERPRINTS IDENTICAL

Here now was a story worthy of publishing, and it spread like wildfire through the country, the Continent, America and Canada. Probably the most dramatic headline came from America. It read:

DESTROYS THEORY OF FINGERPRINTS
Discovery of twins with identical
thumb marks said to discredit
system believed perfect.

As by now the majority of countries had converted their record systems to fingerprints only, one can imagine the consternation caused by these wild reports on the various law-enforcement agencies. The result was a steady stream of letters and messages from all over the world to New Scotland Yard, seeking some form of reassurance that the unthinkable had not happened. Needless to say, they all received the necessary reassurance. The *Lancet* in its edition dated the 5th of February 1927 also put on record that the fingerprints of the twins were not identical. Peace then reigned and memories dimmed – so much so that two years later the same national newspaper which published the original story of the twins published an article under the heading:

ABOUT TWINS: DO YOU KNOW THAT – ?

It included the following paragraph:

> One of the most interesting, as it is one of the most surprising, points of similarity in twins is the fact that not only their fingerprints, but the whole of what is known as the friction surfaces of their hands and feet, are frequently found to be identical.

It was claimed that the article was written by a doctor. If this was correct it is quite apparent that he did not believe in using the *Lancet* when he researched his subject.

Frustrated by the lack of success of the single-fingerprint system devised by Collins – only seventy crimes had been solved by means of fingerprints at New Scotland Yard between 1923 and 1925 – the new head of the department, Battley, directed his talents to finding a more efficient system. Battley chose as his assistant another man who had a considerable ability in fingerprint analysis, Detective Sergeant Cherrill. The fact that they had both worked the Collins system made them very aware of its weaknesses.

Their approach was completely different to that of Collins, inasmuch as they analysed a series of fingermarks collected from various crime scenes to determine how much data was revealed. Their findings discredited previous assumptions regarding the frequency of occurrence of a fixed point called a delta. Deltas normally appear on either side of a fingerprint pattern, and with some patterns they appear on both sides. The analysis by Battley and Cherrill indicated that in fact the delta was present in over 60 per cent of chance impressions. Armed with this vital piece of information they devised a special fixed-focus magnifying glass with a glass base on which seven concentric circles were inscribed with respective radii of 3mm, 5mm, 7mm, 9mm, 11mm, 13mm, 15mm. From the centre each circle was allocated an identifying letter, A, B, C etc. By placing the centre spot on a fixed point – usually the core of the print – they were able to relate delta to core by reading out the concentric circle in which it fell. This information – coupled with special codings for core formations, ridge counts between fixed points and tracings – allowed each print to be very accurately described. As previously mentioned, ten separate collections, one for each digit, were formed. Each collection was initially subdivided by the print pattern – i.e. Arch, Tented Arch, Radial Loop, Ulnar Loop, Whorl, Twinned Loop, Lateral Pocket Loop, Composite and Accidental. Using the new codings, each print was filed in sequence within these subdivisions. As with the Collins system, the fingerprints of those persons who specialized in breaking into premises were placed in these collections.

The results obtained were, by the standards of those days, quite dramatic. During the years 1928 and 1929 over three hundred and sixty identifications of criminals were effected in this new collection. In 1930 Harry Battley's book entitled *Single Fingerprints* was published by H.M. Stationery Office. The invaluable assistance given by the recently promoted Detective Inspector Cherrill was recognized in a preface to the book.

Besides forming a single fingerprint collection, Battley also formed a sub-collection of unidentified fingerprints from crime scenes. These were prints remaining unidentified after normal searching processes. That they remained unidentified was due mainly to one of three reasons:

1. They revealed insufficient data for search.
2. The person responsible had not yet been convicted of an offence which would qualify him or her for inclusion in the specialized collection.
3. The person responsible had not been previously arrested and fingerprinted.

The effectiveness of the unidentified marks collection in relation to the last category was well demonstrated in 1928.

The case began with a run-of-the-mill break-in at a pavilion at Watford on the 21st of July 1928. When local county police officers examined the scene they found a fingerprint on a wine-glass. This print was believed to have been left by the intruder. The wine-glass was sent to New Scotland Yard, where the digital impression was photographed. From its position on the wine-glass the searching officer deduced that the print had been made by a right forefinger, and a search of the right-forefinger section of the single-fingerprint collection was carried out without success. The fingerprint was then filed in the unidentified marks collection.

Shortly afterwards an article from a crime committed on the 12th of August, 1928 at Staple Hill, Gloucestershire, was sent to New Scotland Yard. The digital marks on this article were found to be identical with the fingerprint on the wine-glass from Watford. This meant that there was now proof positive that the two crimes committed in a three-week time scale, and roughly one hundred miles from each other, had been committed by the same person.

This sequence of events was to be repeated many times over the next few months, with marks from scenes of crimes committed many miles apart:

16 August 1928 – Stinchcombe, Gloucestershire.
27 August 1928 – Chipping Sodbury, Gloucestershire.
25 September 1928 – Harpenden, Hertfordshire.
10 October 1928 – Rugby, Warwickshire.
25 December 1928 – Redbourne, Hertfordshire.
1 June 1929 – Loughborough, Leicestershire.
24 July 1929 – King's Langley, Hertfordshire.

Shortly after the King's Langley crime, a man was arrested at Hitchin, Hertfordshire, and charged with housebreaking and larceny. As he was being fingerprinted, he remarked that this was the first time his fingerprints had been taken. The fingerprint department confirmed that this was so, but at the same time informed the arresting force that the man had been identified by fingerprints for a series of crimes committed in four counties. This method of tracking unknown criminals has been repeated many thousands of times since.

By 1930 the fingerprint collection contained the fingerprints of 486,000 persons, and the departmental strength had increased to twenty-seven officers. The number of identifications established by fingerprints since the Department was formed in 1901 then stood at 318,316.

12 Palm-prints, murders and passports

The first palm-print case in England occurred in 1931. John Egan – who had been identified by his fingerprints left at several crime scenes – had been arrested and charged with breaking and entering houses at Watford, Staines and Hendon. He had also been charged with attempting to break and enter a shop in Camden Town. While he was on remand in Brixton Prison his palm-prints were taken and sent to New Scotland Yard. An identification was soon established for a palm-print which had been developed on a plate-glass top of a dressing-table at a crime scene. Egan was committed for trial at the Central Criminal Court from Wimbledon Police Court.

On the day of his trial, Detective Inspector Cherrill attended to give identification evidence in regard to the palm-print. Egan, however, was not disposed to question the evidence. He pleaded guilty to four charges, and asked for nine other similar cases to be taken into consideration. As the prisoner had pleaded guilty, it was not necessary for Cherrill to prove the palm-print. The court was made aware by prosecuting counsel of this new variation of personal identification, evidence of which would have been given if it had been necessary.

The Recorder, Sir Ernest Wild, called Cherrill to the witness-box and asked him if palm-prints were as infallible as fingerprints. Cherrill told him they were, and went on to point out that the patterns on the end of the fingers were simply a culmination of the ridge system which covered the whole of the palmar surface of the hands, and that the ridge structure on the palm of the hand was as immutable as those on the fingertips. His curiosity satisfied, the Recorder then sentenced Egan to fourteen months' imprisonment.

I have little doubt that if Egan had pleaded not guilty the court's attention would have been drawn to the palm-print case of the State *v*. Kuhl, heard in an American Appeal Court thirteen years before.

This appeal case which challenged the admissibility of palm-print evidence, was heard by the Nevada Appeal Court in 1918. It was raised by a man named Kuhl, who had been convicted of murdering Fred. M. Searcey, a Federal mail-stage driver, in Elko County, Nevada. The principal evidence was a partial palm-print in blood found on an envelope recovered from one of the mailbags at the crime scene.

The court in this case stated in part:

Were we dealing here with a fingerprint impression, our course would be easy, for the courts of this country, and of England as well, have paved the way for the recognition of this science as an evidentiary element of criminal prosecution. The main contention here is that the experts who testified were not qualified to give an opinion as to the identity of palm print impressions; and, as we understand the contention of appellant, it is that science has not yet developed this question sufficiently to bear out the conclusion of an expert on the subject. Will the same rule which led the court to recognise experts of fingerprint identification permit such experts to testify as to their conclusions upon palm print identification? This is the vital question here.

The lines of the palms of the human hand and the soles of the feet, which form the basis of individual identification, are the papillary ridges which serve the office of raising the mouths of ducts, so as to facilitate the discharge of sweat, and perhaps perform the additional function of aiding the sense of touch and of giving elasticity to the skin of the hand, and, having a vacuumistic tendency, they assist in preventing against slipping. These papillary ridges form figures, patterns or designs which research, study, and science have divided into classes named after their particular form, to wit, arches, loops, whorls and composites. These patterns as they have been established and named by those who have become devotees to the science of fingerprint identification, while they have been discussed principally in connection with finger impressions, are not confined alone to the human finger but are found with equal importance and equal persistency in the human palm and the sole of the human foot.

All the learned authors, experts, and scientists on the subject of fingerprint identification agree that these patterns, formed by the papillary ridges on the inner surface of the human hand and the sole of the foot, are persistent, continuous and unchanging from a period in the existence of the individual extending from some months before birth until disintegration after death. While most of the experts on fingerprint identification deal most extensively with impressions of the human finger, we find that some, of whom Mr. Galton is first and foremost, have divided the palmar surface of the human hand into what they term well marked systems of ridges.

We have gone at length into the subject of palm print and fingerprint identification, largely for the purpose of evolving the indisputable conclusion that there is but one physiological basis underlying this method of identification; that the phenomenon by which identity is thus established exists, not only on the bulbs of the finger tips but is continuous and co-existing on all the parts and in all sections and sub-divisions of the palmar surface of the human hand.

A masterly summation expressed in simple terms which even the layman can understand.

In the early hours of Sunday the 27th of August 1933 in a house in Moor Street, West Bromwich, Mrs Fox was awakened by the sound of breaking glass which appeared to come from a downstairs room. She woke her husband Charles and told him. While she waited on the landing he went downstairs to investigate the noise. Shortly after she heard sounds of a struggle. Her husband then came slowly back up the stairs, only to collapse on the bedroom floor, with a bowie knife buried in his back.

Mrs Fox's screams were heard by a passer-by, who went for assistance. He found two policemen in the near-by High Street, who when they saw the condition of her husband called a doctor. On his arrival the doctor found the victim was beyond human help, having been stabbed seven times, the fatal blow having penetrated one of his lungs.

The local police were in the early stages of their inquiries when they received news that a butcher's shop in near-by Bromford Lane had been broken into during the night, and some money stolen. From an examination of the shop premises it was apparent that the intruder had remained there for some time. Time enough, indeed, to have a wash and shave, using the butcher's razor. As a needle and some cotton had been removed from a work-basket, he presumably had time enough to effect some kind of repair. Finally, to quench his thirst, he had a drink from a bottle of milk. Shortly after the discovery of the second crime, a third crime in the area came to light. A garage in Bromford Lane had been broken into and a car had been stolen.

Numerous items from the murder scene and the shopbreaking were sent to the Yard, where Detective Inspector Cherrill, assisted by Detective Sergeant Birch, had been deputed to handle this inquiry. They worked steadily through the day and on into the early hours of the following day. Eventually they made the identification they were seeking. On the milk bottle from the shopbreaking were two digital impressions, one from a right thumb, the other from a right middle finger. They were identified as having been made by Stanley Hobday. This result was telephoned to the murder squad at West Bromwich. As Hobday was known to the local police, they went straight to his home to interview him, but he was missing.

Meanwhile the stolen car had been recovered. It had crashed near High Legh, in Cheshire, nearly seventy miles from the murder scene, at 7.30 a.m. on the morning of the murder. It was extensively damaged, but it contained a locked suitcase. The car and its contents were recovered by police from West Bromwich. Items from it – but not including the suitcase – were rushed to Scotland Yard, where a print on the starting-handle was identified as being made by the right ring finger of Hobday.

The need to find Hobday was now most urgent. For the first time in Britain (as far as is known) a description and details of a man wanted in connection with a murder inquiry were broadcast on the ordinary public radio. This shrewd action soon brought results. A herdsman near Carlisle was driving some cows when he saw a man who fitted the description he had heard over the radio. He told his employer, who in turn told the police. Shortly after, P.C. Elder of the Cumberland Constabulary arrested Hobday at a place called Rockcliffe. His left elbow was bandaged with a handkerchief, and a jagged tear in the left elbow of his jacket had been repaired with black cotton.

In the meantime local inquiries in West Bromwich, led by Detective Superintendent Clarke, had traced some of Hobday's movements before the murder to a camp-site known as Warstone Fields. Several campers remembered him, and particularly the sheath-knife which hung from his belt.

When he was interviewed, Hobday was shown the still locked suitcase found in the stolen car. He admitted it was his, but said he had hidden it under some ferns, and that when he went back for it it was missing. He described the contents of the case, which included a sheath-knife. The case was then unlocked in his presence. Every item was there except the sheath-knife.

His trial for murder – to which he pleaded not guilty – was heard at the Stafford Assizes between the 14th and 16th of November 1933. Apart from the many witnesses to events there were the pieces of evidence which required experts to explain their significance. These included the identification of the fingerprints on the milk bottle from the butcher's shop, and on the starting-handle of the stolen car, as those of Hobday. This evidence, ably given by Detective Inspector Cherrill, was strongly attacked by defending counsel. Mr Thomas

Rigby, the Birmingham Public Analyst, gave evidence that the stubble left on the razor in the butcher's shop was darker than that of Mr Newton, the owner of the shop, and that hair from the chin of Hobday (obtained while he was on remand) was identical in colour. He further gave evidence that the cotton used to repair the tear in the sleeve of Hobday's jacket matched that used by the intruder at the butcher's shop. Evidence was given of a footprint in the earth below the window through which the killer had gained access to the house of Mr and Mrs Fox. The footprint had been made by a size-four shoe. Hobday was a small man, and wore a size-four shoe. Evidence was also given about the sheath which had contained the murder weapon – it had been found between the victim's house and the butcher's shop.

When the case for the prosecution was completed Hobday exercised his legal right not to give evidence. He relied on his counsel's submission that the case for the prosecution had not been proved. In his address to the jury, defending counsel said, 'Think it out, gentlemen. Is it conceivable that any man, woman or boy, after foully murdering another human being and with his hands still bearing the stains of blood, could calmly go off to Mr Newton's house and commit a burglary, sit down, and shave himself, his nerves so calm that he could thread a needle and sit down and mend his clothes, and then go off and commit another burglary – the theft of a motor-car? . . . It is a fantastic story – one such as the author of a "penny dreadful" would consider so ridiculous and unreal that he would never find a publisher for it.'

However, the jury did find the case conceivable, and found Hobday guilty of wilful murder. He paid the full price for his crime the following month, on the hangman's trapdoor.

While this drama was being played out the Fingerprint Department was once again engaged in sorting out another misleading statement in a newspaper. A fingerprint had been found at the scene of the break-in at an Army Training Store and sent to Scotland Yard, where it was identified as belonging to one of the two men charged with the crime. The detective inspector giving evidence on the identification added, 'I have been engaged in the identification of persons by means of fingerprints for nearly nineteen years. I have never known impressions taken of different fingers to agree in the sequence of their ridge characteristics.' A local newspaper, when reporting the court proceedings, staggered everyone by headlining it in the following manner:

TWO FINGERPRINTS AGREE
EXPERT AMAZED AT LYDNEY

and reported that Detective Inspector Charles Garrett had said he had been engaged in the fingerprint department for nearly nineteen years, but he had never known a case where an impression taken of different fingers to agree in the sequence of their ridge characteristics as it did in this case. Two national newspapers carried the same story under the same heading:

FINGERPRINT SURPRISE

By now the alleged evidence given was a little more explicit:

> I have been engaged in the identification of persons for nineteen years, but this is the first case I have known where impressions taken of different fingers agree in the sequence of their ridge characteristics.

Although the local newspaper published a correction the next day, it was too late. Messages of concern flooded into the Yard from Australia, Africa, America, Canada and Europe. As on the previous occasion, letters were sent assuring the inquirer that the fingerprint system was still intact.

Even after thirty-four years of continuous use, the fingerprint system still had the 'Doubting Thomas' syndrome within the judiciary. A man whose first criminal conviction had occurred twenty years previously was identified as the intruder at a house in Lee. Several of his digital impressions were found on a cigarette-box. These were subsequently identified in the single-fingerprint collection. The fingerprint evidence of identification was given by Detective Sergeant William Gibson, who had over eleven years' experience. The fingerprints (as happens in so many cases) were the only evidence connecting the man with the crime. As already mentioned, the Appeal Court decided in 1909 that this was quite acceptable. The Chairman of the Quarter Sessions listened intently to the evidence and then asked, 'Could the fingerprint of "A" be made to look like the fingerprint of "B" by means of varying degrees of pressure?' Gibson assured him it could not.

The Chairman in his address to the jury paid tribute to the manner in which Gibson had explained the methods used in fingerprint identification. Then, to the consternation of Gibson, and later of many other people as well, the Chairman said, 'I think it is dangerous to convict the prisoner on the evidence of fingerprints alone.' He then intimated to the jury that he considered the alibi put forward by the defence had been established. After that no one was really surprised when the jury acquitted the prisoner – except, maybe, the prisoner.

MP Rupert De la Bère had no such doubts. On the 17th of November 1937, he asked the Home Secretary in the House whether he was prepared to consider a scheme for the national registration of fingerprints throughout the country with a view to storing them, thus making it easier for the police to trace persons suffering from loss of memory.

The Home Secretary's answer was as follows:

> Fingerprints undoubtedly afford an easy and certain means of establishing identity, but my Right Honourable Friend would not feel justified in considering the question of a national fingerprint registry for the purpose indicated unless he were satisfied that there was a real and general desire for such a system.

De la Bère was not put off by this apparent lack of interest. On the 1st of December 1937 he asked the Secretary of State for Foreign Affairs (Anthony Eden) whether he would consider bringing in regulations to the effect that the print of the right thumb of the holder of a passport should be stamped next to the holder's signature solely for the purpose of identification when travelling abroad.

Eden replied that apart from the objection which exists in the minds of the public to any requirement of fingerprints, there are many unsurmountable difficulties in the way of the adoption of such a system, and he was not convinced that any substantial public benefit would accrue from its adoption.

De la Bère persisted by asking the Foreign Secretary if he was aware that at the International Police Convention which had been held in Copenhagen it was urged that all passports should bear the fingerprints of the owner, with a view to preventing the use of fraudulent passports, and that it was only prejudice which stood in the way of the adoption of a practice which would prove to be a very sound one. Eden batted away this logical piece of reasoning by thanking De la Bère for the information, admitted he had not heard of it, but thought life was complicated enough already.

Once an unidentified finger or palm-print has been found at a crime scene the capability of solving that crime exists as long as the particular print is retained for comparison. As far as serious crimes – such as murder – are concerned this period of retention is almost indefinitely. The value of this long-term retention was well illustrated by a murder case which occurred in 1937.

Just before 6 p.m. on Monday the 16th of August 1937 Mrs Mary Connell, who lived at 304 Euston Road, London, noticed smoke coming out of a second-floor window next door. She raised the alarm by hammering at the front door. At first she received no reply. An old woman named Mrs Shladover, who lived on the third floor of the house, put her head out of the window. Mrs Connell drew her attention to the fire in the room below. The front door was eventually opened by an Indian, Gulum Mustafa, who after looking to see which room the smoke was coming from, went upstairs to the room occupied by a Mrs Torchon. Although the door was slightly ajar, he knocked several times. He had by this time been joined by Mrs Shladover. As there was no reply, they entered the room.

The occupant was lying on the bed with her feet on the floor and a cushion over her face. Mr Mustafa traced the source of the smoke to some cloth smouldering near a table behind the door. He stamped out the fire, and then left the room with Mrs Shladover, both of them firmly convinced that Mrs Torchon was asleep.

About an hour later a young girl called with a message for Mrs Torchon. She was accompanied to the room by Mr Mustafa and Mrs Shladover. This time they tried to awaken her, but without success. Concerned that she was still lying in the same position as when they had previously seen her, Mr Mustafa tried her pulse, and realizing she was dead, called the police.

The police surgeon examined the fully clothed body shortly before 8 p.m., and formed the opinion that death had been caused by strangulation and smothering, and had occurred shortly before the body was first discovered. This cause of death was confirmed three days later at St Pancras Coroner's court.

Newly promoted Detective Chief Inspector Cherrill (who was to dominate the fingerprint scene for so many years) arrived with his assistant shortly after the divisional surgeon. He was faced with the fingerprint expert's nightmare – a bed-sitting room which was both filthy dirty and untidy in the extreme. On one table alone which stood in front of the fireplace were a miscellany of items such as beer-bottles, a glass, a cup, an empty salmon-tin and other food-tins, newspapers and books.

In spite of the deplorable conditions, a number of fingerprints were found, but unfortunately the clearest prints had been made by the victim. These were only fragmentary finger impressions, one on a Guinness bottle, another on the metal rim of a handbag, and finally one on the edge of the empty salmon-tin. The marks were so fragmentary that it was not possible to make a search, in either the single or the main fingerprint collections. It was a question of having to wait to see if inquiries being made would discover a likely suspect, whose fingerprints could then be checked.

As the inquiries continued it was learned that the victim had been born in Croydon on the 15th of December 1889, and named Lottie Asterly. At an early age she had been placed in the care of a foster-mother who resided in Boulogne. She attended a convent school until she was sixteen, and then returned to this country to live with her natural mother. She married Victor Torchon, a Frenchman, in 1905, but left him after a few months for another man, with whom she stayed for six years. At this point she commenced a life of prostitution to supplement her earnings as waitress, kitchen hand or cleaner.

Solving the murder of this type of woman is always difficult, principally because there is no stability in her relationships. On the day of her murder a number of people saw her, for she was well known in the area where she lived, particularly to the staff and habituées of two pubs in the Euston Road – The Goat and Compass and the Adam and Eve. Most of these people thought she was a Frenchwoman, because she spoke either in French or in broken English. A number of these people also remembered seeing a man they did not know, either by himself or later with Mrs Torchon. The unknown man was described as being between thirty and thirty-five years of age, five foot four inches in height, medium build, sallow complexion, dark brown hair brushed back, wearing a shabby dark suit. Two witnesses said he had a Newcastle accent.

Although police inquiries were vigorously pursued no progress was made until February 1939, seventeen months later, when the fragmentary impressions on the salmon-tin, the handbag, and Guinness bottle were found to be identical with a set of fingerprints received from the North of England. As soon as he received the news Detective Chief Inspector Frank Drewe, together with Detective Sergeant Smart, travelled north to interview the man identified. The man denied all knowledge of the murder, and claimed that at the material time he was in Brighton. Nevertheless, he was charged, and was eventually brought to trial at the Central Criminal Court. The prosecution evidence, including the fingerprint evidence, was not challenged.

The accused man then went into the witness-box and admitted being responsible for the death of Mrs Torchon. He claimed it was an accident during a struggle in the course of which he seized a silk scarf she was wearing. This became tight, thereby causing her strangulation. This explanation was strongly challenged by the prosecution.

The jury retired for one and a half hours, during which time they sought guidance from the judge on the points of law relating to murder and manslaughter. They then returned a verdict of not guilty of murder but guilty of manslaughter.

The man's antecedents were then given to the court by Detective Chief Inspector Drewe. He told the court that he had been tried at Durham Assizes earlier that year for the murder of a prostitute named Catherine Maud Chamberlain at Newcastle. His defence had been that there had been an argument over money, and he claimed that the woman had tried to rob him. He had lost his head and pulled a scarf round her neck and left her. The jury found him not guilty of murder but guilty of manslaughter. He had been sentenced on the 3rd of March 1939 to ten years' penal servitude. The Chief Inspector also mentioned that the man had been released from prison on the morning of the day that Mrs Torchon died. The look of astonishment – and in some cases embarrassment – on the faces of the London jury was palpable. As the judge sentenced the prisoner to sixteen years' penal servitude (to run concurrently with the sentence of ten years already awarded at Durham Assizes) he said to him, 'It is as well for you that the jury did not know your past history.'

This case not only illustrates the value of fingerprints in such circumstances but also illustrates how scrupulously fair is the legal system in this country.

I have written earlier about a newspaper which tried to popularize fingerprints by using them as clues in a competition, also about two instances where incorrect information published by a number of newspapers caused slight panics world-wide. One newspaper, however, redressed the balance by showing the public at large, by practical demonstration, that no two people have the same fingerprint. This newspaper was the *News of the World*.

In their issue dated February the 19th, 1939, under the heading 'A Fortune For A Fingerprint', they reproduced ten fingerprints. Five of these had been made by a male, and the other five by a female, both donors being employees of the newspaper. They then issued the following challenge to their readers:

To test the infallibility which is officially claimed for the Fingerprint System the *News of the World* makes the substantial offer of £2,000 today.

The sum of £1,000 will be paid to the man reader who can reproduce a fingerprint identical with any one of the five reproduced at the top of this page.

Similarly the sum of £1,000 will be paid to any woman reader who can reproduce a fingerprint identical with any one of the five reproduced at the bottom of the page.

The paper appointed ex-Detective Chief Inspector William Bell, one-time head of the fingerprint department at Scotland Yard, to examine all the specimens submitted, and such was the response that the paper had to repeat the challenge and extend their closing deadline.

Mr Bell completed his task of comparing tens of thousands of fingerprints on March the 11th. His report was published in the newspaper the following day under the heading:

THE FINGERPRINT SYSTEM IS NOT BOWLED OUT

In his report he said:

> I have been amazed at the enthusiasm of the 'News of the World' readers for this experiment, and also the skill displayed by the majority. . . .
>
> These 'News of the World' specimens have come from all parts of the country – from as far north as Wick, from as far south as Land's End and from every town and village in between. In the mountainous piles of fingerprints with which I have been surrounded hardly a district has been un-represented. . . .
>
> Every print has been compared with those published in the 'News of the World'. Many sent in have borne a superficial resemblance to the prints reproduced in the 'News of the World' but I hereby certify that no print is identical with those published. . . .
>
> In my opinion, in carrying out this test the 'News of the World' has performed a very great service in the interest of justice.

On the 1st of June 1939 Frederick Cherrill was promoted to detective superintendent. He had taken over as head of the department when Harry Battley retired on the 30th of April 1938. The fingerprint collection now contained the fingerprints of over 660,000 persons.

13 The value of fingerprint evidence

Although the first English palm-print case occurred in 1931, it was over ten years later before such evidence was to be given in an English murder trial.

The victim was a pawnbroker named Leonard Moules, a 71-year-old man whose business premises were in Hackney Road. Shoreditch. It was in the basement of these premises, at about 10 p.m. on Thursday the 30th of April 1942, that a patrolling policeman found the unconscious body of Moules. He had been brutally attacked with a heavy weapon such as a tyre lever or a hand gun, most of the blows falling on his head and face. As the shop had been closed at 1 p.m., the badly injured man had probably lain there unaided for about nine hours. He was taken to Bethnal Green Hospital, where eight days later he died without regaining consciousness.

As an intensive investigation, led by Detective Chief Inspector Ted Greeno assisted by Detective Inspector Keen, got under way, the premises were examined for fingerprints by Detective Superintendent Cherrill. All the latent fingerprints he found had been made by either the owner or his assistant. Inside the open safe (from which money and rings had been stolen) he found a palm-print. This print did not match those of the owner or his assistant. The Department did not maintain a palm-print collection in the same manner as the fingerprint collections, so the only action that could be taken with this palm-print was to check it with the few held (which at that time were about 4,000), and then wait for the right person to come under police scrutiny.

The first real break in the investigation came when a soldier remarked that at about the time of the crime he had seen two men (known to him only as George and Sam), examining a revolver. The investigating team concentrated on these two names, and eventually

'George' was identified as George Silverosa, a 23-year-old machinist. In due course Detective Inspector Keen traced this man to an address in Pitsea, Essex. To everyone's relief, his palm-print matched the one found inside the safe. Faced with this damning evidence, Silverosa made a statement admitting taking part in the robbery, but blamed his accomplice, Sam Dashwood, for the vicious attack on the old man. Shortly afterwards Dashwood was arrested, and in his statement blamed Silverosa for the initial attack, but did admit hitting the pawnbroker on the head with his revolver when the old man put his arm round Dashwood's neck as he tried to rise from the ground.

At their trial both men declined to give evidence. In fact, Dashwood dismissed the two counsel appointed to defend him shortly after the trial started. The case for the prosecution went virtually unchallenged. Dashwood took no part in the proceedings, and Silverosa, pleaded guilty to the robbery but not guilty to murder. He argued that there was only a common design to rob, not to kill.

Both men were found guilty and sentenced to death. After their appeals against the death sentence had been turned down their executions were fixed for the 10th of September 1942. While awaiting execution, Silverosa sought and obtained permission to burn two letters in the incinerator. As the letters burned he seized a poker and attacked the two warders accompanying him, severely injuring both of them. After he was restrained he was returned to his cell, where he remained until, together with Dashwood, he kept his appointment with the hangman.

Anyone who knows anything about crime in the late nineteenth century is familiar with the story of 'Jack the Ripper'. On the 31st of August 1888 Mary Ann Nicholls entered the annals of English criminal history. She was the first of the five victims of the unknown murderer. His other victims were Annie Chapman on the 8th of September, Elizabeth Stride and Catherine Eddowes on the 30th of September and Mary Jeanette Kelly on the 9th of November. Such was the ferocity of the killings, which usually took place at night in the East End of London, that many women were too scared to venture out after dark.

Just over fifty years later, another 'Ripper' prowled the streets of blacked-out, wartime West London.

A little before 9 a.m. on the 9th of February 1942 a plumber and his mate were passing through Montagu Place W.1. when they noticed the legs of a woman protruding from a surface air-raid shelter. Divisional Inspector Clare and the police surgeon, Dr Baldie, duly arrived, and after the doctor had pronounced the woman dead, Inspector Clare studied the scene. The body was lying on its back with a scarf over the face. Various items of clothing had been disarranged. Her watch had stopped at one o'clock. Bruising of the throat and a protruding tongue indicated manual strangulation, a diagnosis later confirmed by Sir Bernard Spilsbury. A fingerprint examination failed to produce any useful prints.

The victim was eventually identified as Evelyn Hamilton, a spinster who had died either on or within a few hours of her forty-first birthday. Inquiries revealed that she had been born near Newcastle-on-Tyne, and had studied chemistry at Skerry's College. She later obtained her diploma as a chemist and druggist at Edinburgh University. Shortly before her death she had been employed as a manageress of a chemist's shop in Hornchurch, but due to financial difficulties, this shop had to close. On the day of her death she had left her lodgings with the intention of staying in London overnight before travelling to Grimsby, where she had an offer of employment.

Having booked a room at 76 Gloucester Place, she left for a meal and did not return. Subsequent inquiries revealed that she was carrying a handbag, but this was not found at the murder scene or anywhere else.

The Press were quick to point out that this was the third woman to be murdered in this area within four months, the other two being Miss Maple Church in Hampstead Road on 13 October 1941 and Mrs Edith Humphries in Gloucester Crescent four days later.

The next victim was found at 8.25 a.m. on the 10th of February 1942 by two employees of the Central London Electricity Company. They had called to read and empty the shilling-in-the-slot meters at 153 Wardour Street, W.1. Since they were unable to obtain a reply from a first-floor bed-sitting room occupied by Lita Ward, they asked another resident if it was possible to collect the money from the meter in her room. The resident knocked on the door, and receiving no reply, opened the door, which was not locked. As the room was in darkness, she tried to switch on the light, and realized the switch was in the 'on' position. This indicated that the money in the meter had been exhausted. The meter-reader shone his torch into the room, and to his horror saw the body of a woman with her throat cut lying on the bed. The men went into the street, saw Police Inspector Hennessy passing by, and told him of their gruesome discovery.

Shortly afterwards Divisional Detective Inspector Charles Gray came to the scene. He noted that the scantily clad body was lying on its back, with the head hanging over the side of the bed. A tin-opener was on the bed near the body, as was a safety razor blade. A deep cut in the right side of the neck, which penetrated the jugular vein, was probably caused by the latter, and several cuts on the lower body by the former. Detective Superintendent Cherrill, assisted by Detective Inspector Birch, carried out a fingerprint examination of the murder room, and removed a number of items which included the bloodstained tin-opener and a mirror from a handbag, both of which bore digital impressions.

This 34-year-old victim was identified as Mrs Evelyn Oatley, sometimes known as Lita Ward. Before her marriage in 1936 she had been a chorus girl at the Windmill Theatre. She lived with her husband in Thornton, Lancashire, for a while, but eventually left him to become a night-club hostess in London, and later a prostitute.

The third victim was discovered on the 13th of February 1942. A tailor living in a flat at 9/10 Gosfield Street W.1 became concerned because a parcel left outside Flat No. 4 of the same address had remained untouched for several days. He told Detective Sergeant Blacktop of his concern. The sergeant made inquiries, and was told that it was not unusual for the occupant, Mrs Florence Lowe, a 43-year-old widow, to go away for a few days.

Blacktop left, only to return later that afternoon to see Mrs Lowe's adopted daughter, who was firmly of the opinion that Mrs Lowe should be at home. Sergeant Blacktop managed to gain entry to the flat using a key, but found a bedroom door locked, so he forced it open. He found the body of Mrs Lowe under the bedclothes. When he removed the pillow from over her head he found a tightly tied stocking around her neck. Shortly afterwards Detective Chief Inspector Greeno arrived to take over the investigation of this murder, with instructions to correlate it with the other crimes. As the bedclothes were removed he could see the body had been mutilated. On the bed were four knives ranging from a saw-edged bread knife to a small vegetable knife – all were bloodstained.

Spilsbury arrived, as did Cherrill and Birch. At the end of the fingerprint examination a number of items were taken to the Yard, including a part-used bottle of stout from the kitchen, a used glass, a glass candlestick-holder and a bloodstained candle from the bedroom in which the body had been found. It was later established that Mrs Lowe had last been seen alive in the early hours of the 11th of February 1942.

Detective Chief Inspector Greeno was still with Sir Bernard

Spilsbury at the scene of Mrs Lowe's murder when he received a message stating that another dead female had been found at 187 Sussex Gardens, W.2. When they had finished their inquiries at Gosfield Street they both went to investigate the newly discovered murder.

This latest victim was Mrs Doris Jouannet, a 32-year-old housewife who lived in a self-contained flat at 187 Sussex Gardens. Her husband was the manager of the Royal Court Hotel, Sloane Square, who because of the nature of his occupation had to sleep at the hotel. He did, however, make a point of visiting his wife every evening between 7 p.m. and 9.30 p.m. When he was leaving to return to the hotel on the evening of the 12th of February his wife told him she would like some fresh air, and would accompany him to the Underground station at Paddington. When she left her husband she told him she was going straight home. Had she done so she might still be alive.

The following evening her husband arrived at 7 p.m. as usual and noticed the milk had not been taken in, and that the remains of the previous evening's meal were still on the table. He was unable to gain entry to the bedroom because the door was locked. As the housekeeper did not have a spare key, the police were called in. Two police constables made short work of forcing the door open. Under the bedclothes on one of the two single beds was the body of Mrs Jouannet, with the now familiar stocking around her neck and the hideous mutilating cuts on the body. On the dressing-table was a bloodstained safety-razor blade. Once again Cherrill and Birch examined the premises, but the only fingerprints found had been made by the dead woman.

Four dead women – but at least two other women survived this vicious killer. The previous evening, the 12th of February, at about 8 p.m. Mrs M – was waiting for a friend when a man, dressed in RAF uniform, invited her to have a drink. She accepted his invitation. He later suggested that they went to a near-by restaurant for a meal. She hesitated at first, and then agreed. During the ensuing conversation he told her that he would like to see her again, so she gave him her telephone number on a piece of paper. When they were passing through St James' Market, on the way back to their original meeting-place, he pulled her into a doorway, put his Service respirator on the ground, and said he wanted to kiss her. This she agreed to, but objected when he started to interfere with her clothing. As she pushed him away he grabbed her by the throat and started to squeeze, so much so that she lost consciousness. Fortunately for her, the airman was disturbed by a passer-by, who with a friend went to her aid. When she recovered consciousness they assisted her to West End Central Police Station. They also took the Service respirator – which bore the number 525987, to the station – and inquiries were started to trace the owner.

Meanwhile, at about 10 p.m. on the same evening, the airman had picked up a prostitute, Mrs C –, who took him back to her room after he had given her five pounds. Without any warning he grabbed her by the throat and started to strangle her, but she kicked him and managed to escape from his grip. Her cries for help were heard by two women who went to her assistance. The airman put on his boots, gave Mrs C – another five pounds, and hastily departed at about 11 p.m.

The inquiries about the Service respirator revealed that it had been issued to Leading Aircraftman Gordon Frederick Cummins, who at the time was stationed at St John's Wood, and billetted at St James' Close, N.W.8.

Cummins was arrested on the 13th of February, initially for the attack on Mrs M –. As the days progressed the whole macabre story started to fit together. At the time of his arrest he was searched, and various items in his possession were eventually identified: the piece of paper bearing a telephone number given to him by Mrs M –, a cigarette case identified as belonging to Mrs Lowe, a wrist-watch identified as belonging to Mrs Jouannet. A search of his billet produced more evidence. A green and black propelling pencil was identified as having belonged to Miss Hamilton, as was a handkerchief bearing a laundry mark, a cigarette case was identified as belonging to Mrs Oatley, a fountain pen bearing the intials D.J. was identified as belonging to Doris Jouannet. Even the serial numbers on some of the pound notes given to Mrs C – were traced, and identified as being those given to Cummins when he received his Air Force pay.

However, undoubtedly the most damning evidence were the fingerprints. The fingerprint on the tin-opener found beside the body of Evelyn Oatley was identified as being made by the left little finger of Cummins. The print on the mirror from the same location was made by his left thumb. The fingerprints on the various items removed from Mrs Lowe's flat were also identified as being made by Cummins.

He was sent for trial on an indictment which listed four murders and two attempted murders. He appeared at the Central Criminal Court on the 24th of April 1942 to plead not guilty to all charges. The following day he was arraigned on one charge only – that of the murder of Evelyn Oatley.

While he was giving evidence Cherrill noticed that the jury had been erroneously given the fingerprint charts relating to the murder of Mrs Lowe instead of those of the case in hand. He informed the judge of this. As the jury now had knowledge beyond the case they were trying – which could have prejudiced their verdict – the decision was made to stop the trial and start again before an entirely new jury.

The new trial commenced two days later. Cummins denied the fingerprints were his, and claimed he was with a prostitute at the time Evelyn Oatley was murdered. The all-male jury were not impressed and returned a verdict of guilty. He was sentenced to death. His appeal against the death sentence was dismissed, and his executioner made London a safer place for women at 9 a.m. on the 25th of June 1942.

Although many crimes are solved by fingerprints, the evidence is not always presented at a subsequent trial, usually because of an admission of guilt by the person identified or because other evidence is subsequently found to be available. Having said that, there have been many cases where fingerprint evidence was absolutely vital to the successful prosecution of the case. A case which illustrates this point occurred in 1943.

Shortly after lunch-time on Friday the 19th of November 1943 two employees of the Luton Borough Corporation went to the bank of the river Lea, Luton, to take samples of water from the river. They collected such samples every day, and always from the same position on the bank of the river. On their arrival they found a sack-covered bundle, partly submerged, by the river bank. It had not been there on the previous day. They cut some of the string and sacking, and were appalled when they realized the sacking contained the dead body of a woman. They dragged the body onto the river bank known as Marsletts Path. While one man remained to guard the grisly package, the other went to inform the local police.

The body, still in its wrapping, was removed to the Luton and Dunstable Hospital mortuary, where after it had been photographed the covering (which consisted of four sacks) was removed. The corpse, of a female aged about thirty to thirty-five, was completely unclothed. The head had been severely injured by a wide, blunt instrument. Her fingerprints were taken, but she had no previous criminal record.

The next day the Chief Constable, Mr G. E. Scott, requested assistance from the Scotland Yard murder squad. The guide-lines which allowed provincial Chief Constables to call on this élite group of detectives had been set in 1907 by the then Home Secretary, Herbert Gladstone, who felt that many forces lacked the experience to deal with serious crimes such as murder. Shortly after this request had been made Detective Chief Inspector William Chapman and Detective Sergeant William Judge travelled to Luton. They were accompanied by Dr Keith Simpson.

The post-mortem examination revealed that the body was that of a well-nourished female who had given birth to at least one child, and at the time of her death was five and a half months pregnant. No teeth were present in either jaw, and there was every indication that she wore dentures. She had probably died twelve to twenty-four hours before the body was found. The cause of death was shock from wounds to the head and face occasioned by a blunt instrument. This had occurred before the body had been parcelled up and dumped in the river.

In any murder inquiry it is absolutely vital to identify the victim at the earliest possible moment, because this gives an immediate focal point for all subsequent inquiries. The site chosen by the killer to dispose of the body indicated a degree of local knowledge, so police inquiries were concentrated in the Luton area. A description of the dead woman was sent to all police forces, and thousands of women were checked. Nearly five hundred women reported missing were traced, a pattern which repeats itself monotonously every time the police are trying to identify a female murder victim. Most of these women are not genuinely missing; they just do not want to be found, for a multitude of reasons.

House-to-house inquiries were carried out in Luton and the surrounding area by police officers who carried photographs of the deceased woman. Many people thought they recognized her and attended the mortuary to view the body – unfortunately, to no avail. As well as photographs being published in newspapers, local and national, they were also displayed in shop windows. Cinemas projected a photograph of the victim on their screens, with a message asking for assistance in identifying her. A search for the woman's clothing led to a considerable quantity of garments, hats and shoes being taken to the police station, most of it having been recovered from various rubbish dumps.

Slowly the frustrating weeks passed, but Chapman, who was dealing with his first provincial murder case, kept a sense of perspective and a spirit of optimism.

Two days before Christmas the still unidentified body was buried in a pauper's grave, and two months later Chapman decided to re-examine all the clothing which had been brought to the police station. He then got his first breakthrough. In some loose, shoddy packing believed to have come from a piece of black coat found in Stuart's Place, Luton, he found a dyer's tag No. V1 2247. This was traced to the Sketchley Dye Works in Wellington Street, Luton. Their records indicated that the tag related to a lady's coat brought to them on the 15th of March 1943 with instructions to dye it black. The depositor's name was Manton, who lived in Regent Street, Luton. Inquiries the next day disclosed that Mrs Irene Manton, who lived at 14 Regent Street, had not been seen since the 18th of November 1943.

Number 14 Regent Street was a house with three ground-floor rooms, three bedrooms and a basement, and was normally occupied by Bertie Manton, a forty-year-old fireman with the National Fire Service, his 35-year-old wife Irene and their four children, two boys and two girls aged from ten to seventeen. The two boys had seen the police during their house-to-house inquiries. They failed to recognize the photographs, and satisfied the inquiring officers that their mother was alive.

Bertie Manton was brought to Luton Police Station to be questioned by Chief Inspector Chapman. He was shown the photographs, which he said he did not recognize. He made a statement saying that his wife had left him, as she had on a previous occasion, and that she was probably staying with her mother or with her brother in Grantham. Chapman was far from satisfied with this rather vague and indifferent explanation, so he asked Cherrill if he would examine the house to see if he could find any of the dead woman's fingerprints.

In the meantime, Chief Inspector Chapman obtained from the nearly blind mother of Irene Manton four letters all purporting to have been written by her daughter. They had been posted on the 31st of December 1943, the 7th of January 1944, the 19th of January 1944 and the 2nd of February 1944. If they were genuine, the body could not be that of Mrs Manton, but Chapman still had his doubts.

Cherrill made an exhaustive search of the house, and eventually found a print which matched the left thumb of the dead woman. It was not in the kitchen or the bedroom, where he reasonably expected to find it, but in the basement, on an empty pickle-jar. Armed with this information, Chapman interviewed Manton again. When he was shown the letters obtained from his mother-in-law he said he recognized the handwriting as that of his wife.

Now that the body had been identified Chapman realized the forged letters had been written to prevent Mrs Manton's mother reporting her daughter as missing. To prove the forgeries, he asked Manton to write copies of them at his dictation, and this he did. The copies revealed the same spelling errors, such as 'Hamstead' instead of Hampstead and 'surpose' instead of suppose, as were contained in the original letters.

Shortly afterwards Chapman told Manton that he was satisfied that the dead woman was his wife, and that he would be charged with murdering her. Manton then made a statement admitting killing his wife in a temper. He recounted their tempestuous and quarrelsome life together, and how on the 18th of November 1943 when the children were out they had another argument, and his wife threw a cup of hot tea in his face. The statement went on:

> I lost my temper, picked up a very heavy wooden stool which was quite near my feet, under the table, and hit her about the head and face several times. She fell backwards towards the wall and then on to the floor near the front room and door. This door leads from the kitchen to the front room. When I come to and got my senses again I see what I'd done. I saw she was dead and decided I had to do something to keep her away from the children. I then undressed her and got four sacks from the cellar, cut them open and tied her up in them. I then carried her down the cellar and left her there. I had washed the blood up before the children came home to tea. I hid the bloodstained clothing in a corner near the copper.

He then went on to describe how he disposed of the body:

> After it was dark I brought the wife up from the cellar, got my bike out and laid her across the handlebars and wheeled her down to Osborne Road. I laid her on the edge of the river bank and she rolled into the river.

Manton was arraigned for trial at the Bedford Assizes. He pleaded not guilty to murder, relying on a defence of provocation. The following day the jury took just over two hours to bring in a guilty verdict, and he was sentenced to death.

It was ten days after Manton's appeal against conviction for murder had been dismissed, on the 19th of June 1944, that he was reprieved and his sentence commuted to life imprisonment. Not that he lived long enough to enjoy his escape from the hangman; he died in prison just over three years later.

14 Mass fingerprinting for murder

My first encounter with a murder case involving fingerprints occurred in 1948. Unidentified fingerprints from a provincial murder scene were received at the Yard, with a request that they be searched for in the collections. I was part of the team which received incoming arrest fingerprint forms from all over the country and processed them through the nominal index. We were supplied with copies of the murder prints just in case the murderer were arrested in another part of the country for an unrelated offence.

The murder had been committed in the early hours of Saturday the 15th of May 1948 at the Queen's Park Hospital, Blackburn, Lancashire. The victim of this particularly brutal crime was June Devaney, aged three years and eleven months. She had been admitted to the children's ward ten days before with pneumonia. She had made good progress, and was due to be discharged later that day. She was the eldest of the six young patients in the ward that night.

The night nurse, who had seen June in her cot at 12.20 a.m., noticed she was missing at 1.20 a.m. She also noticed footprints on the highly polished floor, and a bottle containing sterile water under the cot of the missing girl. This bottle – which was normally kept on a trolley at the end of the ward – had not been under the cot an hour earlier. She raised the alarm, and a search of the immediate area was carried out. The police were informed, and soon a number of officers carried out a systematic search of the hospital and the extensive grounds, covering some seventy acres. At 3.17 a.m. a constable found June's body, lying face downward in the grass, near the boundary wall about a hundred yards from the ward.

When the Chief Constable of the Blackburn Borough Police, Mr C. G. Looms, arrived about a half an hour later he did not hesitate to ask for assistance from New Scotland Yard and the Lancashire

County Constabulary. The Chief Constable of Lancashire, Sir Archibald Horden, responded immediately by sending his Assistant Chief Constable, Mr W. W. Thornton, together with officers using radio-equipped cars and the head of the Lancashire Fingerprint Bureau, Detective Chief Inspector Colin Campbell. The latter was at the murder scene by 5.10 a.m., less than two hours after the body had been found.

By coincidence, Detective Chief Inspector Jack Capstick – affectionately known by the criminal fraternity as 'Charlie Artful' – together with Detective Sergeant Stoneman, of the Yard's murder squad, was assisting the Lancashire County Constabulary to investigate the murder of an eleven-year-old schoolboy named Jack Smith, at Farnworth, about seven miles from Blackburn. As there were some similarities in the injuries inflicted, Capstick and his sergeant were also assigned to the new murder, and Detective Inspector Daws and Detective Sergeant Millen were sent from the murder squad to assist.

This, however, was not going to be a case for the skilled interrogators. Instead it was a case for the methodical and persistent slog of the technician. Campbell's painstaking examination of the ward was to take fifteen hours. At the end of it he had recorded many fingerprints, including those found on the bottle from under the cot. He also recorded a number of footprints on the floor, made by a man in socks. They were ten and a quarter inches long, and it was thought that they were male, and not made by a member of the nursing staff.

The check to eliminate the fingerprints of the members of the hospital staff who had immediate access to the ward was completed just before 9 p.m. and by 2 a.m. the following morning, and the only prints remaining unidentified were those on the bottle. By 6 p.m. on the 16th of May a search for these fingerprints had been made through the Lancashire single-fingerprint collection. The search of their ten-finger main collection followed without success.

Meanwhile Detective Chief Inspector Robert McCartney and eleven detectives from the Lancashire Constabulary took over inquiries at the hospital. Their task was to trace and fingerprint anyone who had had legitimate access to the children's ward during the previous two years. By the 19th of May they had traced and fingerprinted over four hundred people. The team's inquiries were so thorough that by the 15th of June they had traced 2,017 people with general access to the hospital, and among these were 642 with specific access to the children's ward.

On the 18th of May the principal investigators held a conference and arrived at a series of conclusions, the most important of these being that the fingerprints on the bottle had been made by the murderer, and that because of the topography of the hospital grounds the latter was a man with considerable local knowledge. These conclusions inevitably led them to take the unprecedented decision to fingerprint all male persons of sixteen years of age and over who were known to be in Blackburn on the 14th and 15th of May 1948.

An appeal for public co-operation in the massive task was made by the Mayor of Blackburn. This appeal was given maximum publicity by the local Press, as was the assurance of the Chief Constable that all fingerprints taken would be either returned to the donor or destroyed. The revulsion felt by the public at this terrible crime virtually guaranteed their complete co-operation.

In order to simplify the taking of these fingerprints, Chief Inspector Campbell designed a special card. It was three and a quarter inches square with facility to take the plain impressions of the left thumb and left forefinger on one side and the four fingers of the left hand, taken simultaneously, on the reverse. The name, address and national registration identity number (a wartime requirement) of the donor was written on each card.

On the 23rd of May twenty officers, under the control of Inspector William Barton of the Blackburn Borough Police, were assigned to the task, which meant visiting 35,000 houses. The electoral register was used to make certain that every house was visited. At that time it only listed persons who were twenty-one years old or older, while today the minimum age is eighteen. At each house, therefore, inquiries were made about any males aged sixteen to twenty years of age who lived there, and had been in Blackburn on the 14th/15th of May 1948.

These inquiries (which were spread over two months) revealed that many people who were in Blackburn at the time of the murder had already moved on. Follow-up inquiries brought fingerprints of these men and boys from Australia, South Africa, the United States, Egypt, Singapore, India, most of the European countries, and of course from many locations in the United Kingdom.

While the mass fingerprinting of the local male population was taking place, other investigations were being made. On the premise that the murderer was a young man and could be serving in, or had served in, the armed forces during the recently ended World War or in the immediate post-war years, copies of the unidentified fingerprints were sent to every major fingerprint bureau in the world. About three and a half thousand men discharged from Northern mental hospitals were traced and fingerprinted, as were three thousand males described as being of uncertain nationality, German prisoners of war and Polish army personnel, all of whom resided in camps within a twenty-mile radius of Blackburn.

Towards the end of July the house-to-house visits were nearly completed. About forty-six thousand cards had been collected and checked without success.

Although these inquiries were being made three years after the end of the war the rationing system for basic commodities was still in operation. This was fortunate for the inquiry, for the local registration office had issued new ration documents in the Blackburn area between the 30th of June and the 18th of July. To obtain their new ration documents, each person had to fill in a reference form from their current ration document. On the reference form was recorded the name, address, date of birth and national registration number of the holder. No new ration documents were distributed without this reference form, and when completed the forms were filed in alphabetical order and retained at the registration office. This index was far more comprehensive than the electoral register.

On the 18th of July all officers involved in the house-to-house inquiries were withdrawn from that activity and used to check the fingerprint card index against the ration document index. Three weeks of patient checking produced a list of about two hundred males who had, for one reason or another, slipped through the net. Armed with this list, the team commenced fingerprinting again on the 9th of August. During the afternoon of the 12th of August a fingerprint expert was checking a batch of fingerprints taken the previous evening when he lifted his head and said, 'I've got him! It's here!' The details on the card gave the name as Peter Griffiths, 31 Birley Street, Blackburn, National Registration Number NBA6917-188. This number indicated that he had served in the armed forces.

At 9.15 p.m. on Friday the 13th of August 1948 Griffiths, a 22-year-old flour-mill packer, was arrested near his home by Detective Chief Inspector Capstick and Detective Sergeant Millen. When told he was being arrested for the murder of June Devaney, Griffiths replied, 'What's it to do with me? I've never been near the place.'

Later he asked, 'Is it my fingerprints why you came for me?' When he was given an affirmative answer he continued, 'Well, if they are my fingerprints on the bottle I will tell you all about it.' He went on to describe how after spending the evening consuming a large quantity of beer, Guinness and rum he had entered the children's ward and picked up a big bottle and carried it part-way down the ward. When he put in on the floor he overbalanced and fell against a bed, and the occupant started to cry. He tried unsuccessfully to hush her, so he lifted her out of the cot and took her outside, but he lost his temper when she wouldn't stop crying, so he banged her head against the wall. He then went back to the veranda outside the ward, put his shoes on, and went home.

Shortly after making his statement Griffiths was charged with murder. He was then finger- and palm-printed. Prints were also taken from his stockinged feet. Ten finger and palm impressions on the bottle were found to be identical with those of Griffiths, and the footprints were identical in shape and size with those found on the floor of the ward.

On Friday the 15th of October 1948 his trial at the Lancaster Assizes began. Griffiths pleaded 'Not Guilty'. The prosecution evidence was rarely challenged. The defence was an attempt to prove that Griffiths was a schizophrenic, but the medical officer from Liverpool Prison rebutted this claim.

It took the jury just twenty-three minutes to bring in a verdict of guilty. The death sentence was carried out at 9 a.m. on Friday the 19th of November 1948 at Liverpool Prison.

Shortly after the arrest of Griffiths it was announced through the Press that any one of the 47,000 men fingerprinted during the inquiry could have their fingerprints returned on application. Only about five hundred men asked for the return of their fingerprints, mainly to be retained as a souvenir. Later the remaining 46,500 fingerprint cards were pulped at a local paper-mill in the presence of the Mayor of Blackburn, news reporters, photographers and a newsreel cameraman.

In 1948 the first piece of 'fingerprint' legislation was introduced. Section 39 of the Criminal Justice Act 1948 made provision for the proof of a previous conviction against any person in any criminal proceedings by the production of the evidence of the conviction, and by showing that his fingerprints and those of the person convicted were of the same person. The Act made provision for this evidence to be produced in a certificated form. It was an improvement on the old system, when it was necessary to trace the prison warder who had taken the fingerprints of a convicted person at some time in the past, and then call him as a witness if the prisoner denied his previous convictions.

Section 40 of the same Act (later continued as Section 40 of the Magistrates' Courts Act 1952) made the provision that where any person not less than fourteen years old who had been taken into custody is charged with an offence before a magistrates' court, the court may if it thinks fit, and on the application of a police officer not below the rank of inspector, order the fingerprints of the person to be taken by a constable, using such reasonable force as may be necessary for that purpose. English legislation still will not allow police officers to fingerprint all persons who have been charged with a criminal offence without reference to a magistrate's court. Police in the majority of countries, including Scotland, have had this right for many years.

The Act works reasonably well within the hazy limits of judicial discretion. Probably the oddest reason for a judicial refusal to grant an order to take fingerprints I ever heard was that the boy's parents objected.

I remember one instance when the facilities of this Act were used as a delaying tactic by a very astute criminal. He had been arrested in the early hours of the morning, and the detective dealing with him was far from satisfied that the name and date of birth he had given on his arrest were correct. The detective asked him to supply his fingerprints, but he refused, saying that he would only agree if the magistrate granted an order for them to be taken.

The following morning, shortly before he was due to appear in court, the prisoner obtained the services of a solicitor. After some discussion, the solicitor told the police that it would not be necessary to obtain a court order to fingerprint his client, as he was now agreeable to have them taken. A few minutes after the fingerprints had been taken the man appeared before the magistrates and pleaded guilty. His solicitor then asked them to deal with the case immediately. The police naturally objected to this course of action (for obvious reasons), but the magistrates agreed to deal with the case there and then. After the hearing the prisoner was sentenced to three months' imprisonment, suspended for two years, and he was released from the court. He took full advantage of his good fortune and disappeared.

His fingerprints were rushed to New Scotland Yard, where to no one's surprise it was found that he did have a criminal record, and had of course given a false name and date of birth. His eagerness to conceal the fact that he had a criminal record was quite understandable, as it further revealed that he was an escapee from one of Her Majesty's

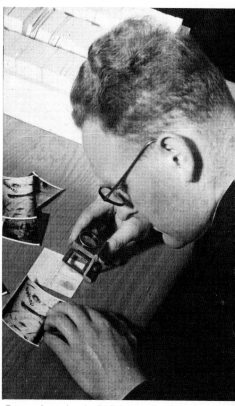

The bottle under June Devaney's cot

Comparing prints in the Devaney case

The evidence against Peter Griffiths

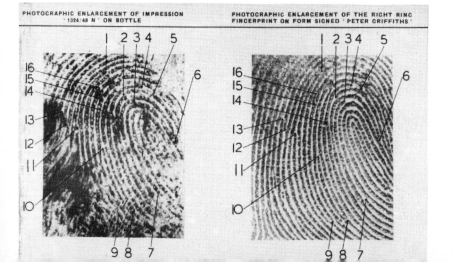

PHOTOGRAPHIC ENLARGEMENT OF IMPRESSION
'1324/48 N' ON BOTTLE

PHOTOGRAPHIC ENLARGEMENT OF THE RIGHT RING
FINGERPRINT ON FORM SIGNED 'PETER GRIFFITHS'

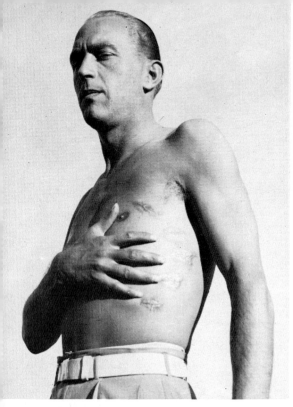

Scars on the chest of Robert James Pitts after a skin-graft

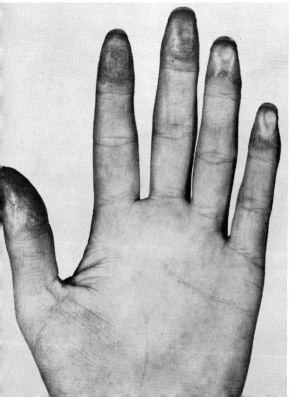

Pitts's fingerprints after the skin-graft

1-23-45-9 10-11   12

19-23 18 14-17 13

lleged right index, second
oint impression of Robert
ames Pitts.

1-23-4 5-9 10-11   12

19-23 18 14-17 13

Known right index, second
joint impression of Robert
James Pitts.

1   2 345-8 9 10-15 16

29   22-28 17-21

Alleged left index, second
joint impression of Robert
James Pitts.

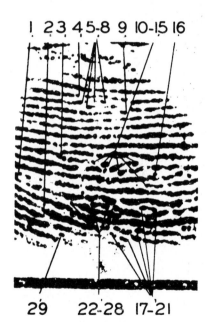

1 23 45-8 9 10-15 16

29   22-28 17-21

Known left index, second
joint impression of Robert
James Pitts.

*The establishment of Pitts's identity through the use of the ridge-structure of his second
finger-joints*

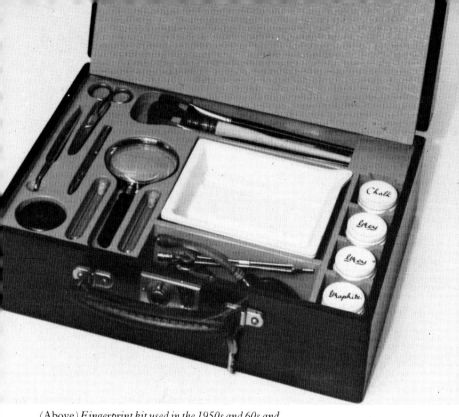

(Above) *Fingerprint kit used in the 1950s and 60s and*
(below) *Modern equipment*

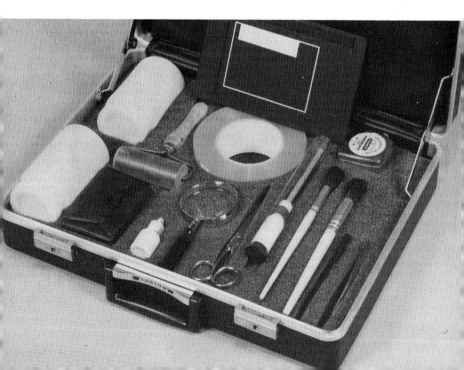

The kitchen at Leatherslade Farm

The ridge structure on an Ancient Egyptian mummified hand (over 2,000 years old)

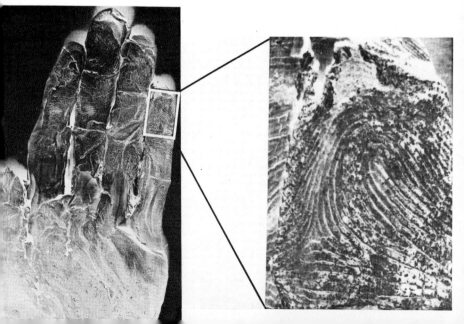

'The Dance to the Music of Time', by Nicolas Poussin

Detail from 'The Dance to the Music of Time' showing the area on the central figure

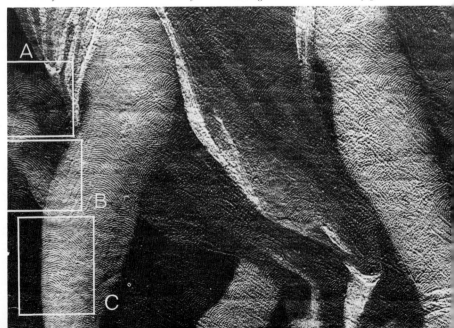

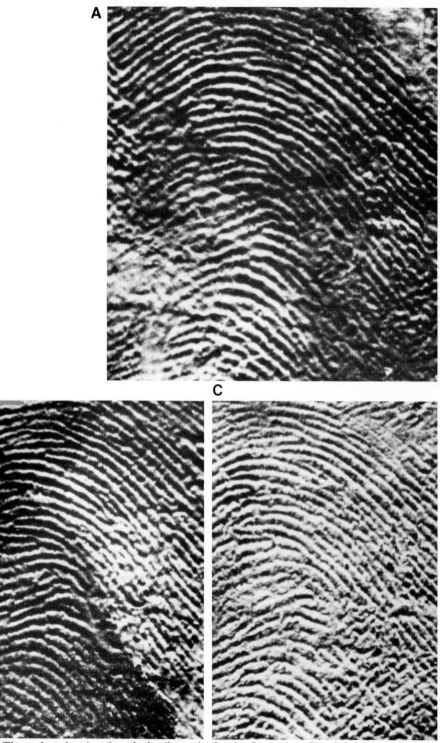

Three enlarged sections from the detail opposite, bearing fingerprints all made by the same digit

Example of Transmogrification before and after

Fixed points on a fingerprint

Prisons and that police wanted to interview him in connection with a murder. The final insult to injury was the address the criminal gave the court: the address of the local corporation's tip.

It had taken forty-seven years at least to obtain legislation to take a person's fingerprints by a court order. It was to take a further nineteen years before the Act was updated by section 33 of the Criminal Justice Act 1967, making it possible to apply for a court order to take a person's palm-prints. No one can accuse British Justice of acting precipitately.

15 The post-war years

The immediate post-war years were difficult ones for the police service in general and the Metropolitan Police in particular. Over two and a half thousand Metropolitan policemen who had been unable to retire during the war were finally allowed to do so in 1946. This, coupled with the departure of a large number of war reserves, left London's force very depleted. The problem was compounded by the fact that no recruiting to the regular force had taken place between 1939 and 1945. Although new recruiting was brisk by pre-war standards, low pay, housing, unsocial hours, and the retention of pre-war attitudes by some senior officers led to resignations which decimated the numbers of new entrants. By the end of 1946 the Metropolitan Police were over five and a half thousand men under strength, and this was against an unrealistically low establishment figure.

The situation did not improve. In May 1948 a committee, under the chairmanship of Lord Oaksey, was appointed to examine the police service, its pay, pensions, discipline, housing, conditions of service, promotion and negotiating machinery. The recommendations fell short of many aspirations, and did nothing to halt the decline.

One paragraph of this report, however, indicated to the Fingerprint Department that covetous eyes were being cast in their direction. Paragraph 89 of the first part of the report, published in April 1949, stated:

> . . . but we think that some posts could equally well be taken over by 'civilians'. In particular, photography and the identification of fingerprints call for skill and experience that have only the remotest connection with police duty proper, and we think it a pity that policemen should be directed to work of that kind.

This was reinforced later in the report in paragraph 394, which stated:

There would be no justification at any time for giving police rates of pay, police pensions and police conditions generally to people who are not engaged on police duty.

This factor alone was to guarantee an exceptionally difficult metamorphosis some years later. The 'Oaksey' Committee either did not know, or totally ignored, the part played by detectives 'with special skills' for nearly half a century in the constant battle against increasing crime. A few months later a Home Office Circular was sent to all Police Authorities and Chief Officers advising them to civilianize all posts currently held by policemen which did not specifically require the use of police powers.

The Fingerprint Department at that time was staffed by sixty-seven police officers, and was seeking an augmentation of strength to cope with a work-load which had increased by 20 per cent during the previous two years. This manpower requirement led a working party to recommend the total civilianization of the Fingerprint Department. The existing police staff would be allowed to remain to effect a smooth transition which it was anticipated would take many years to accomplish. (It has taken twenty-eight!)

No one doubted that Detective Chief Superintendent Cherrill, the head of the Department, was not enthralled with the prospect of civilian staff joining his police-disciplined department. How much this situation figured in his decision to retire will never be known. He retired on the 31st of January 1953 as the last head of an all-police-staffed Fingerprint Department.

Two years previously he had presided over a dinner to celebrate the fiftieth anniversary of the Department's inauguration. Virtually all its members, accompanied by their wives, attended. During the proceedings he read to the assembled company a letter he had received from the first Head of the Department, Charles Stedman:

DEAR MR. CHERRILL,
Many thanks for the invitation to attend your public gathering. I very much regret I am unable to be present. My doctor happened to be here when your letter arrived. He said, 'If you go, I and two nurses must accompany you in an ambulance.'

'What a to-do!' I told him. 'Two nurses would not be enough to go round.'

Your date for the gathering coincided with the date of my retirement – the first Saturday in March 1908, 43 years ago, after being told by my doctor that I had a possible chance of living another three or four years. I had a long record of sickness, the last one being thirteen weeks in hospital.

Although I am a 'Man of Kent,' I came here (Gorleston-on-Sea), and I suppose the North Sea air helped me on a little.

I can picture your work running smoothly now, as I expect all the objectors and obstructionists of my day have all been laid low. . . . I hope you may survive to attend the next jubilee gathering in 2001, and perhaps I may be fit to attend also.

I wish you all a very happy time and a prosperous future, and tell the boys to remember the old saying, 'Be joyful whilst you are young,' then the passing of time and approach of old age is forgotten.

and now believe me,

Yours very sincerely,

C. H. STEDMAN

P.S. I forgot to say that I still have enough strength to draw a cork if I come across one in trouble.

Cherrill's successor was Detective Chief Superintendent Jack Livings, who as a Divisional Detective Inspector had been my instructor. The last two police officers to enter the Fingerprint Department were transferred in on the 23rd of March 1953. Recruiting for civilian staff commenced later that year and the first civilian Assistant Fingerprint Officer took up his post on 4 January 1954.

Later that year a murder in Skegby, Nottinghamshire, added yet another 'stated case' to the growing list. Late on the evening of 15 December 1954, at a house named 'The Hollies' in Old Road, Skegby, an 83-year-old widow named Mary Dodsley was brutally attacked. Her assailant attempted to rape her, then killed her by manual strangulation and suffocation. The Yard responded to a request for assistance by sending Detective Superintendent Ball of the Murder Squad and Detective Superintendent Maurice Ray of the Fingerprint Department.

After a conference with the head of the Notts. County CID, they attended the murder scene, where Superintendent Ray carried out a most painstaking examination for latent prints. He found a number of digital and palmar impressions. Two of the fragmentary palm-prints found were at the point of entry, one on a glazing bar, the other on a piece of glass. As other prints were eliminated as belonging to people with legitimate access, it became very apparent to the investigators that these fragmentary palm-prints would play a decisive role in the investigation.

Suspicion fell on a local resident named James Robinson, a 27-year-old labourer, who lived at No. 6 Sylvan Crescent, Skegby. When questioned Robinson admitted he knew the victim, but denied that he had anything to do with her death. In spite of his protestations, his palm-prints told a different story. The palm-prints on the glazing bar of the window and on the piece of glass had both been made by Robinson's left palm. He was charged with murder, and eventually brought to trial at the Birmingham Assizes in March 1955.

Superintendent Ray said that when he was examining the victim's house he had found a palm-print on the glazing bar of the kitchen window, and that in his opinion heavy pressure had been brought to bear on the bar to produce the print. This was consistent with someone pushing the bar to the left. He added that he had no doubt that the marks on the glazing bar and on the piece of glass had been made by the left palm of the accused.

The defence drew attention to the fact that no fingerprints had been found. Superintendent Ray agreed, and added that the person opening the sliding window had had his fingers flexed back. He made the observation that it wasn't the natural way of opening a window, but the person doing it might have been aware of the value of fingerprints for identification. Evidence was also given by a member of the Home Office Forensic Science Laboratory about a footprint found on the lino in the kitchen. He said the print fitted precisely with an impression taken from the right shoe of a pair of crêpe-soled shoes owned by Robinson.

The defence relied on an alibi. Robinson said he had been working at turkey-plucking, and had got home about 6 p.m. After dinner he went to a public house named The Rifle Volunteer and had remained there until closing time, when he returned home and went to bed. His mother and sister both supported the alibi by saying he had returned home at about 10.30 p.m. and had not gone out again. The defence also produced a consultant pathologist whose findings about the time of death, between 9 p.m. and 10 p.m., did not agree with that given by the pathologist appearing for the prosecution, which was between 11 p.m. and 1 a.m.

In his final speech for the defence counsel said that, if the defence pathologist was right about the time of death, Robinson could not have committed the murder. He claimed that the only cogent facts put forward by the prosecution were the palm-prints on the glazing bar and on the piece of glass. He suggested that the experience of palm-prints was very small, as there were only twelve thousand palm-prints in the Scotland Yard collection. He added, 'You must have doubts whether the whole theory is established to such an extent that you can rely on it in a case of this importance.'

The jury, which included three women, deliberated for six and a half hours before arriving at their verdict. The foreman of the jury announced their verdict 'Guilty', and added 'committed unintentionally during an act of violence, namely rape'.

Robinson heard the sentence of death without displaying any emotion. His appeal against his conviction for murder was heard at the Court of Criminal Appeal before the Lord Chief Justice, and was dismissed.

The Lord Chief Justice said while delivering judgment:

> If this crime had been committed fifty or even thirty years ago this man might never have been convicted. The science of fingerprints and handprints had developed over the last three decades. . . . it had now been shown beyond the possibility of a peradventure that no two human beings had the same fingerprints. It had now been established that no two human beings had the same palm-prints. If an impression could be found those police officers and others trained in fingerprints could find indications whether the print found at the scene of the crime was the fingerprint of any particular person. Those of the judges who had had to study photos of prints could now follow the evidence given by experts which showed the distinguishing marks . . .
>
> . . . the jury were justified in finding that the print was the print of the murderer and that the print was the print of the appellant. . . .

In 1955 another case involving a palm-print occurred, and was guaranteed a place in English criminal history. The victim was a 46-year-old housewife named Elizabeth Currell who lived with her husband, Alfred, in Cranbourne Road, Potter's Bar. Like most contentedly married couples, their lives had fallen into a gentle daily routine. They both worked; he was a driver, while she assisted in a shop. Each evening after the meal had been eaten and the washing-up completed Mrs Currell would take their pet corgi, named Tina, for a walk. On fine evenings she would make her way to the near-by golf-course.

It was such an evening on Friday the 29th of April 1955. She took Tina for a walk just after 8 p.m. When she had not returned by 9.30 p.m. her husband went out to look for her. To his consternation, he found their pet corgi sitting by itself in the front garden. He went out on to the golf-course to search for his wife, but was unsuccessful, so he returned home and phoned his local police station. The police searched the golf-course in the dark, without success, and began again at first light. At 5 a.m. her lifeless body was found near the seventeenth tee. Her coat covered the head of her partially unclothed body, which lay face upward in the grass. The removal of the coat revealed very severe injuries to the head, and a stocking around her neck. Near by, partly hidden by some of her clothing, lay the heavy metal 17th green tee-marker, the top of which measured about eight inches by five inches. It was covered with blood, with some of the victim's hair still adhering to it. At the top of the plate was a fragmentary palm-print – in blood.

Immediately the whole area was cordoned off and soon after, Detective Superintendent Leonard Crawford from the Yard's Murder Squad arrived to take over the investigation. The standard appeal for witnesses was made, but it produced very little response.

In the meantime the fragmentary palm-print had been photographed, and had been examined by the head of the Fingerprint Department, Detective Chief Superintendent Jack Livings, who after consulting his senior officers formed the opinion that the print was the base of a right palm. A search was made through the Yard's palm-print collection. Copies of the palm-print were sent to all the United Kingdom fingerprint bureaux.

Back at Potter's Bar, house-to-house inquiries had begun, and a team of detectives were checking the criminal records of men with convictions for sexual violence. Messages were sent out to various police forces asking that the men be seen, and asked where they were on the night of the 29th of April 1955. At the same time they were asked to obtain if possible the palm-prints of the person being interviewed and to send them to the Yard. As with the Blackburn case, inquiries stretched far and wide, reaching such places as California, Canada, Australia, and Africa. Although such inquiries are standard procedure, the investigators were certain in their own minds that the solution lay with a person who had lived in the area for some time.

At a meeting of the senior investigators, held towards the middle of June, the possibility of carrying out a mass palm-printing exercise, to include all males aged sixteen and over who lived or worked in Potter's Bar, was discussed and agreed. Shortly after, the task of visiting seven thousand houses, numerous factories and other establishments began.

In the Fingerprint Department three teams of checking officers were organized. Because of the very tedious nature of the check each team was only allowed to check for one week, and then they had to revert to normal duties for a week and so on. This was done to prevent eye-strain. Each palm-print received was given a sequential reference number on reception and checked by three different officers. No one had any illusions about the size of the task. Day by day new palm-prints arrived from the house-to-house teams. As they could take them faster than they could be checked, a backlog soon built up. By the middle of August nearly nine thousand sets of palm-prints had been taken.

On the 19th of August the palm-print was identified by a young detective sergeant named Walter Wright. It was palm-print number 4,605, taken several weeks earlier, and bearing the name of Michael Queripel.

Eighteen-year-old Queripel, who lived with his family in Dugdale Hill, Potter's Bar, was arrested at the local town hall, where he was employed as a junior clerk. At first he denied the killing, claiming that Mrs Currell was dead when he found her, but later made a statement which amounted to a confession. He recounted that on that night he had been suffering from a migraine, and as was his usual practice when he had such attacks, he went for a walk. On this occasion he had gone to the golf-course. His statement continued:

> I saw her walking towards me with her dog. She walked along the path and I waited until she was out of sight behind the trees. I walked over to the green and waited behind the trees. She came back. I walked around the hedge and came up behind her and tried to knock her out. She turned just as I was going to hit her on the jaw. Then I tried to strangle her. She was still alive and I had to hit her with the tee iron to kill her. I hit her several times until we were both covered in blood, then I ran across the railway line and home through the wood to the Hatfield by-pass and to Bridgefoot Lane. . . .

When Queripel appeared before Mr Justice Hallett at the Central Criminal Court on the 12th of October 1955 he pleaded 'Guilty', and was ordered to be detained during Her Majesty's Pleasure. He had been saved from the death sentence by a few days. Although he was eighteen years old when he was sentenced, he was in fact only seventeen years of age on the day of the murder.

16 Identification standards and new techniques

I was to serve in the National Collection for nearly seven years. In the middle of 1954 I was transferred to the Scenes of Crime section, where I was posted to the section dealing with unidentified fingerprints recovered from crime scenes. As mentioned previously, these are the fingerprints remaining after normal searching processes. The fingerprints of newly arrested persons, who have been charged with 'breaking' and allied offences, are then checked against these unidentified fingerprints.

I well remember the first identification I made in this collection. The fragmentary print had been found at the scene of a warehouse-breaking in Hounslow. The print did not disclose any pattern detail, and only revealed the bare sixteen ridge characteristics required to 'prove' the identification in a court of law. My thoughts at the time were 'If I can find a print like that, I can find anything.'

At this point I should explain the significance of the sixteen-ridge characteristic requirement for proving an identification in court. I briefly mentioned in the Introduction that identity by finger and palm-prints is established by comparing the ridge detail in two impressions, and although ridge characteristics are common to all hands they only appear in the same sequence when the impressions have been made by the same finger or palm.

These ridge characteristics are named as follows:

A *ridge ending:* This is where a ridge stops short and flanking ridges converge to take its place.

A *ridge forking or bifurcation:* This is where a single ridge divides into two and the flanking ridges diverge to make room for it.

A *short independent ridge or island:* This is a small portion of a ridge lying between two other ridges, which ends in both directions.

A lake: This is where a ridge diverges into two and they converge and join again within a short distance.

A spur: This is a combination of a fork and a short independent ridge.

A crossover: This is a combination of two spurs which meet.

All ridge characteristics are either ridge-endings, bifurcations or combinations of both. On the average finger there are eighty to a hundred such characteristics. Over the years many people have tried to calculate the probability of two people having the same fingerprint – that is, two people with the same sequence of ridge characteristics. One of the first practical calculations was by Sir Edward Henry, who, allowing a very low one-in-four probability for each characteristic, calculated that for any ten characteristics in sequence the probability was one chance in a million.

In the early days of fingerprint identification a strict requirement for a specified number of characteristics was not enforced. The early experts relied on quoting how many sets of fingerprints they had in the collection, and how many comparisons they had made without finding a duplicated fingerprint. It was not until 1920 that Scotland Yard introduced the standard of sixteen characteristics for all fingerprint identifications placed before the courts. Using Henry's calculations, this made the probability of two persons having the same fingerprint 1 in 4,294,967,296. Later calculaitons have, however, put this probability at one in ten (English) billion (10,000,000,000,000).

At a trial some years ago a judge said to me, 'I know that you can explain mathematically what the probability is of two people having the same fingerprint but you must appreciate that the jury are not mathematicians. Will you explain to them in layman's English what the probability is of two people having the same fingerprint?' I replied, 'One person stands more chance of forecasting eight correct draws every week through one football season.' Although that is theoretically possible, I could not think of any other situation which was practicably impossible. Even the judge had the good grace to smile at my explanation, and the jury returned a verdict of guilty.

Although the Fingerprint Department at New Scotland Yard introduced the sixteen standard in 1920, it was not until 1953 that it became the national standard. Varying standards being used by other bureaux gave rise to a meeting, held on the 29th of September 1953, between representatives from the Home Office, the Deputy Director of Public Prosecutions and fingerprint experts from five major fingerprint bureaux – New Scotland Yard, Birmingham City Police Force,

Lancashire Constabulary, Manchester City Police Force and West Riding Constabulary. They concluded that it was desirable that a common shared standard should be observed by all forces whose officers give evidence in court about fingerprint identification, and that in the case of a single print this standard should be a minimum of sixteen points of resemblance.

It was also agreed that it would be of mutual advantage to the police forces whose officers give evidence in court about fingerprint identification if periodic conferences of fingerprint experts were arranged. Shortly after this the first meeting of the National Conference of Fingerprint Experts was held under the chairmanship of Detective Chief Superintendent Jack Livings. In his opening address he said, 'The pooling of the long experience of the members was vital and would be invaluable in resolving controversial issues which arise from time to time, as well as providing the opportunity of discussing methods of improving the efficiency of the system.' The National Conference, which meets annually, has over the years fulfilled his expectations.

The identification standard used in this country is one of the highest in the world; only the French, with a requirement for seventeen characteristics in coincident sequence, is higher. Twelve characteristics only are required in Greece, Switzerland, Yugoslavia, and Spain. In Sweden ten will suffice, if some of the characteristics are uncommon. In Turkey eight characteristics can be accepted. In India the standard varies from state to state, the highest being Mysore with twelve characteristics and Uttah Pradesh the lowest with six.

The United States of America has abandoned any formal standard. A report published in 1973 by the Standardisation Committee of the International Association for Identification stated that there is no valid scientific basis for requiring that there be a minimum number of ridge characteristics present in two fingerprints in order to establish positive identification.

Their findings are totally opposed to my own. In my opinion, certain major factors must be considered when discussing fingerprint standards. Firstly, we must always budget for the weakest link in the chain, usually a recently qualified expert with limited experience. Secondly, the fingerprint system has gained such a world-wide reputation for practical infallibility that this reputation must be protected by placing the standard of identification beyond assumption and doubt. Finally, to us, justice means that the defendant's guilt must be proved beyond reasonable doubt. At all times our concept of a fingerprint standard must equal our concept of justice.

Over the years many ideas have been suggested in an attempt to improve the system of identification by coincident ridge characteristics. One of the most impressive of these was presented to the 22nd General Assembly of the International Police Commission in Oslo in June 1953 by Florentino Santa Maria Beltram, the then Chief of the Technical Police Laboratory, Madrid. His method of evaluation was by a qualitative standard, not (as in use in this country) a quantitative standard. He evaluated characteristics by their frequency, giving low values to common characteristics such as ridge endings and bifurcations, and to moderately rare characteristics such as lakes or combination of characteristics a high valuation. These values were either one, two or three. His arguments in favour of this system were persuasive, but I think the quantitative system practised in this country is preferable.

On the 18th of April 1955 I was promoted to detective sergeant, and six weeks later I was sent to a flat in Buckingham Gate, Westminster, to examine my first crime scene for fingerprints. Unfortunately, the only fingerprints I found (apart from those of the householders) were never identified. This visit was the first of many I was to make over the next few years, and the start of a new series of experiences. These were to teach me a considerable amount about criminals, their behaviour, and that group of people so sadly ignored by those who devote their efforts to trying to excuse and justify the criminals – the victims. It isn't the loss of property and damage that truly disturbs the people whose homes have been broken into, although that alone in all conscience is bad enough, but the average person feels that his or her home has been violated.

A crime-scene fingerprint can be made in one of three ways:

1. As an impression in a soft substance such as putty;
2. As a legible impression made by a finger which has become contaminated with paint, blood, oil, etc.;
3. As a latent or invisible impression which has to be made visible by exploiting the nature of the mark or the substrate it is on.

The first two categories are reasonably straightforward and can be recorded by photography. The third category requires development, by either powders or chemicals, depending on the type of surface on which it has been placed.

A latent fingerprint weighs anything between 4 to 250 micrograms, and consists basically of 98 to 99·5 per cent water and 0·5 to 2 per cent solids in varying forms. The make-up of sweat is so complex that the total spectrum of substances present has still not been fully identified, but the following have been found by scientific investigation: Chlorides, amino acids, urea, ammonia, lactic acids, sulphate, sugars, phosphates and uric acid. The amount of these substances discharged by a person is not static; they differ not only between individuals but also from hour to hour and season to season within the same individual.

The fingerprint kit I carried in my early days contained the standard fingerprint powders which had been in use for over forty years. There was a grey powder called Hydrargyrum cum creta, which consisted of one part metallic mercury and two parts chalk, by weight, not measure. This powder was mixed in the Branch, and I well remember how fascinated I was the first time I saw it being mixed in a mortar. The mercury was placed in the mortar and the chalk was added gradually, while it was being thoroughly pounded by a pestle. It took about an hour and a half to mix one pound of mercury and two pounds of chalk. This powder was suitable for developing latent prints on non-porous surfaces such as glass, dark-painted or lacquered surfaces and silver-plated objects. Eventually it was withdrawn from operational use in 1967 because it was alleged that the mercury content could be a health-hazard.

Latent prints on light-coloured non-absorbent surfaces were developed with finely powdered graphite. This powder gave excellent results but was very messy to use, particularly if the examination was out of doors and a high wind was blowing. Finely powdered chalk was also carried for use when examining gold objects, because the mercury in the grey powder reacted to gold, and marred its surface. The kit also contained trays for the powders, brushes, an insufflator, scissors, a probe, tweezers, tape-measure and of course that item so loved by the fiction-writer, a magnifying-glass.

Any porous items such as paper, cardboard and untreated wood found at crime scenes which required a fingerprint examination were brought back to the Yard and treated by one or more of the three methods available for this particular type of surface. The first two, silver nitrate and iodine-fuming, had been in use for a number of years. Silver nitrate reacts with the chloride content of sweat, and iodine-fuming reacts with its grease-content.

The third method, ninhydrin, was a recent addition to the fingerprint-development techniques. The discovery that ninhydrin reacts on the amino acids in sweat was made in Sweden, in 1954, by Svante Odén of the Institute of Pedology, Royal Agricultural College,

Uppsala. Having made the discovery, he joined forces with Bengt Von Hofsten of the Institute of Biochemistry, University of Uppsala, and eventually a workable system suitable for general fingerprint development was produced. This one discovery was to revolutionize technical crime investigation in general, and fraud investigations in particular.

The original method was to spray the article for examination with a 0·2 per cent solution of ninhydrin in acetone, followed by its heating in an oven at 80 degrees centigrade for a few minutes. This accelerated the development of the strongest marks, which were pink in colour. However, the reaction was so good that over a period of days other prints would gradually appear. Today, although the solution has been somewhat altered, ninhydrin is accepted world-wide as the finest general developer of fingerprints on porous surfaces, and has led to the solving of many thousands of crimes.

In 1954 the system of crime-scene examination varied. Previously, officers from the Department would usually only attend the scenes of the more serious crimes. For example, a mere 368 visits were made to crime scenes by fingerprint personnel in 1952, and 411 in 1953. In other cases detectives from all over London used to transport an array of exhibits – such as broken glass, bottles, drinking-glasses and so forth – to the Fingerprint Department for examination.

As more successes were achieved the demand for more support from the Fingerprint Department grew. CID officers were given basic training in examining crime scenes for fingerprints, and four detective sergeants from the Department were posted to outside duties. They checked fingerprints found by the divisional CID officers, carried out further examinations, eliminated the prints of persons having legitimate access to the crime scene and arranged for fingerprints to be photographed, either at the scene or at Scotland Yard.

This procedure was so successful that the number of fingerprint experts posted to outside duties was increased gradually until 1968, when each of the twenty-four land divisions in London had a fingerprint expert.

In the eight years I served as a detective sergeant I became involved in thousands of investigations, ranging from theft to murder. Many of the cases were repetitive, varied only by premises and location. Some cases are more memorable than others because of some unusual twist. Such a case occurred at Notting Hill in 1960. A young mother answered a knock on the door of her basement flat. The man at the door told her he had come to do some decorating. (By a quirk of fate she had recently been discussing with her husband the possibility of doing some decorating.) She invited him in, and he then seized her and demanded a kiss. When she screamed he forced her into the bedroom and pushed her across the end of the bed, at the same time threatening that if she did not keep quiet he would harm her baby daughter. He closed the wooden shutters over the windows and placed the baby on the bed before he raped the mother. Before he left the flat he took her husband's pyjamas and went round the flat, wiping away his fingerprints.

My fingerprint examination shortly afterwards confirmed that he had in fact wiped away all his *finger*prints – but fortunately he forgot his thumbs. I found a thumb-print on the shutter, and another thumb-print on the inside of the footboard of the bed. These thumb-prints were later identified as those of a 22-year-old father of two children. When arrested he denied the allegation and demanded to be confronted by his victim. This was arranged, and when she identified him he said, 'I don't know what to say. I'm ashamed. I must have gone mad. She was wearing tight trousers and something came over me.' He pleaded guilty when he appeared at the Old Bailey and was sentenced to three years' imprisonment.

Finger and palm-prints are not only used for criminal records and identifications at crime scenes, they also are used to identify the dead who cannot be positively identified in any other way.

On the 29th of August 1960 the body of a man was picked up by a ship passing through the English Channel. It was believed that the corpse was that of a nineteen-year-old English seaman who had been reported missing on the 21st. Because of the condition of the body the identification needed to be confirmed by fingerprints. Although the hands were badly macerated – that is, covered with deep wrinkles with partial epidermal separation – identifiable prints were obtained from both fingers and the palms. A search of the National Fingerprint Collection showed that the man did not have a criminal record. It was known that the seaman stayed at an address in Chiswick when he was on leave. I went to this address in the hope that I would find latent prints which would match those of the body.

A charming middle-aged woman answered the door, and was most distressed when I told her the reason for my visit. She looked upon the young seaman as a surrogate nephew, but explained that it was unlikely that I would find any of his prints because since his last visit the whole house had been redecorated from top to bottom, and none of his personal property remained in the house. She invited me in for a cup of tea, and as we drank our tea she talked about the young man and described when he was last there, including how he climbed into the loft to get his case. I asked her if I could look at the entrance to the loft, and when I examined the trapdoor I saw that the paintwork on the inner surface of the framework was not quite the same colour as the rest. This must have been about the only place in the house not freshly painted. As I applied graphite to this surface a fragmentary palm-print became visible. This print – to my satisfaction but to the distress of the woman – had been made by the left palm of the dead seaman. As I left the house she said quite philosophically, 'Well, at least we know what happened to him.' A sentiment I was to hear repeated many times in my service.

It has been said that one fingerprint is worth more than a thousand eye-witnesses, a view with which I would not quarrel. The value of a fingerprint, as against that of an eye-witness, can be demonstrated in the following cases, where two separate and totally unrelated bodies were visually identified. On the 20th of December 1961 a 39-year-old Australian woman, Miss B –, who had lived in this country for a number of years, was reported missing from her Bayswater home. On the 30th of December 1961 the body of a woman was recovered from the river Thames at Chelsea. Fingerprints were taken from the body and checked in the female fingerprint collection but no identification was established. It was later thought that this body could be that of the missing Australian woman, so on the 16th and 17th of January 1962 I carried out a fingerprint examination of her home. A number of personal documents, including a birth certificate and army records in the name of Miss B –, were found. I found numerous fingerprints, none of which were identical with the 'Chelsea' body.

When I returned to the Yard I compared the fingerprints I had found with those of other unidentified female cadavers, and established an identification for a body recovered from the river Thames at Greenwich on the 1st of January 1962.

An inquest on the 'Greenwich' body had been held six days previously on the 12th of January 1962, where it had been identified as Miss M – by a male friend. Her Majesty's Coroner had returned an open verdict, and issued a burial certificate. Needless to say, we now had a conflict of identification. The Coroner was informed of the new development on the 18th of January, and by all accounts he was far from pleased. Fortunately, the body had not been buried, and as it was not I who had fingerprinted it in the first instance, the Coroner requested, as a safety precaution, that I should do so. This I did on the 24th of January at Deptford mortuary, and although the body had deteriorated considerably since it was originally printed there was no doubt that it was that of the missing Australian woman.

The Coroner held an inquiry into the matter on the 31st of January 1962. In the interim Miss M – had been traced, and was most certainly alive. When I discussed the situation with her she asked if a person who was officially 'dead' still had to pay income tax. An interesting point to which I did not have an answer!

She attended the inquiry, and satisfied the court that she was in fact Miss M –, and the hearing was adjourned. The Coroner then applied for an order of *certiorari*, as was necessary to bring Miss M – 'back to life', and to hold another inquest on the body which was undoubtedly that of Miss B –.

On the 13th of March 1962 the Queen's Bench Divisional Court quashed the inquest verdict and ordered that a new inquest be held. During this hearing the Lord Chief Justice, Lord Parker, asked Mr Cumming-Bruce (who appeared for the Coroner), 'You clearly have leave to quash, but what is the procedure? Has anyone to be served with notice?' Mr Cumming-Bruce replied, 'There is nobody to serve. The person who was pronounced dead cannot, if dead, have an interest in the proceedings, and if alive cannot have any interest in opposing the quashing of the inquest.'

The new inquest on the 'Greenwich' body was held on the 23rd of March 1962. The identification of the body as that of Miss B – was accepted after the fingerprint evidence had been given. By coincidence, a dental surgeon, who had treated Miss B – in Australia in 1958, was in London. He attended the inquest and produced her dental record, which agreed with the work done on the teeth of the dead woman. Evidence was produced that indicated that Miss B – was in a depressed state and exhibiting suicidal tendencies. The Coroner recorded a verdict of suicide.

It is strange to relate that the 'Chelsea' body which was originally thought to be Miss B – was also wrongly identified. On the 19th of January 1962 the 'Chelsea' body was visually identified by her landlady as Miss H –, a German art student who had been reported as missing since the 17th of December 1960. To substantiate this identification the landlady produced Miss H –'s German identification card, issued in the American sector of West Berlin on the 27th of December 1949, which bore the holder's photograph and right forefinger impression – but when I made the comparison I found it was not identical with the 'Chelsea' body.

To allow for the possibility of a forged identification document, I

asked if any of the girl's personal effects were available for examination. I was told that all the girl's property had been returned to
Germany except a large bin of modelling clay which had been used by
the missing girl. I arranged for this to be brought to the Yard, where I
examined it. As modelling clay is an ideal medium for recording
impressed fingerprints, I was not surprised when I found a large
number of them. None of these fingerprints were identical for the
'Chelsea' body, but one impression was identical with the right-
forefinger impression on Miss H –'s German identification card.

In the face of this fingerprint evidence, Her Majesty's Coroner
rejected the physical identification of the landlady. The dead woman
was recorded as 'unidentified', and an 'open' verdict returned. Sad to
say, the 'Chelsea' body was never identified, and is still known today
as: Body reference 452, January 1962, Western Division.

One case I was involved in at this time, and which made me smile,
appeared to have more clues than the average fictitious crime novel.
For the purposes of the story I will call the chief participants Cain and
Abel.

In early May 1962 Cain and Abel were walking past an art gallery
when they stopped to look at paintings by Bonnard and Renoir and
they decided to steal them. The gallery was on the ground floor of a
building which also housed a number of other businesses. Access to
them was by the same street door. The entrance to the gallery was by a
door off the main entrance. Shortly before closing-time at 1 p.m. on
Saturday the 26th of May 1962, Cain hid himself on the premises.
When all the employees had left the building he let Abel into the
building. They then broke into the gallery and stole paintings by
Matisse and Renoir, eight drawings by Degas and two by Picasso.
They left the premises with their haul and took a taxi to a flat they were
sharing at Hampstead.

As there were no external signs of breaking in at the premises the
crime went unnoticed until the late afternoon of the following day,
when an employee of one of the other organizations in the building
paid a security visit and noticed the smashed glass panels in the door to
the gallery. When a detective sergeant visited the scene he found a
number of empty frames and pieces of glass scattered around on the
floor as well as various items presumably left behind by the thieves: a
large jemmy, twelve skeleton keys, rubber gloves, a glove packet and
an invoice.

When I examined the scene I could not believe that anyone would
be so stupid as to use rubber gloves and then to leave behind their

paper container. In all probability it had been handled by someone not wearing gloves. This, as it happened, was the case.

The invoice (which had nothing to do with the gallery) was traced to a firm who had cut a piece of glass for a table-top, but had no record of the customer in question. They did, however, have the template made by him from two sheets of newspaper. On one sheet was some almost indecipherable writing. This was eventually recognized as Abel's.

Meanwhile Cain and Abel were getting increasingly worried as they had been unable to dispose of the pictures. One drawing, *Le Berger* by Degas, had in any case been badly damaged during the theft, and had been destroyed. They decided to return them in such a manner that they could claim the reward offered. In the early hours of the 1st of June, Cain informed a national newspaper that the paintings and drawings had been placed in a left-luggage locker at Leicester Square underground station. A similar message was given to a detective at Tottenham Court Road Police Station at about the same time by Abel.

A detective sergeant, accompanied by other officers, went to the station and searched the left-luggage lockers. In locker number thirteen – 'unlucky for some' – he found two parcels. One parcel, wrapped in a torn sheet, contained the two paintings. The other, wrapped in a sheet bearing a laundry mark M138, contained the remaining nine drawings. These were taken back to the police station, and later brought to me for examination. I could not treat the paintings and drawings, because a powder or chemical fingerprint examination would have caused irreparable damage, but I decided to examine the backing boards of the drawings, and I treated them with ninhydrin. Eventually two particularly clear fingerprints did appear.

While I was dealing with the technical aspects of the investigation Cain and Abel were being interviewed by a superintendent. Both claimed that they had not been involved in the crime, and that they had been told the whereabouts of the paintings and drawings by a person who had given them the information as a means of repaying a good turn. Naturally, they would not divulge the name of their informant.

Although far from satisfied, the superintendent released both men and asked me to check to see if either had a criminal record. Abel did not, but fortunately Cain did. I withdrew his master fingerprint form and checked the fingerprints developed. The print on the rubber-glove packet and one of those on a backing board had been made by his right thumb, and the print on the other backing board had been made by his left middle finger.

With his suspicions confirmed the superintendent, accompanied by other detectives, went to the flat in Hampstead and arrested Cain and Abel. When the flat was searched, a sheet bearing an identical laundry mark to the one wrapped around the pictures was found, also a card addressed to Abel relating to a broken coffee-table top. When Cain was searched a key, which fitted the left-luggage locker number thirteen, was found.

On the 26th of July 1962 the two men appeared at the Central Criminal Court. Cain pleaded guilty to breaking and entering the gallery and stealing the pictures, and guilty to maliciously damaging the Degas drawing *Le Berger*. He was sentenced to eighteen months' imprisonment on each count, the sentences to be served concurrently. Abel only faced one count, that of breaking into the gallery and stealing the pictures, to which he pleaded not guilty. The jury, having heard the evidence, decided otherwise. He also was sentenced to eighteen months imprisonment.

17 The Great Train Robbery

On the 1st of August 1963 I was promoted to detective inspector, but seven days later a far more newsworthy event took place.

When at some point in the twenty-first century someone writes the history of twentieth-century crime in England there is one crime in particular that will undoubtedly feature largely, the Great Train Robbery. The train involved was the Royal Mail from Glasgow to London. On the night of the 7th of August 1963 it stopped en route at various stations to pick up mail. The train left Rugby at 2.17 a.m., the last official stop before London.

Twelve coaches of the train consisted of a baggage van which was at the front, then the high-value packet (HVP) coach, which held 128 mailbags containing money from various banks in Scotland, Wales and northern England sent by registered post to head offices in London. Post Office staff in this carriage – which was in the charge of Frank Dewhurst – worked through the night sorting the mail. The remaining ten coaches carried ordinary mail, some sorted and bagged, the remainder being sorted by more post-office staff. Although the ten coaches had a communicating corridor throughout, there was no access from these coaches into the HVP coach. The whole train was pulled by a diesel engine numbered D.326, driven by Jack Mills, who with his fireman, David Whitby, had taken the train over at Crewe at 12.30 a.m. on the 8th of August.

Two and a half hours later as the train, travelling at seventy miles an hour, approached Sears Crossing the driver was vaguely surprised to see the distant signal showing amber, and reduced speed in anticipation that the next signal would show red, which it did. As he brought the train to a halt at Sears Crossing he noticed that the next signal down the line was showing green. This indicated to him that a signalling fault might have occurred, so he asked his fireman to use the telephone on the signal gantry and query the red signal with the signalman.

David Whitby, the fireman, could not use the telephone because the wires had been cut and was returning to the train when he was seized by two men dressed in boiler suits and face-masking balaclavas. They returned to the waiting train with him, where he saw that Driver Mills was bleeding from a head-wound and was surrounded by a number of men similarly dressed. Both Mills and Whitby were pushed into a passageway behind the driver's cabin and handcuffed.

While this happened other members of the gang had disconnected the rear ten coaches from the front two. Shortly afterwards, the driver was brought back into the cabin and told to drive the abbreviated train forwards. As he was already suffering from the initial attack on him, and fearing a further assault, he felt he had little alternative but to comply. He was told to stop the train about a half a mile farther down the track at Bridego Bridge. The stopping-point was clearly marked with a piece of white material stretched across it. Mills and Whitby were taken from the train, handcuffed again and told to lie face downward on the embankment.

The HVP coach was then attacked by the gang, armed with coshes and an axe. The resistance of the postal staff was soon overcome, and they were made to lie face downward on the floor. The robbers formed themselves into a human chain and passed the mailbags from the coach, down the embankment, to vehicles alongside the road below. In this way 120 mailbags, holding 630 packets which contained over £2,500,000, were stolen. The driver and his fireman were then taken to the plundered coach, and together with the postal staff, told not to make a sound for half an hour.

Half a mile back up the track, the guard, Mr Miller, puzzled by the long delay, eventually left his compartment and walked along the track towards the diesel unit, only to discover it was missing, along with the two front coaches. Like Whitby, he also found he could not use the telephone. Realizing the vulnerability of the ten remaining coaches, he wisely placed detonators on the track to their rear to warn any oncoming train about the obstruction, and then set out to walk to Cheddington station. On the way he came across the hijacked front portion of the train. By good fortune he was able to stop another train which took him to the station, where at 4.15 a.m. he raised the alarm which started one of the most intense police manhunts seen up to that time.

It was soon discovered that the robbers had interfered with both the distant and home signals. The green light of the home signal was shrouded in a man's glove, and the red light was connected to portable dry batteries which could be operated by a simple on/off switch. The distant signal had been similarly tampered with to produce the cautionary amber signal, the only difference being that the bulb for the green light had been removed.

When police searched the embankment at Bridego Bridge they found the white marker, a mailbag, a pickaxe handle, some crowbars and a railwayman's cap. It was later established that the latter items had been stolen from a ganger's hut.

Realizing the size and scope of the crime committed in his county, the Chief Constable of Buckinghamshire, Brigadier John Cheney, after a discussion with his head of CID, Detective Superintendent Malcolm Fewtrell, asked for the Yard's assistance. Later that afternoon a conference, attended by representatives of all the interested investigative agencies, was held in London.

There was little doubt that the train-robbers were London criminals, nor was there any doubt that they had a hideout somewhere in the vicinity of the robbery. The first assumption was based on the skill and cunning employed to effect the robbery. The second was that such an experienced team of criminals would know that a series of road blocks would have been set up once the police knew the crime had been committed. The longest time the gang could guarantee before the alarm was raised was about thirty minutes, and thirty minutes did not leave very much time to remove about two tons of mail from a crime scene.

After the meeting the acting Assistant Commissioner for Crime, George Hatherill, sent a most experienced officer, Detective Superintendent Gerald McArthur, to the Buckinghamshire Police Headquarters at Aylesbury to take charge of the search, and handle the county end of the inquiry. He was accompanied by Detective Sergeant Pritchard. The London end was initially shared by Detective Chief Superintendents Ernie Millen and Tommy Butler. As a result of a request for a fingerprint examination, Detective Chief Superintendent John Godsell, who had taken charge of the Fingerprint Department on New Year's Day 1960, directed Detective Superintendent Maurice Ray, Detective Inspector John Chaffe and myself to undertake this task. Our examination of the train and signals failed to produce any fingerprints which would assist the inquiry, and we returned to the Yard to await the next development. We did not wait long.

Three separate rewards, totalling £260,000, were announced for information leading to the arrest of the robbers and the recovery of the money. As can be imagined, the police in London and Aylesbury were inundated with calls offering various forms of information. One call among many hundreds to the police at Aylesbury was made by John Maris, a 33-year-old herdsman, who lived at Oakley, some twenty miles from the scene of the robbery. He had become suspicious of a number of people who had been to and from a place named Leather-slade Farm during the few days immediately before and after the crime. On the 13th of August he told the local policeman at Brill of his suspicions, and together they made a closer examination of the farm, which at that time was unoccupied. The policeman entered the farm-house, and in the cellar found mailbags and bank wrappers. Almost immediately a number of policemen arrived and threw a cordon around the main farm buildings. Shortly after lunch we loaded our equipment into our transport, and together with our photographer, Ken Creer, made our way to Aylesbury.

The location of the farm buildings was ideal for a hideout. They were set in a hollow on rising ground, and could not be seen from the few roads in the vicinity. The ugly farmhouse was a functional two-storey building consisting of five rooms of varying sizes, a kitchen, a bathroom and a cellar. Outside, opposite it, was a large covered open-fronted barn-like structure. Inside was an Austin lorry, which had been crudely painted yellow. It was covered with a large tar-paulin. To the side of the lorry, in an enclosed area under the same roof, was a generator which was used to provide the farm with electricity. To the right of this structure were the remnants of a bonfire. Many half-burned tin cans which had contained a variety of substances from soup to beer still remained recognizable. In a shed, behind the farmhouse, was a khaki-coloured Land-Rover. It had been driven so far into the shed that it had pushed out the back. Just down the drive was another shed, also housing a Land-Rover, only this one was green in colour. For some reason best known to the robbers, both Land-Rovers carried the same index-number – BMG 757A

When we had completed our preliminary inspection, it appeared logical to us to start our examination in the farmhouse, but the weather made it necessary to check the outbuildings and vehicles first. When we removed the tarpaulin from the lorry we found that a secret compartment had been built between the chassis members. Our examination revealed a number of prints, both finger and palm, on all three vehicles, including a palm-print on the outside of the nearside door of the green Land-Rover and a palm-print on the tail-board of the yellow-painted lorry (which incidentally had a pickaxe-handle stowed away behind the passenger's seat).

As we were examining the vehicles, laboratory officers removed all the mailbags, wrappers etc. from the cellar. Included in this material were various newspapers whose front pages were devoted to graphic descriptions of the robbery. A number of games were also found.

The external examination completed, we turned our attention to the farmhouse. Considering that a large number of men had been using the kitchen, it was strangely tidy, almost as though a woman had been keeping it under control. It appeared from the amount of provisions in the larder that the recent occupants had intended to stay longer than they did. All the items were neatly laid out: thirty-four tins of fruit salad, thirty-eight tins of soup, eighteen tins of pork luncheon meat, sixteen two-pound packets of sugar, forty tins of baked beans, seven wrapped loaves, fifteen tins of condensed milk, nine tins of corned beef, eighteen one-pound packets of butter, as well as cakes, jam, biscuits, tea, coffee, potatoes, apples, seventeen double packets of toilet rolls, forty candles, a Johnson first-aid travel kit, and tomato ketchup. As one senior officer put it, the shelves were stacked like a supermarket. In the kitchen cupboards were eating and cooking implements, plus dozens of eggs. On the floor was a two-ringed camping stove. Two metal containers with water in them stood in the bath, and in other rooms were sleeping bags, lilos, pillows, various items of clothing and towels.

Although we were to find a miscellany of prints throughout the house, there is no doubt that as far as fingerprints were concerned, the kitchen and larder were to be our 'Aladdin's cave'.

It was to be claimed later that someone let the robbers down by not destroying the evidence at Leatherslade Farm after they had departed, but there was strong evidence that the occupants themselves had tried to wash away traces of fingerprints, using two large sponges we found in the kitchen. In fairness to them, they were at a disadvantage: they could not see their prints, but we could.

The first arrests came when we were still at the farm. The information came, ironically, from a policeman's widow who lived in Bournemouth. Her suspicions were aroused when a man came to rent her garage. He insisted on paying three months' rent in advance, and pulled a thick roll of banknotes from his pocket to pay her. After he had left she phoned the police. By the time the police arrived, the man had returned with a friend and driven his vehicle into the garage. Both men were questioned by the police officers, who detained them both. At the police station they were searched. On William Boal they found £118 and a receipt which indicated that he had recently purchased a car and paid for it in cash. On the other man, Roger Cordrey, they found £160. When police returned to the rented garage and opened the car they found two bags filled with banknotes. They then went to a flat where Cordrey had been staying, and to a garage where he kept his car, and more money was found. From the three locations a total of £141,000 was recovered.

We completed our examination of the farm on Saturday the 17th of August and returned to the Yard to start the mammoth task of sorting out the prints we had accumulated. During the sorting we noticed that some prints were repeated on different articles. A fingerprint on a blue-edged plate, found in a cupboard, had been made by the same finger that had left a fingerprint on the Cellophane wrapper of a Johnson's travel kit which had been on a shelf in the pantry. From their positions it was deduced that they had been made by a right middle finger. A search was made in the Single Fingerprint Collection, and the owner of the fingerprint was identified as Roy John James, a 28-year-old silversmith. A second pairing up of marks, one on a part of a *Monopoly* box-lid, the other on a Heinz tomato ketchup bottle, were searched in a similar manner, and led to the identification of a 34-year-old carpenter named Ronald Biggs.

We set up two teams. The first dealt with the chemical treatment of all the torn wrappers and packages recovered from the cellar at the farm. They eventually added many hundreds of finger and palm-prints to those we already had. The second team dealt with all the checking of finger and palm-prints, both for persons suspected and for those with legitimate access to whatever the prints were on. For instance, the fingerprints of over two hundred railway employees who had access to either the diesel unit or the railwayman's cap found at Bridego Bridge were checked, as were the prints of over two hundred postal employees who either had access to the HVP coach or had received postal packets at various post-offices. Over two hundred bank employees from various banks in the north of the country, Wales and even the Isle of Man were fingerprinted for checking with the prints developed on the torn wrappers and packages – all told, over eight hundred sets of elimination finger and palm-prints were taken and checked.

It was apparent from the outset that the robbers were highly skilled, top-echelon criminals. At any one time it is extremely unlikely that there are more than two hundred criminals of this calibre operating in the British Isles, outside Her Majesty's Prisons. The detectives investigating the crime soon started to suggest various members of this criminal hardcore as possibilities. One by one the people who had been at Leatherslade Farm were identified. There was Charles Wilson, a 31-year-old bookmaker and greengrocer, whose right palmprint was on the window-sill in the kitchen, and whose right thumbprint was on both a drum of salt and the Johnson's travel kit, the latter being the same article which bore the print of Roy John James. Marks on a torn envelope stamped Barclays Bank Ltd, Pwllheli were identified as being made by the right middle and right ring fingers of Ronald Edwards, a 32-year-old club-owner. The palm-mark on the nearside door of the green Land-Rover had also been made by his left palm. James Hussey, a 31-year-old painter and decorator, was identified by his right palm-print on the tailboard of the Austin lorry. A palm-print on the handrail of the bath was identified as being made by the left palm of Thomas Wisbey, a 34-year-old bookmaker. Palm-marks on a pipkin of Friary Draught Bitter, found in a cupboard next to the back door, were identified for the left and right palms of 35-year-old Robert Welch. A palm-mark on a copy of the *Oxford Mail*, dated the 9th of August 1963, which had been in one of the mailbags was identified as being made by the left palm of James White, a 44-year-old café proprietor. Prints developed on two *Monopoly* tokens and on the Heinz tomato ketchup bottle previously mentioned were made by various fingers of Bruce Reynolds, a 32-year-old antique dealer.

While we were busy finding out who was involved other officers were finding out about the manner of their involvement. The history of the farm and the vehicles was well and truly probed. The Austin lorry had been purchased at an auction in July for £300. The purchaser (who paid in cash) gave a false name and address. While one of the Land-Rovers had been purchased quite legitimately, the other had been stolen in London eighteen days before the robbery and fitted with false plates.

It was pure chance that Leatherslade Farm had become available to the robbers. Earlier in the year the owner, Mr Rixon, having decided to sell the farm, gave instructions to three estate agents. On the 27th of June 1963 Leonard Field, who professed an interest in purchasing the farm, and Brian Field (not related), a managing clerk to a solicitor named John Wheater, viewed it. The owner was pleased when a purchase price of £5,500 was agreed, and a cheque for the deposit of

£550 was sent from Wheater to his agent. He was later informed by his solicitor that the balance of the money would be made available on the 13th of August. However, the purchaser was keen to take possession of the farm some two weeks earlier, if some suitable settlement could be arrived at. This took the form of an agreement to pay 7 per cent interest on the balance until the completion of the purchase. Satisfied with this, Mr Rixon vacated the farm on the date agreed. Although they were to claim that their actions were quite innocent, the two Fields and the solicitor Wheater were at a later date found guilty of conspiring to obstruct the course of justice.

When photographs of some of the wanted men were published in the Press they created bedlam for the fingerprint staff. Members of the public phoned police in all parts of the country to say that they had seen this wanted person or that wanted person. Police responding to these calls ordered where necessary a fingerprint examination of the premises or vehicle, and sent the prints to the Yard for checking. After nearly two million fingerprint comparisons had been carried out the first of a number of trials – which were to take place during a five-year period – commenced at Aylesbury on the 20th of January 1964 and lasted three months.

Of the ten men convicted for the actual robbery (as distinct from those found guilty of conspiracy to rob), only one did not leave his finger or palm-prints behind in Leatherslade Farm. An interesting aspect of all these trials was that not one defendant denied his finger-prints. Several even went so far as to confirm that the finger or palm-print were indeed theirs, and then explained that they had been left at the farm either before the robbery (when they had taken provisions there) or after the robbery (when they went to the farm to destroy the fingerprint evidence).

Two post-robbery, but related, occurrences made me wonder about our human values. The first took place on Tuesday the 4th of February 1969 when a public auction was held at Measham in Staffordshire of the equipment discarded by the robbers, most of it from Leatherslade Farm. The prices paid for some of the items bore no relation to their value if purchased new. For instance, a frying-pan was sold for £30, and an aluminium teapot fetched £60. Even the Austin lorry which had been purchased at an auction just before the robbery for £300 was sold for £1,150. It was reported that one person said after making a purchase, 'My wife will be proud that I have bought this. We shall be able to boast about it all our lives and then pass it on to our grandchildren.'

The other incident related to the driver of the train. Jack Mills never fully recovered from his injuries, and died in February 1970 from leukaemia. It is sad but true that quite a number of people made a lot of money out of the Great Train Robbery but the notable exception was its victim, Jack Mills.

18 Computerization

A slow but sure escalation in the crime-rate caused more arrests, which in turn increased the size of the National Fingerprint Collection and the number of inquiry searches. At the end of 1963, 1,813,156 sets of fingerprints were housed in the national collection. Approximately 200,000 inquiry fingerprint forms were received by the Department annually. About half of those were linked to a previous criminal record using the nominal index. These only required checking against the master set of fingerprints in each case to prove identity. Of the remaining hundred thousand inquiries, only about 5 per cent were identified as of persons having a previous criminal record. This meant that a tremendous effort in skill and manpower was being expended to prove that ninety-five thousand out of the original hundred thousand had no previous criminal record.

'Can fingerprints be computerized?' I was asked by the Head of the Department in February 1964, and replied, 'Yes, I have no doubt they can be computerized.'

He then asked, 'Who should work it out – a fingerprint expert with computer knowledge or a computer expert with fingerprint knowledge?'

Again I had no doubt, and expressed the view that it should be a fingerprint expert with computer knowledge.

He then posed a final question, 'Are you prepared to take the task on?' When I agreed I began a most satisfying period of my service.

I chose as my assistant a very promising young fingerprint officer named John Seymour, and together we got to grips with the challenge. At each stage we asked our colleagues for their views. By sampling a large number of officers we obtained a reliable consensus. It was interesting to see how people reacted to the new concept. Most gave us enthusiastic encouragement, even though they had certain reservations, but a few resisted any thought of change. In fairness, I think we all shuddered at the prospect of converting a collection of over two million fingerprint forms to produce the computer data base.

We had no doubt that the key to successful computerization was an expanded pattern structure analysis closely allied to ridge counts. For some time a vast amount of information available on fingerprint forms was not being used in the existing 'Henry' system. Although group charts, based on counts and tracings, had been introduced into the densest areas of the collection some years earlier, this had only gone part-way in utilizing this data. A good example of wasted data was the whorl section. In this all multi-delta patterns were grouped together under one general heading; the only subdivisions in general use were the three tracings, inner, meeting and outer, and these were only used when they formed part of the 'Henry' secondary or tertiary classification, or where they had been incorporated in a group chart. They took no account of the widely accepted multi-delta patterns: twinned loops, lateral pocket loops and composites. Plain loops, nutant loops and converging loops were also grouped together under the general category of 'loops'. Counts obtained from them were only used when they appeared in the 'Henry' classification or where they had been grouped.

The more we studied the collection the more we realized that whatever system we designed, the patterns would require very close definition. Sir Edward Henry in his original system had obviously realized that not all fingerprints would fit neatly into the general descriptions of the five main patterns then recognized. When any of his officers came across such a pattern he encouraged them to discuss it with his colleagues, and of course himself. Many early fingerprint forms had pencilled drawings of such patterns, drawn in such a way that the reason for the eventual pattern diagnosis would be apparent to anyone looking at it. As the collection, and the staff, grew this practice unfortunately ceased.

We eventually settled on a structure of twenty-seven patterns, twenty-five of which described patterns and two of which dealt with scarred and amputated digits. After many trials this was reduced to twenty-two patterns. To each pattern, with the exception of arches, scarred and amputated, we added a ridge-count, which is obtained by counting the number of ridges crossed by an imaginary straight line between two fixed points – a delta and the associated core. We worked on the theory that with two descriptors, a pattern and a count for each digit, if all ten fingers were recorded in this way each individual finger would subdivide the data obtained from the other nine, thus making it possible to isolate one form from many thousands.

The theory sounded all right, but would it work on a collection of over two million forms? The only way to find out was to test it. In the mid-sixties computers were not as freely available as they are today, so we had to simulate a computer data base. To demonstrate that people could be trained to code sets of fingerprints using the new system, we trained four relatively junior fingerprint officers in the new technique. For our test we selected two of the sections of most frequent occurrence in the male collection. The first, and major part of the test, consisted of all ulnar loops, the most prolific of all fingerprint patterns. The second was the all multi-delta pattern section. We chose them because we were certain that if the system worked in these two areas it would work anywhere in the collection. Our newly trained officers had to code two hundred thousand fingerprints and enter the new codings on specially prepared cards, one card for each record.

The test consisted of four hundred searches, picked at random and coded by our young officers. The manual searches carried out in the collection of coded cards were long and laborious, because as a safe-guard we had built a count-allowance factor into the system. This was to counter the vagaries of ridge-counting, which is brought about by the varying pressures used when taking a set of fingerprints. These varying pressures have no effect on the sequence of ridge character-istics used for identification, but can cause a count variation, depend-ing on the number of ridges which end on or near the imaginary count line.

The results were beyond our wildest expectations. All the searches were correctly identified, and over two hundred reacted only with the correct form. This was almost unbelievable, because to carry out the same searches manually would have required for each search consul-tation with a minimum of a hundred forms and a possible maximum of more than four thousand.

The test indicated that if the system was applied to the whole collection only an average of six fingerprint forms would have to be consulted for every fingerprint record inquiry. More importantly, it showed that under a computerized system half the searches carried out would not require any comparisons at all to determine that no criminal record existed.

To prevent any suggestion that it was only our enthusiasm and special skills that had produced such an excellent result, we persuaded

Manual searching in the National Fingerprint Collection (1965)

Fingerprint officers retrieving and comparing scenes-of-crime data on the Videofile system

A fingerprint officer making a comparison on a split-screen VDU

A fingerprint expert coding fingerprints, using Datapad

The author discussing a glove-print identification with senior fingerprint officer Chris Coombes

The Press heralds the advent of glove-prints

Now glove prints will trap criminal

GLOVES NOW NO PROTECTION FOR CRIMINALS

By T. A. SANDROCK

FOR the first t criminal law on the evi oves.

The break-thro hieved mainly by (Scotland Yard's many years in resear chances of one matching another small, whatever ma they are made of.

Mr COLIN HART-LE prosecuting counsel, Inner London Sessions means that from criminals will receive tection from gloves th wear when committing

"This is due to the l researches of Scotland ing gloves were " the s

Glove prints put finger on crime

CRIMINALS who wear gloves to hide their fingerprints are in trouble—for the police can now match up glove prints.

For the first time in Britain's history a man was convicted today on the evidence of marks left by his gloves.

Mr. Colin Hart-Leverton, prosecuting, told the London sessions: "From now on criminals will receive no protection from gloves when committing crimes."

Mr. Hart-Leverton, said the breakthrough had followed years of research by Supt Gerald Lambourne, head of Scotland Yard's fingerprint branch.

He said: "The Superintendent has been able to establish that the chances of one glove matching another are very small, the same as or a pro-

the broker, latched the tley.

added:
I ground in ' ime in the vestigation d possibly brought to ts."

AVELL said, deputy Hartley in s, or a pro-

'Glove prints' catch a criminal...

For the first time in Britain's history a man was convicted yesterday on the evidence of marks left by his gloves, and rosecuting counsel, Mr Colin art-Leverton, told the Inner London Sessions: "From now criminals will receive no protection from gloves they may wear when committing crimes. This is due to the forensic researches of Scotland Yard." The police to

new ground in the detection of criminals because it is the first time in the history of criminal investigation, in this country and possibly throughout the world, that an offender has been brought to trial, and convicted solely on the evidence of glove prints.

It applied to all k whether of rubber.

Sydney Noakes chairman, or he remanded in May 20 for a p

Scotland Yard's Branch, had been able ish the the chances very small, as in the fingerprints and th

Man trapped by glove prints for first time

For the first time in Britain a man was convicted yesterday on the evidence of marks left by his gloves.

Mr Colin Hart-Leverton, for the prosecution, told Inner London Sessions: "This means that

been left on the broken window".

He added: " This case breaks new ground in the detection of criminals because it is the first time in the history of criminal investigation in this country, and possibly throughout the world, that an

Prints from various fabrics

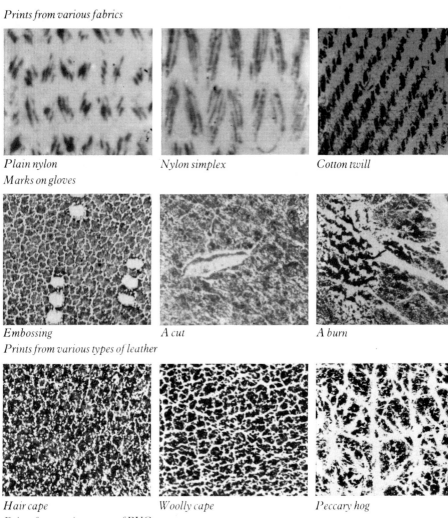

Plain nylon

Nylon simplex

Cotton twill

Marks on gloves

Embossing

A cut

A burn

Prints from various types of leather

Hair cape

Woolly cape

Peccary hog

Prints from various types of PVC patterns

Prints from various types of rubber gloves

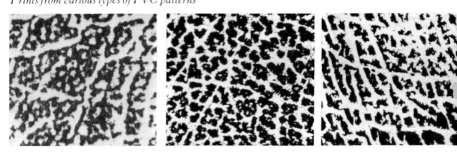

(Above) *Control print and* (below) *Scanned print*

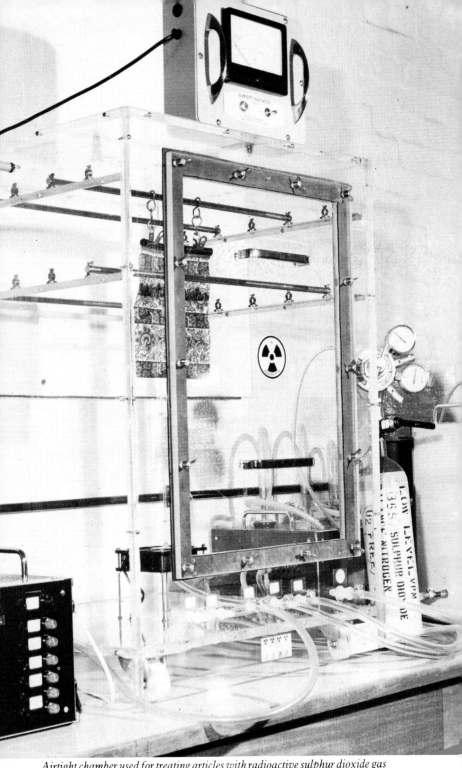

Airtight chamber used for treating articles with radioactive sulphur dioxide gas

(Above and right) *Postage stamps displaying fingerprints, all issued in 1973 to celebrate the fiftieth anniversary of Interpol*

(Below) *Stamp issued in 1976 to denote the Arab 'Day to Eliminate Illiteracy'. (The crossing out of the fingerprint is significant, because the fingerprint is used instead of a signature in the case of illiterate Arabs.)*

(Below) *A stamp issued in 1957 in honour of Juan F. Steegers, a Cuban fingerprint pioneer*

(Above) *Nineteenth-century 'New Scotland Yard' (1890) and*
(Below) *Twentieth-century 'New Scotland Yard' (1967)*

our friends in the Joint Home Office and Metropolitan Police Automatic Data Processing Unit (JADPU) to put our test on a computer and then carry out four hundred searches. The test was carried out on an ICT 1301 serial processing computer, normally used for pay and statistics. Although it was unsuitable for a live fingerprint system, the computer gradually ground its way through the test. When we compared the computer print-out with our own manual results, we were pleased to find they coincided exactly.

Eighteen months later specially trained fingerprint officers made a start on the monumental task of coding the whole of the national fingerprint collection in preparation for the day when it would form part of the data-base on the Police National Computer.

Any large fingerprint collection will contain a few sets that cannot be dealt with in the same way as the vast majority. These aberrations are caused by a malfunction during foetal growth. Polydactyly means extra – literally, 'many' – digits. Quite often they appear as an appendage on the thumb or to the side of the little finger. There are, however, instances of six or more fully grown digits being perfectly integrated on one hand. Each bears normal ridge configurations. Syndactyly or 'webbed-fingers' is the fusing together of one or more digits. The degree of fusing is variable, and can range from just a skin union to a bone union. The extent of the fusion is also variable: it can apply only to the lower joints of the affected digits or extend the full length of the fingers. Extreme cases of total fusion of all four digits still bear normal ridge structure.

Other digital abnormalities are: brachydactyly, abnormally short digits; ectrodactyly, the congenital absence of one or more digits; macrodactyly, abnormal largeness of a digit.

Abnormalities which interrupt the natural flow of the ridges are also encountered occasionally. The most common of these is a condition known as dissociated ridges. The ridges, instead of following the normal parallel tracks, break up into a series of fragments, and although each fragment does not relate to any other fragment the total configuration still bears a resemblance to a recognized pattern.

One other rare condition is worth mentioning – that is, the 'ridges of the end' syndrome, sometimes referred to as cuspal patterns. In these cases the ridges, instead of flowing horizontally and forming recognizable patterns, flow vertically and form no such patterns.

During our computer study we naturally took a close look at scarred fingers. Scars are either temporary or permanent. A temporary scar occurs when the epidermis, the surface layer, is damaged. The damage will in time be replaced with new cells, and no sign of it will remain. The ridge data will, of course, remain unaltered. A permanent scar will only form if the injury penetrates the epidermis and damages the more sensitive dermal layer below.

As a side-issue we kept an eye open for instances of people who had deliberately mutilated their fingers to avoid identification. We already knew of various instances where people had tried to damage their prints after they had been arrested, but the damage they inflicted – either by rubbing their fingers on an abrasive surface or picking the epidermis with something sharp like a pin – was of a superficial nature, and did not result in permanent scarring. In spite of assurances by fiction-writers that such mutilations are carried out by master-criminals, we only found two instances where all ten digits had been mutilated in this manner. Both were Canadians. They were prisoners in a Canadian penitentiary in 1957, and together with a number of other inmates they had attempted to mutilate the pattern core of each digit by using a sharp instrument and acid. Their success was limited because these two men were later identified by their fingerprints when they were next arrested.

Probably the most spectacular mutilation to remove fingerprints occurred in the United States of America. It came to light in October 1941 when officers of the Texas Highway Patrol arrested a hitch-hiker at El Paso, Texas, for vagrancy and possible violation of the Federal Selective Service Act. As he was being fingerprinted, the officer noticed that the end digits of his fingers did not have any friction ridges. When questioned the man (who claimed his name was Paul Cline) said that he had had a surgical operation to remove the friction ridges on the ends of his digits in May 1941. Five portions of skin, all about two inches in diameter, were cut from both sides of his chest, leaving each portion attached by one side of the flap. Most of the flesh on the end-joints of each of his fingers and thumbs was then cut away. His arms were folded comfortably across his chest. The fresh-cut side of the flaps were then sewn to the fresh-cut portions of his finger-tips. His arms and fingers remained in this position until his fingers had grown to the skin of his chest. They were then cut apart, leaving the end-joints of his fingers free from papillary ridges. After further questioning he admitted his true identity was Robert James Pitts. His identity was confirmed by using the ridge-detail of his second joints.

In the late 1950s and early 1960s a number of instances of deliberate transmogrification of fingerprint patterns were noted in Hong Kong. In the main these cases involved people who had been deported from

Hong Kong to the near-by Portuguese colony of Macau. Fingerprints of all deportees are taken by the Hong Kong authorities just prior to their deportation. It would appear that some of these were persuaded by a person in Macau that he could alter their fingerprints in such a way that they would not be recognized if they made another attempt to enter Hong Kong illegally. The 'alteration' was achieved by cutting out the core area of each finger and repositioning it – usually upside down – and then leaving it to heal. As no attempt was made to align the ridges of the removed segment with the ridge-flow on the rest of the finger, the displacement was immediately noticeable.

The people concerned in the cases of transmogrification recorded in Hong Kong did not have a criminal history of prolonged or serious crime. They just wanted to become permanent residents of Hong Kong!

As we were busy preparing for the computerized future, the rest of the department was still coping with an ever increasing case-load. One murder case in particular, dealt with in 1964, will be long remembered. I cannot remember any other case where so much fingerprint evidence was produced against one person for one crime.

The unfortunate 67-year-old victim was Joseph Hayes, the managing director of two engineering firms. It was very much a family concern, employing about 150 people. His wife Elsie was the secretary of both companies, and their son Peter was a director. It was company practice to collect the employees' wages from a local bank every Thursday morning. When the pay packets had been made up they were handed to those employees who were immediately available. The pay packets for workers on outside contracts were taken home by Mr Hayes and his wife for safekeeping until they could be paid out next day.

Thursday the 23rd of July 1964 was no different to any other Thursday. The money for the wages had been collected, the pay-packets made up and fifty-five wage-packets paid out. The remaining pay-packets, containing just over £1,878, were placed in an old brown briefcase. At about 5.30 p.m. Mr Hayes and his wife collected the briefcase and were driven to their home in Longbridge Road, Barking, by their son, arriving there at about 6.30 p.m. When they entered the house Mr Hayes took the briefcase to the kitchen while his wife went upstairs to change. While she was doing this, she heard a knock at the front door, and thought it was probably the little girl next door. To her horror she heard a shot and her husband say, 'Let him have the money, Elsie.'

As she reached the landing she was confronted by a man coming up the stairs shouting, 'I want the money!' He followed her down the stairs and in the hallway she had to step over the body of her dead husband. Once in the kitchen, she started to shout for help. The murderer hit her over the head a number of times, shot her as she lay helpless on the floor, then seized the briefcase and fled.

Mrs Hayes, covered in blood, managed to get to her kitchen door and call for help. Quickly her sister, who lived near by, police and an ambulance were at the scene of the murder. Mrs Hayes was fortunate that she did not die with her husband. The bullet fired at her passed through her arm, entered her chest and finally lodged against her spine. Although she was in considerable pain, she managed to describe the assailant as being aged between twenty and thirty, fairly tall with dark hair, a good-looking man with a longish face and smartly dressed in a dark suit.

The murder investigation was conducted by Detective Superintendent Ernest Williams, who got there shortly after the attack. He was closely followed by Detective Superintendent John Robertson of the Fingerprint Department. His meticulous examination revealed numerous finger and palm-prints, including some on the stairs handrail. At the top of the stairs on the landing he found a copy of the *Evening News*, with holes in it. It had been published between 3.40 p.m. and 4.5 p.m. on the day of the murder. He took possession of this for fingerprint examination. It was later deduced that the gunman had fired his first shot through the newspaper, which had been folded in four at the time. The .38 'wad-cutter' bullet had carried fragments of the paper into the fatal wound.

The newspaper was treated with ninhydrin and a number of finger and palm-prints were developed, some of which were identical with those found on the handrail. These prints were checked against the finger and palm-prints of all those people who had legitimate access to the murder scene, and found not to be identical with any of them. This confirmed earlier speculation that the prints had been made by the murderer.

A massive search of the National Fingerprint Collection was arranged. Even allowing for certain parts of the collection being automatically eliminated by virtue of the pattern data we had available, it was calculated that over half a million comparisons would have to be made if it turned out to be an abortive search. This type of search – which had been carried out many times with successful results – could not be conducted during normal working hours because of the limited manpower available. The staff, as always, rallied round and made themselves available for this daunting search out of normal hours. Just seven days after the murderous attack, a young fingerprint officer made the vital identification. The fingerprints on the newspaper and handrail had been made by 25-year-old Ronald John Cooper.

It is interesting the effect of making such an identification has on the fingerprint officer concerned. I saw it happen many times. Two very strong emotions are invariably involved. The first is the almost utter disbelief that he has made such an important identification, and he is momentarily stunned. This, however, soon gives way to satisfaction followed by elation.

Now that Detective Superintendent Williams knew the name of the suspect, his task was to find him. The last time that Cooper had come to the attention of the police was during street disturbances in Notting Hill some six years earlier. Gradually the investigators gathered information about him. He had had various types of contrasting employment. He had worked both as a salesman in a gentlemen's outfitters and as a car-breaker. In August 1963 he attended a school for croupiers, and in December 1963 he signed a two-year contract with the casino of the Lucayan Beach Hotel, Freeport, in the Bahamas. This had lasted until early July 1964, when he was involved in a disagreement with one of his supervisors and immediately dismissed. His fare back to England was paid by his ex-employers, and he arrived back in this country on the 10th of July 1964. His movements were traced to a number of gambling clubs in London and Liverpool. Then a real break occurred. A sales clerk at London Airport remembered selling a return ticket to the USA at about 9 a.m. on Friday the 24th of July 1964, some fifteen hours after the murder. The passenger's name was given as R. J. Cooper.

Urgent messages were sent to the police in the USA and the Bahamas, and on the 14th of August Cooper was detained at Nassau Airport. It took several weeks to complete the extradition procedures, but finally Cooper was formally arrested at Nassau Prison by Detective Superintendent Williams and Detective Sergeant Rutland. He was brought back to England, and charged the next day with murder and attempted murder.

On the 3rd of December Cooper appeared at the Central Criminal Court, where he pleaded not guilty to four counts: the murder of Joseph Hayes, the attempted murder of Elsie Hayes, wounding Elsie Hayes with intent to do her grievous bodily harm, and robbery with violence.

Detective Superintendent Robertson produced as evidence nineteen comparative charts relating to various of Cooper's fingers and portions of his palms, all enlarged and each marked with sixteen ridge characteristics in coincident sequence. The defence, during cross-examination, tried hard to make Robertson contradict himself without success.

One interesting development in the trial occurred when the defence introduced a witness to rebut the fingerprint evidence. He turned out to be one of those witnesses – occasionally produced by the defence in such cases – who has never worked in a fingerprint bureau making fingerprint comparisons, and most certainly does not meet the exacting standards of police fingerprint experts. These standards state that before a person can be considered competent to give evidence of a finger or palm identification in a court he/she must have served at least five[1] years whole and continuous service in making finger and palm comparisons in a bureau of such size and case-load to enable him/her to gain such experience in all aspects of fingerprint work. At the end of five years that person may, with the recommendation of his/her Chief Police Officer, take an advanced fingerprint course at a centre approved by the Secretary of State. It is only when a person has passed this advanced course that they qualify to give expert evidence relating to finger and palm comparisons.

It is quite noticeable that this kind of witness is usually loath to advance an opinion that 'the prints are identical' or 'the prints are not identical'. They rely on casting doubt either on the quality of the photographic images or the clarity of individual marked characteristics. The defence witness in this case was no different. He opted to attack the photographic quality, and to claim that some marked characteristics were too near the edges in some of the exhibits. Although he was given ample opportunity to express an opinion as to whether certain marks were identical, he steadfastly declined to give an opinion.

The trial continued until the 14th of December 1964, when the jury found Cooper guilty of murder, wounding with intent to commit grievous bodily harm and robbery with violence. He was sentenced to death for murder. Because capital punishment was in the process of being abolished, Cooper escaped the hangman's noose and his sentence was commuted to one of imprisonment for life.

[1]Prior to the 4th of January 1964 this period of time was seven years.

19 Glove-prints and 'lifting'

Over the next few years a number of changes in command, working practices and even location were to occur within the Fingerprint Department. On the 22nd of May 1966 its head, Detective Chief Superintendent John Godsell, after thirty-six years in the Department, retired from the Force and accepted the post of fingerprint adviser to the Home Office within the Police Scientific Development Branch (PSDB). The PSDB is an integral part of the Home Office Police Department which recruits most of its staff from among qualified scientists. Technical specialists and technical support staff are also employed. The Branch, headed by a Director, consisted then of six independent groups, each dealing with a different aspect of police duty: matters affecting the uniformed branch; traffic; crime; human factors; equipment; and of course fingerprints.

The fingerprint group really started with Godsell's appointment. Gradually, as people realized the effectiveness of fingerprints, the group recruited more specialists, including physicists and chemists. Their projects ranged from a thorough chemical analysis of perspiration to automatic fingerprint retrieval by the use of scanners. Many contracts were placed with universities, industry and government agencies to enhance the use made of fingerprints within a criminal environment. The full value of their work came to the fore during the IRA mainland bombing campaign in the mid-seventies.

Mr Godsell's successor was Detective Chief Superintendent Harold Rodden Squires, who had joined the Department in 1931, shortly after Godsell, and still holds the record of the longest-serving officer in the Fingerprint Department, with thirty-seven years' service.

The increased number of fingerprint experts examining crime scenes produced spectacular results, from 414 crime scenes examined by fingerprint personnel in 1955 to nearly 9,000 in 1965. At that stage all fingerprints found at crime scenes were being photographed, and the photographic department was overwhelmed. This was partially countered in April 1965 when all fingerprint officers, operating at crime scenes, were equipped with, and trained to use, CRL fixed-focus fingerprint cameras. This camera was only suitable for flat surfaces and the photographic department still had to deal with prints on any other surface, either by attendance at the scene or – if the property was portable – by having it transported to the Yard in specially equipped vehicles.

The other area to suffer from the deluge of work coming in from the field force was the scenes-of-crime section. The backbone of this section had been until then the single-print collection, the pride and joy of the Department for nearly forty years. It became apparent that this system (which had been excellent in its day) no longer had a place in a department dealing with an ever-increasing case-load, so early in 1967 the decision was taken to scrap it, and replace it with a series of easily maintainable collections. The results of this major surgery within the first year quelled any lingering doubts about such a decision. In this period 30 per cent more crime cases were handled, resulting in a 26 per cent increase in identifications.

Crime identifications not only identify people who have committed specific crimes, but also lead to numerous other crimes being solved. Many criminals arrested for a particular crime, following a fingerprint identification, often admit other crimes they have committed in order that the judge can take them into consideration when they are sentenced. In this way one fingerprint identification can in fact solve more than one crime.

This is well illustrated by the case of an itinerant burglar who was identified for fourteen cases of burglary and housebreaking in north London between October 1966 and June 1967. When he was finally arrested he was charged with four of these offences, and at his trial he asked for 357 similar cases to be taken into consideration.

Sometimes fingerprints of one person are found at a number of crime scenes. Occasionally sufficient data is obtained from these fingerprints to justify a search in the national records. Such a case occurred in 1960. Fingerprints from a series of housebreakings in south London were searched in the national records without success. The housebreaker obviously had no previous criminal history. The housebreakings continued, and he became such a nuisance that fingerprint staff (including myself) spent many evenings with the local CID officers checking on various people found in the alleyways behind houses, or carrying bags and parcels late at night. Each person stopped in this way was told the reason for it, and asked to show his fingers to the accompanying fingerprint expert. Most people we spoke to were co-operative, and appreciated the efforts we were making to catch this troublesome housebreaker. The man had a charmed life, because he continued his activities for five years.

By 1965 we had amassed sufficient fingerprint evidence to prove over a hundred break-ins. Eventually a man was seen acting suspiciously near some unoccupied houses. He assaulted the police officer who questioned him and ran away, but he was soon detained and arrested. His fingerprints proved that he was the person we had been seeking for five years. Before sentence was passed on him at his trial he admitted committing over six hundred similar offences.

During 1966, following my promotion to Detective Chief Inspector in December 1965, approval was given for the fingerprint computerization programme to proceed. John Seymour and I immediately set to work preparing an instruction manual and training schedule for the staff who would be involved in the task of coding the national records. We realized the back conversion programme – and by this, I mean converting the existing two million non-computerized fingerprint records to make them compatible with the incoming computer system – would not be easy. Because of the arduous nature of the work, staff were only used for a limited period at any one time. In this way, by the time the conversion was completed all members of the staff had been instructed in the new system.

1967 was a memorable year, not only for the fingerprint staff, but also for everyone at Headquarters because, early in the year, New Scotland Yard was moved, lock, stock and barrel, from the site it had occupied for over seventy years to a new, glossy, marble-clad office block in Westminster. While it was possible to transfer people, and the paraphernalia for policing the capital, into a hygienic, air-filtered edifice with one and a half miles of corridors set in eleven acres of floor space, it was not possible to transport the atmosphere and memories from the old building. I had spent twenty years of my life in that old, draughty edifice, and like so many of my colleagues, I disliked the move to the new, anonymous building which looked like so many other office blocks springing up in London. Undoubtedly other people, in another time, will feel the same way when in turn the new premises are eventually vacated.

The move of the fingerprint department in February was masterminded by Detective Superintendent John Robertson in an operation aptly named 'Crowbar'. The transfer of the national records, protected by a strong police escort, started at the close of business on Saturday, and they were installed and operational again on the Monday morning.

On the 13th of June 1968 Detective Chief Superintendent Squires retired as head of the Fingerprint Department and was succeeded by Detective Chief Superintendent Robert Peat. At the same time I was promoted to Detective Superintendent and took over the scenes-of-crime operations.

I spent my first year in this new post continuing the reorganization started by my predecessor to improve the searching capability of the section. The new collections still needed streamlining. A study of the criminal records of those people whose fingerprints were in the specialized collections revealed that the period between the last occasion they had been arrested for crime, or released from prison, and the next time they were arrested averaged out to two years and four months. This meant that it was safe to reduce the ten-year retention period in the collection to three years providing a very strict updating policy was maintained. This allowed us to concentrate all our effort on the most active section of London's criminals.

The scenes-of-crimes staff were divided into a number of teams. Six of the teams each had a responsibility for a geographical section of the Metropolitan Police District. Four of these teams had boundaries which joined Home County police forces and they made liaison arrangements with these forces. Specialized teams were also formed. One of these teams dealt with serious crimes like murder, rape and armed robbery. The fact that criminals were gradually finding out that cheque fraud was a less risky method of unlawfully obtaining someone else's property led to the formation of a fingerprint team specializing in all forms of fraud.

When a crime scene is examined and fingerprints are found it is essential that the fingerprints of all people having access to the place where the prints are found are checked. An increase in the number of crime scenes being examined led obviously to an increase in the amount of elimination checking. A separate team was formed for this purpose. The team had a number of experienced officers assigned to it as well as a number of junior officers, and became an ideal training-ground.

More crime scenes examined meant more fingerprint identifications, which in turn led to more requests for fingerprint evidence. So much so that it became necessary to form a special court section to collate, check and generally oversee all court cases where fingerprint evidence was required.

In June 1969, in recognition of increased responsibility, all super-intendents and chief superintendents were upgraded. The head of the Fingerprint Department became a Commander, so for the first time in its history the department was headed by a man with chief police officer status and membership of the prestigious Association of Chief Police Officers. John Robertson and I became detective chief super-intendents at that time.

The success achieved by increasing the number of fingerprint officers assigned to examine crime scenes fired the imagination of the policy-makers. Consequently, in 1969 arrangements were made to recruit a special force of scenes-of-crime officers (SOCO). They were to be trained to examine crime scenes for fingerprints and other forensic evidence such as blood, fibres, hair etc. Their skill was to lie in the recovery of forensic evidence, not in its analysis. The initial seventy officers required were recruited in small batches, trained and then assigned to their divisions.

I realized that the additional fingerprints found by this new force of SOCOs would overwhelm the storage space available, which already could hardly cope with the many thousands of articles bearing finger-prints which were being transported to the Yard each year. The same problem faced the Photographic Department, with its limited number of skilled photographers. There were three solutions to this particular situation. The first was to increase the number of photo-graphers available. This was not possible due to a freeze in staff numbers. The second was to increase the storage space available. This was not possible as space in the new 'New Scotland Yard' was already at a premium. The third and final solution was to change our technique for recording fingerprints at crime scenes.

I decided to concentrate on option three. From the inception of the fingerprint system in this country all fingerprints found at crime scenes had been photographed. This was not so elsewhere. In America, for instance, fingerprints have been 'lifted' for many years. A 'lifted' fingerprint is one which has been developed normally with a fingerprint powder and then lifted from the surface on which it was developed by using a low-adhesive tape (so described to differentiate it from the high-adhesive tape normally used in offices and homes). The lifted mark is then mounted on a backing to preserve it.

The lifting of fingerprints had been considered taboo by all my predecessors. Two previous heads of the Department were quite outspoken in their condemnation of the technique. They warned of dire consequences if it were used, by suggesting that it would not be acceptable to judges and juries. I was puzzled by their dogmatic rejection of the lifting method and I could not help wondering whether they had really bothered to test legal reaction to such a method.

I researched the use of various powders and low-adhesive tapes until I was satisfied that I had the right combination. I then produced a report outlining the need for change and discussed it with the commander. He was a far-sighted man, and recognized the need for change.

The first hurdle was to test legal opinion. Happily, the Solicitor and Deputy Solicitor at New Scotland Yard supported this new venture, and arranged for me to demonstrate the system to the Chief Magistrate, most of the London magistrates, Her Majesty's judges at the Royal Courts of Justice and the Central Criminal Court, the Director of Public Prosecutions and his deputies, the Commissioner of Police for the Metropolis, and the Assistant Commissioner for Crime. I was heartened by their combined reaction. Their unanimous opinion was that they considered the lifting technique provided better evidence than the photographic method by producing the actual fingerprints in court, and wondered why it had not been done before.

Having got the principle of lifting accepted, the next stage was to implement it. The photographers were most enthusiastic, and one of them, Ernie Whatmore, a very competent technician, suggested putting the lifted impression on a transparent backing. In this way photographs of the lifted prints, required for internal checking purposes, could be made directly on to bromide paper without recourse to an intermediary negative, using a technique known as reflection printing. Subsequent trials proved this to be a most satisfactory method. The lifted fingerprint, of course, became the court exhibit when required. All the staff involved in crime-scene examinations were then trained how to use the new method, and the manner in which such evidence should be presented to a court.

In the meantime, the Photographic Department prepared themselves by obtaining a reflection-transmission projection printer, more commonly known as a 'Kenprinter'. This type of equipment is normally used to produce commercially printed holiday photographs. Once it had been modified to print lifts it could print four copies of each of one hundred lifts an hour. Each photograph not only showed the fingerprint but also the address where the print was found, and the unique reference number allocated to it. It was certainly quicker than sending photographers to crime scenes just to photograph fingerprints, and a lot cheaper. It was calculated that the cost of recording fingerprints found at crime scenes had been reduced by a staggering 75 per cent.

Finally, on Monday the 11th of May 1970, the lifting of fingerprints became official Force policy. After we had trained their officers, every major fingerprint bureau in the country adopted the lifting system. For many months we monitored each court case involving a lifted fingerprint. No adverse reaction occurred. Eventually lifting became a matter of routine.

With lifting safely established I concentrated on a research project I had started fourteen years earlier, glove-prints. People wear gloves for a measure of protection, protection from cold or heat, protection from dirt or disease, protection from chemicals or protection for whatever is to be handled by them, be it a patient or a precious metal surface – and, of course, protection from detection when committing crime. There is nothing more frustrating for a fingerprint officer than to examine a crime scene where he finds glove marks and consequently to be unable to help the investigating officer.

It was this frustration, which generated a strong desire to turn the tables on the criminal, and led me to become absorbed in a most fascinating line of research. Over the years I watched gloves being cut, sewn and moulded, but probably the most important aspect of the research was the study of the various materials used in their manufacture, which are as varied as their uses.

From the constant handling of objects such as door-knobs or handles, banisters, shop-doors, rails on buses or trains, on which people have deposited large quantities of perspiration, a glove soon becomes impregnated with grease and dirt. Even during the putting on and removal of a glove, a layer of perspiration is placed on it. Consequently, when it comes in contact with a smooth, hard surface a layer of this grease is sometimes deposited, in much the same way as an unprotected finger will leave a fingerprint. As with fingerprints, the grease-deposit from the glove can be made visible by the skilful application of a fingerprint search powder. The layer of grease left by the glove is by its mere nature not as strong and dense as a fingerprint, but it is nevertheless detectable, recordable and in certain cases can be as reliable as a fingerprint when it comes to identification.

Each glove can be individualized in many ways: the material it was made from, the way it was put together – machine-stitched, hand-stitched, knitted, moulded, its embossing, perforations; the creases and contours formed when it is worn constantly; the accidental damage caused by the wearer. Some or all of this data can be revealed in a glove impression left at a crime scene.

I recognized that to claim individuality for one particular type of glove could raise doubts. The rubber household glove is manufactured by the thousand from the same formers or moulds. Such gloves are made, inside out, on porcelain formers. The grip pattern is indented in the former. This is dipped in a tank containing latex which adheres to it. When the latex has solidified the completed glove is removed from the former. Slight uneven adhesion of the latex can mutilate what should be a regular pattern. Air bubbles can occur in the pattern area when the former is dipped into the latex, or a piece of latex from a previous glove can contaminate a portion of the pattern. All of these factors can be detected in a glove-print. The user of such gloves would not be aware of these slight variations, which are only revealed under magnification.

I asked a very co-operative manufacturer of rubber gloves if they would supply me with a series of gloves all made on the same former. I printed each of the gloves, and then compared each series of prints with all the others. Although all the gloves looked the same, minute variations between each of them was detectable, all of which had occurred during manufacture.

By early 1971 I was satisfied that a glove-print could be positively identified, and that the only stage that remained was to test this thesis in a court of law.

The scenario for my first operational glove-identification had its origins just over a mile away from New Scotland Yard. At 1.55 a.m. on Friday the 29th of January 1971 an alarm bell at 62 Wilton Road, London S.W.1 brought police hurrying to the scene. As the premises backed on to a large enclosed car-park, some officers went to the front of the building and others went to the other side of the car-park in case the suspect attempted to escape across it. Shortly after their arrival a man was seen climbing over the wall of the car-park between a house and a hoarding. After a short chase he was detained. He vehemently denied that he had just come from the car-park or that he had anything to do with an office-breaking. He claimed that he had been drinking in a local public house most of the evening, and that he had just gone to a nearby mews to urinate. The officers questioning him were far from satisfied with his explanation, so they arrested him and charged him with being found in an enclosed yard for an unlawful purpose.

When the premises at 62 Wilton Road were examined it was

discovered that a pane of glass in a first-floor window at the rear had been broken. This window was immediately above a flat asphalt roof, from where it was possible to drop into the car-park. The premises were examined by a fingerprint officer, and on the outside of the broken window he developed a glove-print which was across some cracks in the glass.

The lifted mark was brought to me, and after I had examined it I was satisfied that it had been made by a left-hand glove. The texture of the print indicated a glove with a suede finish, the surface of which had been damaged. I inquired if the prisoner was in possession of a pair of gloves, and when I was told that he had, I asked for them so that I could carry out a comparison. They turned out to be a pair of sheepskin leather gloves with a suede finish. The left-hand glove showed signs of surface damage which matched the glove-print on the window. As a result of this evidence the prisoner, a 26-year-old painter and decorator, was further charged with breaking into the office at 62 Wilton Road with intent to steal. I was told later that when he found out the evidence was to be his glove-prints he thought the officer was joking.

On the 6th of May 1971 the accused appeared before the Inner London Quarter Sessions. The scene was set to test this new form of identification. The charge of entering 62 Wilton Road as a trespasser with intent to steal was put to him, and he was asked to plead. Despite all his previous protestations of innocence, he pleaded guilty. This was an anticlimax. The prosecution then informed the court of the type of evidence that had made the charge possible. The Press had a field day the next morning.

Although I trained a small team of officers in glove-print identification techniques, and passed over to them the day-to-day running of the system, I presented all glove-print evidence for the next two years to ensure that the system became well established. In that time I successfully gave evidence about gloves made from leather, PVC, rubber and cotton twill. The fact that juries were prepared to convict on glove-print evidence afforded me considerable satisfaction. I owe grateful thanks for the unstinted co-operation I received from the members of the National Association of Glove Manufacturers, the members of the British Plastic Federation and the Leather Institute. Without their co-operation this project would still be an idea – not a reality.

20 Scientific developments

The fingerprint section of The Police Scientific Development Branch[1] concentrated a large part of its research programme on producing techniques for developing fingerprints on surfaces which were resistant to the fingerprint detection methods then available. A number of their discoveries are now standard operational systems.

For some years researchers were engaged in the development of latent fingerprints by the vacuum deposition of thin metal films, as it was known that fingerprints inhibit the condensation of metal films. Many metals were examined as to their suitability for use in this context. As a result of these examinations, a number of metal and metal combinations were found to delineate fingerprint ridges on paper and fabric substrates. The most promising results were obtained with lead as a single-method treatment, or with silver or gold followed by cadmium or zinc.

To develop fingerprints by the gold/zinc metal deposition technique, the article is placed in a chamber with the surface to be treated facing a pair of molybdenum boats which are loaded, one with a small amount of gold wire and the other with a quantity of zinc. The chamber is then evacuated, causing a vacuum, and by heating each metal in turn to the point of evaporation a layer of each metal is deposited on the surface of the article under examination. This process may be used on a variety of materials for which conventional techniques do not yield good results, such as most forms of plastic.

The use of radioactive sulphur dioxide is being exploited primarily for two applications. The first is the fingerprint examination of coloured adhesive tapes of the type quite often found at crime scenes

[1] Now known as the Scientific Research and Development Branch of the Home Office.

on such articles as axe handles, gun-butts and terrorist explosive devices. Secondly, as this technique is non-destructive, it can be used on valuable articles. The article to be examined is placed in a very low concentration of radioactive sulphur dioxide gas in an airtight chamber. The sulphur dioxide reacts selectively with the constituents of the fingerprint. Although it is radioactive, the fingerprint is not visible, and must be imaged by sandwiching it with X-ray film for a predetermined time. This film is then developed, and the fingerprint is revealed.

A process known as a physical developer was produced to meet the needs of two problem areas often encountered in case-work, the fingerprint examination of papers which have been wetted or subjected to high humidity, and papers with highly patterned surfaces. In the case of the wetted papers, conventional reagent systems were ineffective because most of the reagent-sensitive components of the fingerprint, such as amino acids, chlorides, and urea, had been washed away. In the case of the highly patterned papers, the conventional reagent systems did not easily lend themselves to subsequent intensification to allow sufficient contrast between the print and the patterned background.

The physical developer causes selective deposition of silver on the components of the fingerprint which are highly water-insoluble and location-stable, and are therefore unaffected by wetting. The developed print is grey in colour, and in most cases can be recorded by normal photographic processes. With heavily patterned surfaces, however, photography is sometimes ineffective due to pattern interference. In order to obtain an image of the fingerprint, the silver which has been deposited on the fingerprint from the physical developer solution can be made radioactive. As with the radioactive sulphur dioxide gas, the fingerprint is imaged using X-ray film, thus producing a fingerprint free of pattern interference.

By 1973 the National Fingerprint Collection contained the fingerprints of over two and a half million criminals. In spite of drastic pruning, the collection continued to grow in size. Paper records are extremely bulky, and consulting and handling them was time-consuming. Each individual record could only be used by one officer at a time, and was susceptible to possible error of misfiling. It was these problems, coupled with an ever-increasing demand for its services from police forces throughout the country, which led to an in-depth study of the storage and retrieval systems available on the market. The most promising of these was a system known as

Videofile, produced by the Ampex Corporation of Redwood City, California. Research led to the development of high-density, mass-storage tape systems and digital 'disc' storage devices. The use of magnetic tape as the bulk-storage media for Videofile provides several graphic and logic flexibilities, such as instant replay without processing, erase and re-record capability for file purging and updating, automatic copy processes for file maintenance and reorganization, and computer-controlled research routines.

In August 1973 a project team of Metropolitan Police specialists entered into a two-year joint study with representatives of the Ampex Corporation. The head of the Fingerprint Department, Commander Peat, was placed on detached duty and seconded to the project team for a two-year period. I became acting commander in his absence. The joint study led to a contract being awarded to the Ampex Corporation in June 1975 for a customer-designed system at a cost of just under three million pounds.

Terrorism, which had lain dormant in this country for some years, had once more manifested itself in all its ugliness on the streets of London in the late sixties. Attacks on premises with Spanish connections, by dissidents opposed to the Spanish Government; domestic 'establishment' premises attacked by the self-styled 'Angry Brigade'; the attempted hijacking of an aircraft by the 'Popular Front for the Liberation of Palestine'; the machine-gunning of the Jordanian Ambassador's car by the 'Black September' group – it was all happening.

Following a resurgence of 'the troubles' in Ireland in 1969, the IRA opened their mainland attack on the 22nd of February 1972, when they set off explosions in the officers' mess of the Parachute Regiment at Aldershot, killing an army chaplain and six civilians. On Thursday the 8th of March 1973, the day of the Ulster Border Referendum, the IRA car bombers came to London. The first car bomb was parked opposite New Scotland Yard. The second was parked in Great Scotland Yard near the Army Recruiting Office. The third was parked in Westminster, and the fourth was parked outside the Central Criminal Court. They were all set to explode at about 3 p.m. Fortunately, the one opposite New Scotland Yard was discovered and defused long before a telephoned warning was received. The police search for the remaining cars was hampered by the extra large number of cars in London caused by a railway strike. The Westminster car was found and successfully defused, but the others exploded, causing over two hundred casualties.

Because of the early discovery of the car outside New Scotland Yard by two vigilant Special Patrol Group officers, Commander Huntley, of the Bomb Squad, was able to issue his now famous 'close England' order. By the time the two cars exploded the people believed to be responsible (nicknamed the 'Belfast Ten') were already in custody.

After a few months' respite the campaign (which was to be bloody and brutal) gained impetus. Although it was mainly centred on London, many provincial towns and cities such as Birmingham, Manchester and Guildford were to suffer from the bombs of the IRA. Indiscriminate killing and maiming by means of time bombs, throw bombs and shootings from cars were aimed at the general public. The other type of attack aimed at selected persons consisted of book bombs and letter bombs. Their targets were as varied as their weapons, and included departmental stores, pubs, clubs, hotels, places of public interest like Madame Tussaud's and the Tower and public transport. Victims were invariably innocent bystanders of all ages, who probably knew very little about the four-hundred-year Irish wrangle.

During this time the staff of the Fingerprint Department were tested and extended as never before, and acquitted themselves in a most exemplary manner. Fingerprints from scenes of terrorist activity, bomb factories, and safe houses, not only in London and provincial cities, but also from abroad, as far away as Zaïre, Portugal, Gibraltar and the United States of America, flooded into the Department. Many fingerprints came from terrorists' bombs, rendered safe by the expertise and dedication of the Metropolitan Police Explosive Officers. The fingerprints recovered not only identified the participants but also linked groups of people with particular incidents, their respective safe houses and bomb factories. Well over thirty million fingerprint comparisons were made, resulting in over three hundred identifications, which linked a hundred terrorists to their acts of aggression. During the lengthy campaign some two hundred and fifty fingerprint officers were engaged for the part or whole of it, which all added up to a massive concentrated effort.

There was one incredible period in 1975 when besides the fifty fingerprint officers engaged in the IRA investigation, another forty officers were assigned to the inquiry relating to the kidnapping and subsequent murder of Lesley Whittle. Over seven million fingerprint comparisons were carried out during the latter investigation. Apart from these two major inquiries, fingerprints had been recovered from two London murders. In each case, sufficient fingerprint data was available to justify searches being made in the National Fingerprint Collection. The staff were working under intolerable pressures, but, despite this a large number of them volunteered to give up their rest day on two consecutive Sundays in order to carry out these searches. Much to the satisfaction and relief of the hard-pressed detectives, they were successful with both searches.

One of these cases related to the murder of Mrs Lilian Johnson, a 65-year-old widow who lived alone in a ground-floor flat at Norwood Road, London S.E.24. Her body was found in a bed in the rear ground-floor bedroom of her flat by police who had been called because of a gas-leak. A pipe had been fractured when the gas meter had been forced open and its contents stolen.

The victim, almost completely nude, had received extensive facial injuries from what appeared to have been a frenzied attack. Furniture and other articles in the living-room had been broken, and there were bloodstains on the floor and walls. This scene greeted the investigating officer. An extensive examination of the murder flat by a team of fingerprint officers revealed many finger and palm impressions, most of which were subsequently identified for either the victim or her known associates. Attention was eventually focused on fingerprints found on the larder door and kitchen cabinet door, partially in blood. The fingerprints had been made by three fingers of a right hand. On Sunday the 6th of April 1975 the fingerprint officers began the task of making an estimated three hundred thousand comparisons with these fingerprints. Their efforts were rewarded when Charles Henry Derry, a 28-year-old fairground attendant, was identified. Derry was later arrested some seventy miles away from the crime scene, in Northamptonshire. Although he pleaded not guilty at his trial, he was found guilty, and sentenced to life imprisonment.

The other murder inquiry, the following weekend, resulted in the identification of a man who subsequently pleaded guilty to three cases of manslaughter due to diminished responsibility, and was later sentenced to life imprisonment.

On the 29th of August 1975, following the retirement of Commander Peat, I was promoted to commander, and became head of not only the Fingerprint Department but also the Photographic Section and other technical support groups. Together they all added up to a formidable collection of experts and supporting staff, numbering over six hundred.

Syd Draper, as he had forecast all those years previously, became my deputy. Sadly, he died at a comparatively early age, and was sorely missed by all those who knew him.

By late 1975 the computerization of the National Fingerprint Collection was well advanced. Information from every fingerprint record was on the computer data-base, and the computer programmes were being tested in preparation for a period of parallel running. Only one part of the whole operation was causing concern. Every aspect of data-preparation, interrogation and interpretation was controlled and carried out by fingerprint officers. The exception was the interface between the Department and the Police National Computer. This was in the hands of a limited number of data-processors.

Fortunately, a device then known as 'Datapad' and now known as 'Micropad' came on to the market. It consists of a pressure-sensitive writing surface linked to a microprocessor. Data for computer input is written on to a prepared input document placed on the pressure-sensitive surface. As the data is written it is recognized and converted, character by character, into normal computer input. At the same time a small visual display shows graphically the information being accepted for the computer. A period of intense activity by the manufacturers, in close co-operation with the Fingerprint Department, produced a customized version, with inbuilt validation routines, in time for the computerized fingerprint system going fully operational on the 17th of May 1976.

The 'go live' date for the introduction of the computerized system coincided, fortuitously, with the 75th anniversary celebrations of the Fingerprint Department, which took the form of a banquet, cabaret and dance held at the Royal Garden Hotel, Kensington, on the 22nd of May 1976. It was a most enjoyable occasion, and in my address to that happy gathering I made a comparison between crime in 1901 and 1976:

> In 1901 the number of indictable crimes known to Police in England and Wales was just under eighty-one thousand. The latest figures I have for indictable crimes known to Police in England and Wales is well over one and a half million. This is a sad comment indeed about the prevailing attitude among elements of our present day society. A society which is enjoying a higher standard of living than it has known previously, even in the climate of our present economic difficulties. A society where it is seemingly more important to know your rights than to know your responsibilities toward your fellow men. It is to be hoped that by the time the Fingerprint Department celebrates its centenary, in 2001, that this same society will have reached a point in civilized living and thinking

where their need of this Department in the fight against crime will not be as great as it is today. . . .

In March 1977 the Videofile equipment was delivered to New Scotland Yard. We had the equipment and now we had to record over two and a half million sets of fingerprints on videotape. The scenes of crime database was recorded first, followed by the National Collection. Running parallel to this was a massive training programme for the staff.

The New Scotland Yard Videofile system is in fact made up of two systems, one of which deals with the National Fingerprint Collection and the other with scenes-of-crime operations. Each system has its own controlling computer, its own tape library, filing, storing and displaying equipment. A front end processor acts as an index to the combined complex, keeping its records in digital form on disc drives. This index maintains the videotape location of every graphic image stored, and also the descriptive digital data of all scenes-of-crime records. The front end processor also controls the system's autonomic function, together with filing, selective copy and display functions.

By displaying data on VDUs using a split-screen technique it is possible to show the suspect's print on the upper half of the screen for direct comparison with a probable matching print on the lower half of the screen, Videofile can screen responses to fingerprint inquiries suggested by the Police National Computer, or by a nominal index which is maintained in the Fingerprint Department. Additionally, it files and stores the graphic images of fingerprints found at the scenes of crime, fingerprints of persons known to commit 'breaking' offences, and maintains a digital data-base of information relative to the crimes committed and the people who commit such crimes. In the same way that the Police National Computer selects the records to be viewed in the National Fingerprint Collection, basing its selection on the parameters selected by fingerprint officers, so the scenes-of-crime digital data-base is used to select responses to be viewed for any given inquiry in the scenes-of-crime collection.

The responses are selectively limited, both by the systems-inbuilt programmes and by the selected parameters of a fingerprint officer, so that the only record viewed – and the only parts of those records viewed – are those which are strictly relevant to a specific scene-of-crime incident. A simple example of this is that if a left-thumb impression bearing a twinned loop pattern is found at a crime scene the comparative responses which will be subsequently viewed against it will only relate to those criminals who commit that particular type of offence, and whose left thumbs reveal a twinned loop pattern.

The first crime-scene identification made, using the Videofile system, was on the 27th of October 1977. The identification related to a burglar, who when breaking into a house in Earlsfield carelessly left impressions of his right middle and ring fingers on the inside of a sash window. Such was the judgment used by the fingerprint expert when he formulated the search parameters to interrogate the computer that out of many thousands of possibilities only eleven criminals were selected for comparison. The Earlsfield burglar was one of them.

In 1977 I became the permanent chairman of the National Conference of Fingerprint Experts. At the annual conference great concern was expressed by many delegates about the increasing practice of prosecuting counsel requesting fingerprint evidence to be included in statements when prints were below the confirmed standard agreed in 1953. After considerable ventilation of opinion it was agreed that the Home Office be asked to convene a conference similar to the 1953 conference to discuss this very disturbing aspect.

The conference was held in April 1978, and was attended by representatives of the Home Office, the Police Scientific Development Branch, H.M. Inspectorate of Constabulary, the Association of Chief Police Officers, The Police Superintendents Association, the Director of Public Prosecutions Office, the Prosecuting Solicitors Society and of course fingerprint experts. Many interested observers also came. A very lively meeting ensued, which reflected a wide diversity of opinion and attitude. At the end of the conference I was asked to invite the next National Conference of Fingerprint Experts to consider what safeguards would in their view be required to enable a standard of twelve points of resemblance to be safely adopted, and whether there was a case for presenting supporting evidence which fell below the accepted standard.

I discharged this obligation the following month. After considerable discussion the conference voted that there was no case for 'probable' identifications to be used, and that in their view no safeguard in checking and other procedures would be sufficient to justify a reduction to twelve points. They then voted overwhelmingly to retain our present standard of sixteen points in agreement. This was an interesting decision, particularly as most of the delegates had between twenty and thirty years' fingerprint experience.

From its conception the Fingerprint Department had been an integral part of the Criminal Investigation Department, but in 1978 the decision was made to transfer both the Fingerprint Department and the Criminal Record Office out of the orbit of the Crime Department and into a group embracing technical support services. The Fingerprint Department became known as B.12. The police officers involved were, however, allowed to retain their detective status.

In June 1978 a small team of fingerprint experts commenced the final phase of the massive programme of computerization which had begun in 1964. Their task was to search fingerprints recovered from crime scenes against the enormous data bank of fingerprint information from the National Fingerprint Collection. Their instructions were to search suitable fingerprints which still remained unidentified after being searched through the specialized collections. In the first six months they completed 288 such searches and established sixty identifications, which in turn led to many other cases being cleared up.

In this age of technology people automatically look forward to the next progressive step. All present fingerprint systems rely on human participation, either wholly or in part, for their input, but technology has advanced to the point where it is possible to scan a fingerprint automatically, reducing data to a numerical code.

In 1978 a joint project team of seven scientists from the Police Scientific Development Branch and four New Scotland Yard fingerprint officers commenced work on a trial Automatic Fingerprint Recognition System (AFR), based on an experimental system developed by the PSDB. Within a few months they had a system ready for an operational trial.

I should make it clear that although the searching of scanned fingerprints is effective and efficient, the computer does not give the final answer to an identification. It does, however, provide a print-out which lists, in priority order, those persons whose fingerprints could possibly provide an identification with the inquiry fingerprint. The fingerprints of each respondent then have to be checked with the inquiry fingerprint.

The operational trial took the form of a direct comparison between the newly developed AFR system and the operational NSY system. To accomplish this, part of the operational collection, both criminal fingerprints and unidentified crime-scene fingerprints, were duplicated on the AFR data-base. Once this data-base had been established, all the searches which had to be carried out in the selected portion of the operational collection were duplicated on the AFR system. The results obtained from both systems were closely monitored, and after six months it became quite apparent that the AFR system was a resounding success.

As anticipated, the ability to scan and search a greater range of crime-scene fingerprints, plus the ability of the AFR computer to apply greater discrimination to a scanned fingerprint, meant that the AFR system was able to produce more identifications than the existing system. It was interesting to note that when an identification was established on the AFR system it was usually found within the first ten respondents on the print-out. The report of the AFR project team was placed before the Steering Committee and I was pleased that the committee recommended that a full AFR system for scenes-of-crime operations be installed at New Scotland Yard.

A change of emphasis

Having seen the Fingerprint Department progress from a totally manual system to the threshold of the ultimate in fingerprint processing, I retired on the 7th of September 1980. My deputy, Detective Chief Superintendent Martin O'Neill, was appointed as my successor.

In my final year of service three events gave me considerable pleasure. The first came in October 1979. During that year the Metropolitan Police celebrated their 150th anniversary. The celebrations took many forms, starting with a magnificent service at Westminster Abbey, attended by H.M. Queen Elizabeth the Queen Mother, and concluded with a Police Tattoo at Wembley Arena, the final performance of which was attended by H.M. the Queen and H.R.H. the Duke of Edinburgh. Every Metropolitan Police station and district entered into the celebrations, and involved the general public as much as possible, with open days at police stations, concerts, carnivals, flower-shows, sports-days and a boxing match. Fingerprint officers enthusiastically attended most of these events to take the fingerprints of the public on special commemorative cards. The public response to having their fingerprints taken was overwhelming. Even known criminals queued to obtain a memento bearing their own fingerprints. Such was the response that the Queen and the Duke of Edinburgh were invited to record their thumb-prints on a specially prepared illuminated address. To my delight, they both gave their consent.

On the 17th of October 1979 – which coincidentally was my fifty-fifth birthday – I attended the gala performance of the Tattoo. During the interval I was presented to the Queen and the Duke of Edinburgh. I recorded a thumb-print of both of them on the illuminated address to which they added their signatures. This was later framed and presented to the Queen as an unique memento of her visit.

The second event also occurred during the Tattoo, and took us all by surprise. Around the concourse of the arena were display stands which depicted many aspects of police work, Naturally, one of these stands related to the Fingerprint Department, and one of the many thousands of visitors to it was Mrs Dorothy Crow, who told us that her father, Detective Inspector Hunt, had been one of the original members of the Fingerprint Department. Delighted that she had made herself known to us, I invited her to visit the Fingerprint Department. To our utter amazement, she told us her mother would be pleased to hear about the invitation. I immediately extended the invitation to include her mother, who was a hundred and one years old. Over lunch in the Senior Officers Mess I was impressed with Mrs Hunt's remarkable memory about the early days in the Fingerprint Department. She talked of those early days as though it all happened yesterday.

The third event which gave me pleasure was to be awarded The Queen's Police Medal for Distinguished Service in the New Year's Honours list for 1980.

I have been more fortunate than some people, inasmuch that since retiring from the police service I have been able to continue my interest in fingerprints. Of course, I have made myself available as an independent fingerprint expert; and, contrary to public opinion, fingerprints are not restricted to criminal use. The non-criminal study of fingerprints is referred to as dermatoglyphics, which name is formed from two Greek words, *derma* and *glyphē*, meaning basically skin carvings. Dermatoglyphic studies cover a wide spectrum, including anthropology, genetics, medicine, and oddly enough, art, so the areas for research are considerable.

I have in my time been involved in many aspects of fingerprints. I have fingerprinted an Egyptian mummy, and examined 5,000-year-old antlers, recovered from an old flint-mine at Grimes's Graves, for traces of hand-prints of the long-dead users. The antlers had apparently been used as mining-instruments. I have assisted various hospitals who required confirmation that various sets of twins were in fact identical before they embarked on transplant operations, and as I have a particular interest in the fingerprints of multiple-birth families, I have fingerprinted a number of such families. Probably the most difficult one of these to deal with was the fingerprinting of seventeen-day-old quintuplets. After the completion of this task, the consultant paediatrician commented that the taking of the finger-prints of five babies, each little more than two pounds in weight, by two hulking great policemen was the funniest thing he had seen for a long time.

Another area of interest is to be found in the world of art, and relates to fingerprints on, or in, old oil paintings. I have already examined quite a few of these, and it has occurred to me that this is an area which has been neglected by the researchers when trying to establish the authenticity of a particular painting.

In 1978 I became a member of the British Association for the Advancement of Science, and, seventy-nine years after Sir Edward Henry read a paper entitled 'Fingerprints and the detection of crime in India' to the Association at their meeting in Dover I was invited to present a paper to the same august Association at their annual meeting in Bath. The title of my paper was 'Forensic aspects of dermatoglyphics'. I felt particularly privileged, as to the best of my knowledge no one since Sir Edward Henry had spoken to the British Association on the subject of fingerprints.

With so many areas of fingerprint interest available, and my intention to continue my historical researches into this fascinating subject, I do not think I have really retired – I have merely changed the emphasis of my life slightly.

Appendix

Letter from Charles Darwin to Henry Faulds.

> Via Brindisi,
> April 7th. 1880.
> Down, Beckenham, Kent.
> Railway Station,
> Orpington, S.E.R.

Dear Sir,

The subject to which you refer in your letter of February 16th. seems to me a curious one, which may turn out interesting; but I am sorry to say that I am most unfortunately situated for offering you any assistance. I live in the country, and from weak health seldom see anyone. I will, however, forward your letter to Mr. F. Galton, who is the most likely man that I can think of to take up the subject to make further enquiries.

> Wishing you success,
> I remain, dear Sir, Yours faithfully,
> Charles Darwin

Letter from Charles Darwin to Francis Galton.

> Via Brindisi,
> April 7th. 1880.
> Down, Beckenham, Kent.
> Railway Station,
> Orpington, S.E.R.

My Dear Galton,

The enclosed letter and circular may perhaps interest you, as it relates to a queer subject. You will perhaps say hang his impudence. But seriously the letter might possibly be worth taking some day to the Anthropolog. Inst. for the chance of someone caring about it. I have written to Mr. Faulds telling him I could give no help, but had forwarded the letter to you on the chance of it interesting you.

My dear Galton,
Yours very sincerely
Ch. Darwin.

P.S. The more I think of your visualising enquiries, the more interesting they seem to me.

Letter from Francis Galton to Charles Darwin.

42, Rutland Gate, S.W.
April 8/80

My Dear Darwin,
I will take Faulds' letter to the Anthro. and see what can be done; indeed, I myself got several thumb impressions a couple of years ago, having heard of the Chinese plan with criminals, but failed, perhaps from want of sufficiently minute observation, to make out any large number of differences. It would I think be feasible in one or two public schools where the system is established of annually taking heights, weights etc., also to take thumb marks, by which one would in time learn if the markings were as persistent as is said. Anyhow I will do what I can to help Mr. Faulds in getting these sort of facts and in having an extract from his letter printed. I am so glad that my 'visualising' inquiries seem interesting to you. I get letters from all directions and the metaphysicians and mad-doctors have been very helpful.

Very sincerely yours,
Francis Galton.

Our united kindest remembrances to you all.

Letter from Henry Faulds to the Editor of *Nature*, published 28 October 1880 (Vol. XXII p.605).

On the skin-furrows of the hand

In looking over some specimens of 'prehistoric' pottery found in Japan I was led, about a year ago, to give some attention to the character of certain finger-marks which had been made on them while the clay was still soft. Unfortunately all of those which happened to come into my possession were too vague and ill-defined to be of much use, but a comparison of such finger-tip impressions made in recent pottery led me to observe the characters of the skin-furrows in human fingers generally. From these I passed to the study of the finger-tips of monkeys, and found at once that they presented very close analogies to those of human beings. I have here few opportunities of prosecuting the latter study to much advantage, but hope to present such results as I may attain in another letter. Meanwhile I would venture to suggest to others more in this connection, as an additional means of throwing light on their interesting genetic relations.

A large number of nature-prints have been taken by me from the fingers of people in Japan, and I am at present collecting others from different nationalities, which I hope may aid students of ethnology in classification. Some few interesting points may here be mentioned by way of introduction.

Some individuals show quite a symmetrical development of these furrows. In these cases all the fingers of one hand have a similar arrangement of lines, while the pattern is simply reversed on the other hand. A Gibraltar monkey (Macacus innus) examined by me had this arrangement. A slight majority of the few Europeans I have been able to examine here have it also.

An ordinary botanical lens is of great service in bringing out these minor peculiarities. Where the loops occur the innermost lines may simply break off and end abruptly; they may end in self-returning loops, or, again, they may go on without breaks after turning round upon themselves. Some lines also join or branch like junctions in a railway map. All these varieties, however, may be compatible with the general impression of symmetry that the two hands give us when printed from.

In a Japanese man the lines on both thumbs form similar spiral whorls; those of the left fore-finger form a peculiar oval whorl, while those of the right corresponding finger form an open loop having a direction quite opposite to that of the right fore-finger in the previous example. A similar whorl is found on both middle fingers instead of a symmetrically reversed whorl. The right ring-finger again has an oval whorl, but the corresponding left finger shows an open loop.

The lines at the ulno-palmar margin of this particular Japanese are of the parallel sort in both hands, and are quite symmetrical, thus differing from the Englishman's considerably. These instances are not intended to stand for typical patterns of the two peoples, but simply as illustrations of the kind of facts to be observed. My method of observation was at first simply to examine fingers closely, to sketch the general trend of the curves as accurately as possible, recording nationality, sex, colour of eyes and hair, and securing a specimen of the latter. I passed from this to 'nature-printing,' as ferns are often copied.

A common slate or smooth board of any kind, or a sheet of tin, spread over very thinly and evenly with printer's ink, is all that is required. The parts of which impressions are desired are pressed down steadily and softly, and then are transferred to slightly damp paper. I have succeeded in making very delicate impressions on glass. They are somewhat faint indeed, but would be useful for demonstrations, as details are very well shown, even down to the minute pores. By using different colours of ink useful comparisons could be made of two patterns by superimposition.

These might be shown by magic lantern. I have had prepared a number of outline hands with blank forms for entering such particulars of each case as may be wanted, and attach a specimen of hair for microscopic examination. Each finger-tip may best be done singly, and people are uncommonly willing to submit to the process. A little hot water and soap remove the ink. Benzine is still more effective. The dominancy of heredity through these infinite varieties is sometimes very striking. I have found unique patterns in a parent repeated with marvellous accuracy in his child. Negative results, however, might prove nothing in regard to parentage, a caution which it is important to make.

I am sanguine that the careful study of these patterns may be useful in several ways.

1. We may perhaps be able to extend to other animals the analogies found by me to exist in the monkeys.

2. These analogies may admit of further analysis, and may assist, when better understood, in ethnological classifications.

3. If so, those which are found in ancient pottery may become of immense historical importance.

4. The fingers of mummies, by special preparation, may yield results for comparison. I am very doubtful, however, of this.

5. When bloody finger-marks or impressions on clay, glass, &c., exist, they may lead to the scientific identification of criminals. Already I have had experience in two such cases, and found useful evidence from these marks. In one case greasy finger-marks revealed who had been drinking some rectified spirit. The pattern was unique, and fortunately I had previously obtained a copy of it. They agreed with microscopic fidelity. In another case sooty finger-marks of a person climbing a white wall were of great use as negative evidence. Other cases might occur in medico-legal investigations, as when the hands only of some mutilated victim were found. If previously known they would be much more precise in value than the standard mole of the penny novelists. If unknown previously, heredity might enable an expert to determine the relatives with considerable probability in many cases, and with absolute precision in some. Such a case as that of the Claimant even might not be beyond the range of this principle. There might be a recognisable Tichborne type, and there might be an Orton type, to one or other of which experts might relate the case. Absolute identity would prove descent in some circumstances.

I have heard, since coming to these general conclusions by original and patient experiment, that the Chinese criminals from early times have been made to give the impressions of their fingers, just as we make ours yield their photographs. I have not yet, however, succeeded in getting any precise or authenticated facts on that point. That the Egyptians caused their criminals to seal their confessions with their thumb-nails, just as the Japanese do now, a recent discovery proves. This is however quite a different matter, and it is curious to observe that in our country servant-girls used to stamp their sealed letters in the same way. There can be no doubt as to the advantage of having, besides their photographs, a nature-copy of the for-ever-unchangeable finger-furrows of important criminals. It need not surprise us to find that the Chinese have been here before us in this as in other matters. I shall be glad to find that it is really so, as it would only serve to confirm the utility of the method, and the facts which may thus have been accumulated would be a rich anthropological mine for patient observers.

Henry Faulds
Tsukiji Hospital, Tokio, Japan.

(Some very interesting examples of nature-printed finger-tips accompanied this letter. —ED.)

Letter from Sir William Herschel to the Editor of *Nature* published 25 November 1880 (Vol. XXIII p.76).

Skin furrows of the hand

Allow me to contribute the information in my possession in furtherance of the interesting study undertaken by your Japan correspondent (vol xxii, p.605).

I have been taking sign-manuals by means of finger-marks for now more than twenty years, and have introduced them for practical purposes in several ways in India with marked benefit.

The object has been to make all attempts at personation, or at repudiation of signatures, quite hopeless wherever this method is available,

(1) First I used it for pensioners whose vitality has been a distracting problem to Government in all countries. When I found all room for suspicion effectually removed here, I tried it on a larger scale in the several (2) registration offices under me, and here I had the satisfaction of seeing every official and legal agent connected with these offices confess that the use of these signatures lifted off the ugly cloud of suspiciousness which always hangs over such offices in India. It put a summary and absolute stop to the very idea of either personation or repudiation from the moment half a dozen men had made their marks and compared them together. (3) I next introduced them into the jail, where they were not un-needed. On commitment to jail each prisoner had to sign with his finger. Any official visitor to the jail after that could instantly satisfy himself of the identity of the man whom the jailor produced by requiring him to make a signature on the spot and comparing it with that which the books showed.

The ease with which the signature is taken and the hopelessness of either personation or repudiation are so great that I sincerely believe that the adoption of the practice in places and professions where such kind of fraud are rife is a substantial benefit to morality. I may add that by comparison of the signatures of persons now living with their signatures made twenty years ago, I have proved that that much time at least makes no such material change as to affect the utility of the plan.

For instance, if it were the practice on enlisting in the army to take (say) three signatures – one to stay with the regiment, one to go to Horse Guards, and one to the police at Scotland Yard – I believe a very appreciable diminution of desertions could be brought about by the mere fact that identification was become simply a matter of reference to the records.

And supposing that there existed such a thing as a finger-mark of Roger Tichborne, the whole Orton imposture would have been exposed to the full satisfaction of the jury in a single sitting by requiring Orton to make his own mark for comparison.

The difference between the general character of the rugae of Hindus and of Europeans is as apparent as that between male and female signatures, but my inspection of several thousands has not led me to think that it will ever be practically safe to say of any single person's signature that it is a woman's or a Hindoo's, or not a male European's. The conclusions of your correspondent seem, however, to indicate greater possibilities of certainty. In single families I find myself the widest varieties.

W. J. Herschel
15, St. Giles, Oxford, November 13

P.S. It would be particularly interesting to hear whether the Chinese have really used finger-marks in this way. Finger-dips (mere blots) are common in the East, as 'marks.'

Letter from Henry Faulds to the Editor of *Nature*, published 4 October 1894 (Vol L. p.548).

On the identification of habitual criminals by fingerprints

A Parliamentary Blue Book on 'The identification of habitual criminals.' which has recently been issued, reports on The Fingerprint System, stated to have been 'first suggested, and to some extent applied practically, by Sir William Herschel.'

The chairman of the committee appointed by Mr. Asquith, whose report contains the above statement, refers me for his evidence on this point to Mr. Galton's work on 'Fingerprints' (Macmillan and Co., 1892).

My 'careful study' of the subject is mentioned there, and an article of mine in NATURE, October 28, 1880 (vol xxii, p. 605), is referred to. It is correctly indexed in the "Index Medicus" for the year, published in 1881, although Mr. Galton spells and indexes my name incorrectly. That article, I believe is absolutely the first notice of the subject contained in English literature, and the conclusion I reached therein was that the patterns of the skin-furrows, with their distinctive loops, whorls and lines, breaking and blending like the junctions in a railway map, were capable of being readily used as a reliable and permanent basis for the 'scientific identification of criminals.' I conclude my paper with the statement that 'There can be no doubt as to the advantage of having, besides their photographs, a nature-copy of the for-ever unchangeable finger-furrows of important criminals.'

Sir William Herschel wrote in NATURE, November 25 of the same year, alleging that he had 'been taking sign-manuals by means of fingermarks for more than twenty years.' It does not yet appear that anything had been published on the subject by that gentleman till my contribution called forth his letter a month afterwards. The collections made by Sir W. Herschel were recently placed in Mr. Galton's hands, and that writer states that 'they refer to one or more fingers, and in a few instances to the whole hand, of fifteen different persons.' ('Fingerprints,' p. 9).

It is not stated how many of these had been imprinted prior to my first calling attention to the subject. At present it would seem that Sir W. Herschel had not accumulated the impressions at a more rapid rate than that of one person in two years! As we are informed in the letter to NATURE, referred to above, the identification of pensioners had been secured in this way, that the method was in use in all the registration offices of the district, and that 'on commitment to gaol, each prisoner had to sign with his finger,' I should have expected that a somewhat more extensive collection might have been secured. As priority of publication is generally held to count for something, and as I knew absolutely nothing of Sir W. Herschel's studies, nor ever heard of anyone in India who did, some little evidence on the point of priority would be of interest even now.

Mr Galton says, of Sir W. Herschel, 'He informs me that he submitted, in 1877, a report in semi-official form to the Inspector-General of Gaols, asking to be allowed to extend the process; but no result followed.' (p. 28) A copy of that semi-official report would go far to settle the question of priority, as its date is nearly two years previous to my having noticed the finger-furrows. No reference to them was then to be found in any anatomical work that I could find access to, and no writer on identification had ever thought of them as a means to that end. My interest, like that of Purkenje, arose from a special study of the sense of touch, and I was then lecturing to medical students on the 'Physiology of the Senses.' Having myopic eyes which enable me to write with ease the Lord's Prayer three times in the space of a sixpence, I soon noticed the unique patterns which the papillary ridges formed. I happened to be studying the prehistoric pottery of Japan at the same time, and became interested in observing that these patterns were similar, but, I thought, finer and more slender than those of the present day, which pointed, I conjectured, to the employment of children in early fictile art. However that may be, my knowledge of the subject had a natural and independent genesis.

The subject of identification by this means has been brought under the notice of the authorities on criminal matters of different countries by me from time to time, and some years before Mr. Galton's work was published, Scotland Yard placed one of its most enlightened officers in communication with me during a forenoon. Even in 1880, I prepared copper-plate outlines of the two hands, accompanied with instructions as to obtaining fingerprints, and some two chief points on the palm, where the rugæ are characteristic. Sir W. Herschel's letter mentions prints of one finger only as being obtained from prisoners on commitment. On page 79 of the Blue Book mentioned above 'Instructions for taking Fingerprints' are given for the benefit of prison warders, and the ten fingers are to be printed from, as I have advocated. I may add that I have not the slightest wish to diminish the credit that may be due to Sir W. Herschel. What I wish to point out is that his claim ought to be brought out a little more clearly than has yet been done, either by himself or by Mr. Galton. What precisely did he do, and when?

Letter from Sir William Herschel to the Editor of *Nature* published 22 November 1894 (Vol LI, p. 77).

Fingerprints

I have been quite unable, since I saw Mr. Faulds' letter in your issue of October 4, to take the matter of it in hand hitherto; and I do so now only because I think Mr. Faulds is entitled to raise the question if he pleases. To the best of my knowledge, Mr. Faulds' letter of 1880 was, what he says it was, the first notice in the public papers, in your columns, of the value of fingerprints for the purpose of identification. His statement that he came upon it independently in 1879 (?1878) commands acceptance as a matter of course. At the same time I scarcely think that such short experience as that justified his announcing that the finger-furrows were "for-ever unchanging."

How I chanced upon the thing myself in 1858, and followed it up afterwards, has been very kindly stated on my authority by Mr. Galton, at whose disposal I gladly placed all my materials on his request. Those published by him are only part of what were available. (See his 'Fingerprints,' page 27, and his 'Blurred Fingerprints.') To what is there stated I need now only add at Mr. Faulds' request, a copy of the demi-official letter which I addressed in 1877 to the then Inspector-General of Jails in Bengal. That the reply I received appeared to me altogether discouraging was simply the result of my very depressed state of health at the time. The position into which the subject has now been lifted is therefore wholly due to Mr. Galton through his large development of the study, and his exquisite and costly methods of demonstrating in print the many new and important conclusions he has reached.

I take the opportunity, in reference to a late article on Anthropometry (In the 'Nineteenth Century' of September 1894, p. 365) to deprecate, as being to the best of my knowledge wholly unproved, the assertion that the use of fingermarks in this way was "originally invented by the Chinese." I have met no evidence which goes anywhere near substantiating this. As a matter of fact, I exhibited the system to many passengers and officers of the P. and O. steamship 'Mongolia' in the Indian Ocean, during her outward voyage in February 1877; and I have the fingerprints of her captain, and all those persons, with their names. It is likely enough that the idea, which caught on rapidly among the passengers, may have found a settlement in some Chinese port by this route, and have there taken a practical form; but whether that be so or not, I must protest against the vague claim made on behalf of the Chinese, until satisfactory evidence of antiquity is produced.

Littlemore, November 7

Also published was the demi-official letter, generally referred to as the 'Hooghly letter' the full text of which is contained within Chapter 3.

Letter from Edward Henry to Francis Galton.

July 19 1900

Kitcombe,
Alton,
Hants

My dear Mr. Galton,
I send you a copy of my book on fingerprints, what is valuable in it is based upon your labours and had it been anything more than a short manual written to order, I would have asked for it the distinction of being dedicated to yourself.

They wish now to introduce the system in Siam and I hope to introduce it into Africa. I feel sure you will be gratified and realise that I have done my best to 'stand upon your shoulders' – very broad shoulders they are.

Lord Belper's committee are impressed with the rapidity of search under the Bertillon system, but the search is made without adequate allowance to discount the 'personal equation' error and doubtless they will realise this.

In India we have proved by the results of actual working of the two systems side by side that when our allowance of 2 millimetres either way, not withstanding the skill of the measurers is insufficient and with this 2 millimetres limit as many as 12, 24 and even more pigeon holes must be searched when measurements are near the 'medium' margin. Actual experiment even will not demonstrate the degree of error to be allowed when skilled measurers are overworked, careless, overtired and a wrong measurement once recorded cannot be rectified in the Central Office whereas if fingerprints are wrongly classified this would be detected when the record is overhauled as we guard against the possibility of their being impressed in a wrong sequence by taking simultaneously the plain dabbed impressions of their digits impressed on a metal guard. If by misadventure right hand digits are impressed in the spaces for left and vice versa, this attracts immediate attention when the prints are being classified.

The saving of time in taking the data, the greater certainty and rapidity of search, and the fact that the subject has not to take off his coat, boots, etc. are all considerations and then there is the advantage of keeping slips in open files which enables them to be handled easily and carried about if necessary in small space.

I have explained this not at great length for time is against me. I venture to hope that I have your good wishes with me. I sail on Saturday. If you care to keep the palm impressions they shall be sent back to you. Remember me kindly to Mrs. Lethbridge. If any of her sons are in my neighbourhood out there I hope I may make their acquaintance.

Yours very truly,
E. R. Henry

Extract from the paper by Edward Henry presented to the British Association for the Advancement of Science at Dover in 1899.

Finger prints and the detection of crime in India

The employment of the new system has not been restricted to the Police Department, but has been introduced into all branches of public business, being particularly well suited to the requirements of a country where the mass of the people are uneducated, and where false personation is an evil which even the penalties provided by the penal laws are powerless to control. It is believed that, on the death of pensioners, friends or relations have personated them and have continued to draw allowances which should have lapsed with the death of the persons to whom they were originally granted. All military and all civil pensioners are now required to give their finger impressions, and this precaution is effective against fraud. The Courts have to deal with numerous contested cases in which transfers of proprietary or other rights, purporting to have been duly admitted in the presence of witnesses before a registrar of deeds, are repudiated, and evidence is adduced on either side, often of the most conflicting and indecisive nature, both parties not hesitating to rely upon suborned testimony. In all registration offices in the Province of Bengal, persons who, admitting execution, present documents for registration, are required to authenticate their signature or mark by affixing the impression of their left thumb both on the document and in a register kept for the purpose. Should an executant repudiate as not genuine a deed which purports to be a transfer by him of certain rights, the judicial officer can require the person repudiating to give his thumb impression in open court, and this is compared with the impression on the document and in the register, and can be proved to be either the same or a different impression, and this settles the point at issue. In this way, during the last three years, several cases of false personation have been detected and prosecuted to conviction, and the deterrent effect has been so marked as to justify the belief that the volume of work with which the Courts have to cope will be sensibly reduced in amount. In the Opium Department, large advances are made on account, to the cultivators through middlemen, the poppy crop being hypothecated as security. If the middleman or cultivator proves dishonest, the issue is raised whether particular sums reached the persons they were intended for. Formerly the cultivator could disown his mark or signature, or the middleman could put forward as the cultivator's mark or signature one that had been fraudulently made, but as the finger impression of the payee is now required to authenticate acknowledgment of receipt, a check has been introduced, the efficacy of which both cultivators and middlemen fully appreciate. The employer who makes advances to labourers, or pays them salaries, or enters into contracts with them, now protects himself by taking their fingerprints on the receipt or agreement. All emigrants signing contracts under the Emigration Act are required to give the impression of their left thumb on the contract and on the registers. With large establishments, such as are employed by the Survey of India, this system is used to prevent the re-employment of undesirable persons whose services have been dispensed with. The thumb impressions of the employees are taken and registered, and if a particular man is dismissed for misbehaviour, a photo-zincograph of his impression is sent to all working parties, which ensures that he cannot again get taken on, even by assuming a false name. Since April 1899 the system has been adopted by the Director-General of the Post-offices of India, and has been made applicable to all present and future non-gazetted officers, who number many thousands. In the Medical Department of the Bengal Presidency, the local Medical Officer and the Medical Board, when giving certificates, invariably take the thumb impression of the person examined. There is believed to be much false personation at public examinations in India, the candidate who appears in the Examination Hall not being the person who secured the certificate entitling him to compete. In examinations for employment in one branch of Government service this check has been introduced, and is working excellently, and it will no doubt be extended. In connection with the administration of the Rules for preventing the spread of Plague, and for regulating the Pilgrimage of Mussulmans to Mecca, certificates are authenticated by bearing the thumb impression of the persons to whom they are granted. . . . It must be recognised that the introduction of finger impressions in proof or disproof of identity where the person in question is known and accessible, and has given his mark on a previous occasion, is an extraordinary efficient method of preventing perjury and personation. . . . The Government have been so fully convinced of the effectiveness of this new system, and of the certainty of the results it yields, that within the last few months the Indian Legislature has passed a special Act amending the law of evidence to the extent of declaring relevant the testimony of those who by study have become proficient in finger print decipherment, such testimony not being admissible under the unamended law.

Index

N.B. With regard to the policemen cited below, the individual ranks given are the highest achieved during the period of these entries. In some cases they will subsequently have attained higher rank. Judges or counsel may have risen similarly in their profession.